Jews on Trial

Typeset in Minion by Jerusalem Typesetting, www.jerusalemtype.com

Distributed by KTAV Publishing House, Inc., Jersey City, NJ

Library of Congress Cataloging-in-Publication Data

Jews on Trial / edited by Robert A. Garber
   p. cm.

ISBN 0-88125-868-7
   1. Anti-Semitism – Case Studies. 2. Jews – Legal Status, laws, etc. – Case Studies. 3. Europe – Trials, litigation, etc. 4. United States – Trials, litigation, etc. I. Garber, Robert A.

BJ1285.M44 2004
364.1'089'924–dc22

2004019254

JEWS ON TRIAL

by

BRUCE AFRAN • MICHAEL J. BAZYLER •
PHILIP S. CARCHMAN • REBEKAH MARKS COSTIN •
MICHAEL CURTIS • ROBERT A. GARBER • C.M. SILVER •
SALLY STEINBERG-BRENT • JOYCE USISKIN

EDITED BY ROBERT A. GARBER

KTAV Publishing House, Inc.
Jersey City, New Jersey

Bruce Afran (*The American Republic vs. Julius and Ethel Rosenberg* © 2004)

Michael J. Bazyler (*The Holocaust on Trial*: Irving v. Lipstadt © 2004)

Philip S. Carchman (*The Confirmation of Louis Brandeis* © 2004)

Rebekah Marks Costin (*Mendel Beilis and the Blood Libel* © 2004)

Michael Curtis (*The Hilsner Case and Ritual Murder* © 2004)

Robert A. Garber (*Preface, Dr. Lopez and* The Merchant of Venice, *and The Case of Alfred Dreyfus* all © 2004)

Moshe Silver (C.M. Silver) (*Universal Remote: Justice and Injustice in Shakespeare's* Merchant of Venice © 2004)

Sally Steinberg-Brent (*The Leo Frank Murder Case* © 2004)

Joyce Usiskin (*The Punishment of Jonathan Jay Pollard* © 2004)

Typeset in Minion by Jerusalem Typesetting, www.jerusalemtype.com

Distributed by KTAV Publishing House, Inc., Jersey City, NJ

Library of Congress Cataloging-in-Publication Data

Jews on Trial / edited by Robert A. Garber
   p. cm.

ISBN 0-88125-868-7
   1. Anti-Semitism – Case Studies. 2. Jews – Legal Status, laws, etc. – Case Studies. 3. Europe – Trials, litigation, etc. 4. United States – Trials, litigation, etc. I. Garber, Robert A.

BJ1285.M44 2004
364.1'089'924–dc22

2004019254

Contents

Preface

The meaning of the term "trials" in this book's title should be understood in the widest sense – these trials were investigations that
became ordeals. The trials to which the Jewish defendants were
subjected took place not only in courtrooms but in other venues
as well. Unlike the lawsuit against Deborah Lipstadt, the trials
of Hilsner and Beilis, for example, were not courtroom dramas
played out before a conventional bar of justice. Alfred Dreyfus
did appear before judges but, more important, he underwent
trial by popular sentiment. Indeed, many of these cases were
largely tainted by crowd influence – less, perhaps, in the cases of
Jonathan Pollard and Louis Brandeis and more in the matters of
the Rosenbergs and Leo Frank.

Most of those tried were well assimilated into the society in
which they lived. So they believed. Assimilated or not, the relevant
feature of every one of these trials remains the religious heritage
of the defendant. In some cases the reader may decide that the
accused did, in fact, bear some guilt. Nevertheless, either in the
bringing of the case in the first place or in the ultimate verdict and
punishment, the defendant's Jewishness – and with it, inevitably,
the taint of anti-Semitism – was involved. These Jewish defendants
were subjected to judgment, at least in substantial part, because
they were Jewish.

It should not be supposed, simply because of their victimization, that each of the accused was heroic. Dull Leopold Hilsner was certainly not a valiant sort. And the attitudes of some truly courageous characters in these cases may come as a surprise. Neither Georges Piquart in the case of Dreyfus nor Thomas Masaryk in Hilsner's was ever partial to Jews, individually or as a group. But Piquart and Masaryk were partial to the cause of justice.

While many people, both Jews and non-Jews, may have rallied to their cause, ultimately the defendants (except for the Rosenbergs as a couple) stood accused alone. The trials of those we describe were not subsumed in vast pogroms or genocidal frenzy. They were not among the millions who suffered and died as part of some homicidal program. They have the individual faces that rightly belong to every victim of prejudice.

The trials depicted in the following pages are certainly not history's only significant cases that carry the taint of anti-Semitism. They may be taken simply as illustrative of a resurgent historical phenomenon that has lasted two millennia, from postpagan to postmodern times. It long antedates the term "anti-Semitism" itself, which was coined in Germany as recently as 1873. Before that, "Jew hatred" sufficed. The hatred itself has been traced as far back as Antiochus IV Epiphanes, before the common era. Some see significant origins in the politically infused synoptic gospels of Matthew and John. Within the century following the composition of the gospels, Melito, bishop of Sardis, issued an indictment against all Jews on the charge of deicide. The record of the malevolence can be followed through history with such events as the Crusades, the recurrent blood-libel cases like that of Little St. Hugh of Lincoln, the Inquisition, the Iberian expulsion, the venomous writings of Martin Luther, the rantings of the 1930s "radio priest" Charles E. Coughlin on to the Shoah and after until the most recent events, including the rise of a new European anti-Semitism. Indeed, the Passover Haggadah, read in Jewish homes each year, recalls that "in every generation there are those that seek to destroy us."

Geography is not determinative (though our survey ends,

coincidentally, in London, where it began). One would not be surprised to find anti-Semitism in Ruritania or Spoon River if they were actual locales. The trial of the Marrano physician Rodrigo Lopez, described in this book, is an example of the antipathy in the England of Elizabeth i. The old blood-libel tale was repeated in Ukraine in the case of Mendel Beilis, also described herein, and it was repeated yet again, along with other lies, in the notorious tsarist forgery, *The Protocols of the Learned Elders of Zion*. That virulent propaganda was republished by Henry Ford of Dearborn, Michigan, and then propagated by the Nazis. The specious text now can be found in bookshops throughout the Islamic world and in the world of the Internet as well.

The execution of Lopez in Shakespeare's England took place during a period of emerging enlightenment. Technology advanced. It was then that Britons finally retired the longbow in favor of weapons of more modern mass destruction, and it was then that an innovative water closet was installed for the use of Gloriana, Queen Elizabeth i. But, of course, technology did not result in the amelioration of prejudice. Amid badges of a brave new world, "Kill the Jew!" was the demand of the Elizabethan crowd. Three hundred years later, the same call was uttered by the Parisian crowd at the degradation of Dreyfus. It is still heard in much of the world. From Dreyfus to the case of the Holocaust denier in 2000, not much longer than a century elapsed. With the immediacy of contemporary times, these cases are not artifacts of a past age.

Some of the representative trials examined in our symposium were more notorious than others. Because the specifics of these cases may not be familiar, each essay sets forth the salient facts together with suggestions for further reading. The authors may offer some personal views as well. And inevitably, certain questions emerge: Was Leo Frank entirely blameless in his relationships with his employees? Of what, exactly, was Ethel or Julius Rosenberg guilty? Were the political opposition to Brandeis and the punishment imposed on Pollard attributable to their beliefs? Finally, one may ask, will we ever see the end of trials tainted because of the defendants' religion or heritage? Those who subscribe to the cause of social justice can work for that result. Learning about potent cases like the ones that follow and remembering their lessons may be a small start.

*   *   *

This book originated in a series of lectures, also entitled "Jews on Trial," presented from the spring of 2003 through the following spring as part of the ongoing adult education program at the Jewish Center of Princeton, New Jersey. Most of the following essays were first presented in the series. Some of the authors are members of the synagogue who are lawyers. However, as the book took form, other uniquely qualified writers soon joined the project. Each author's conclusions, of course, are his or her own. All the essays that follow have been contributed by the authors to the Jewish Center of Princeton, and any proceeds from *Jews on Trial* will be contributed for the Center's charitable causes. The devoted efforts of the individual contributors are an ongoing testament to their dedication to the cause of learning and understanding.

Robert A. Garber

August 2004
Princeton, New Jersey

Dr. Lopez and *The Merchant of Venice*

ROBERT A. GARBER

There were scarcely any Jews in England during the two centuries after they were driven out in the year 1290. Upon their expulsion from Spain and Portugal in 1492, however, a few Marranos, outwardly professing Christianity, found their way to the island nation. Jewish refugees, often doctors or traders, settled in Bristol and London.[1]

It is not known whether Doctor Rodrigo Lopez, a Marrano born about 1525, was born in Portugal, as some sources assert, or was a native Englishman. The name Lopez, a venerable one, was known in England.[2] It is established that Dr. Lopez was member of the College of Physicians and a senior doctor at St. Bartholomew's Hospital. He, his wife, Sarah, and their children were living in London in 1559. By 1584, the doctor was appointed body-physician to the earl of Leicester.[3] The earl was accused, on occasion, of resorting to poisoning his enemies, aided by his appointed physician.

Dr. Lopez discharged his duties so well that in 1586 he attained the post of chief physician to Her Majesty, Queen Elizabeth. At court, Lopez became acquainted with the unrestrained Robert Devereux, second earl of Essex, twenty-two years old in 1589 and no less than forty years the doctor's junior. Through Essex, Lopez was introduced to both Antonio Perez, former secretary

1

to Philip II of Spain, and Don Antonio, the dimwitted pretender to the Portuguese throne. Don Antonio spoke only Portuguese, and Lopez, fluent in several languages, served as interpreter. Thus Lopez involved the queen in an ineffective scheme to invade Portugal.

About this time, rash Essex quarreled with the venerable physician, accusing him of speaking too freely about the young earl's medical problems.

Intrigue mounted. A messenger from the Spanish king presented a ruby-and-diamond ring to Lopez as an inducement to gain his aid in removing Don Antonio. Lopez, known to be irritable at this stage of his life and having tired of Essex and his friends, offered the ring to the queen. Her Majesty refused the proffered gift, perhaps because she knew it had originated with Philip, the Catholic king.

In 1593, foreign conspirators against Don Antonio were arrested at the home of Dr. Lopez. He was believed to be in league with the foreigners, one of whom had letters mentioning the "price of pearls." This was thought to be a coded reference to a conspiracy against Elizabeth, one of several supposed plots against the crown in those days.[4]

Lopez was arrested and was interrogated by his antagonist, the earl of Essex. The questioning proved fruitless, and the queen admonished Essex for making accusations he could not prove. Essex was spurred to work harder to make a case against the doctor. Meanwhile, Lopez was taken to the Tower.

A month later his trial took place. The celebrated solicitor general, Coke, spoke for the prosecution, laying particular emphasis on the fact that the defendant was Jewish. Essex, by special appointment, presided in conjunction with others. He, too, referred to the doctor's religious background. Threatened with the rack, Lopez confessed to hearing proposals to poison the queen for 50,000 ducats, but he had only intended, he said, to cozen Philip. A jury found him guilty of plotting against Her Majesty. Most historians believe that the verdict was not justified.

The queen hesitated to sign the death warrant, and Lopez spent more than seven weeks in the Tower before she finally agreed to the sentence.

Dr. Rodrigo Lopez, at the end of his seventh decade of life, was hanged, drawn and quartered on June 7, 1594. The crowd at the regular place of execution, Tyburn, was unruly. On the gallows, the condemned man cried out that he loved the queen and Don Antonio as well as he loved Jesus Christ. The crowd thought this was hilarious, shouting "He is a Jew!" as the executioner did his work. [5]

Lopez is often taken to be the model for Shakespeare's Shylock. Much of the plot of *The Merchant of Venice* can be traced to sources not original to the playwright, as is true, of course, with much of the work of the Bard. But Shakespeare's Jew has been traced to Dr. Lopez for several reasons.[6]

The name of Shylock's adversary is Antonio, not a common one in the play's setting. The personality of the fictional moneylender mirrors that of the actual physician. The play refers pointedly to the use of the rack,[7] and there is an odd reference to a wolf ("*lopez*") on the gallows.[8] Shylock seems different from other characters brought to life by Shakespeare. It is not that he is Venetian; he could be English as well. It is that he is Jewish. And, with much being written contemporaneously about him, Lopez was the best-known of the few Jews in England when the play was written.

Shakespeare is known to have written quickly to meet demand, and much is made of the first appearance of the play not long after the execution at Tyburn. Although the exact date of composition of *The Merchant of Venice* remains uncertain, it is certain that the case of Dr. Lopez was very well known when the play was performed at Shakespeare's theater. And that may be the best argument that Shakespeare, the quintessential showman, used him as the model for a Jew. Surely the famous trial and death of Dr. Lopez stimulated the Bard to place his Jew in a courtroom.

Notes

1. It was not until 1655 that Jews were allowed back by Cromwell and resident Marranos declared themselves Jewish after all.

2. Dan Rottenberg, *Finding Our Fathers* (New York: Random House, 1977): p. 278, notes that the name is Spanish for "wolf" and that two unidentified Jewish encyclopedias have Lopez biographies beginning in 16th century England. (Entries in *The Jewish Encyclopedia* and *The Encyclopaedia Judaica* on Roderigo Lopez, of course, go back to the 16th century).

3. The Earl often employed traveling actors, including the father of Richard Burbage, the star performer who created the role of Shylock in *The Merchant of Venice*. It is not unlikely that Burbage met the Jewish doctor in his youth and remembered him.

4. There may have been such a conspiracy, and Lopez may even have heard of it but, as he later asserted under duress, he kept his counsel in order to unravel the plot.

5. The doctor's assets, according to law, escheated to the Crown after his execution. Elizabeth, however, returned his property to his family – except for the ruby and diamond ring. That she kept and wore until she died. Alison Weir, *The Life of Elizabeth i* (New York: Ballantine Books, 1998), p. 419. A painting, "Queen Elizabeth I holding the Garter George" *circa* 1575, now in the possesion of her namesake, the present monarch, depicts the old Queen wearing such a ring on her thumb. It is reproduced in Roy Strong, *The Cult of Elizabeth* (London: Pimlico, 1999), p. 163.

6. See: S.L. Lee, The Original of Shylock, *The Gentleman's Magazine*, Feb. 1880, pp. 185–200, for a full sketch of the doctor's life and a strong argument for his identification with Shakespeare's character.

7. Act III, ii, 25–29

8. Act IV, i, 132

Universal Remote: Justice and Injustice in Shakespeare's *Merchant of Venice*

C.M. SILVER

Jews in the News

The single most famous trial of any Jew is certainly that of Jesus. The second-most famous trial of a Jew, at least in the Western world, is that of Shylock and his pound of flesh in Shakespeare's *Merchant of Venice*. The mention of Jesus is not gratuitous: Shakespeare may have not had the parallels uppermost in mind while crafting the scenes of Shylock's downfall, yet the tales intersect in one key aspect: they share with each other, as well as with the common practice of Shakespeare's own time, the element of public spectacle. A significant point overlooked by both the champions and the detractors of Mel Gibson's film *The Passion* is that public executions in ancient times were noisy, bloody, gruesome, and long-drawn affairs, largely in order to maximize their entertainment value. In a day when we lapse into deathly ennui because there is nothing worth watching on any the 200-plus channels available on our cable television, we can barely appreciate a life before mass communication media made Entertainment On Demand possible. Citizens of Jerusalem under Roman rule did not have available to them the luxury of channel surfing; the biblical counterparts of couch potatoes were denigrated in the Mishnah (in *Pirkei Avot*, for example, the tractate known in English as "Ethics of the Fathers") as "sitters-around on street corners" (*yoshvei kronot* in Mishnaic Hebrew). These good-for-nothings did the pre-electronic equivalent of channel surfing by standing about in the middle of town and watching life and commerce unfold around them.

For all the terror unleashed in the wave of crucifixions under Roman rule, it must be remembered that not every Jew was automatically a partisan of every crucified man. The rule of Rome was abominable, every bit as inhuman and devastating as the Nazi program nearly two millennia later. In the Roman wars of conquest and subjugation of the Jews, and in the famine and general destruction that followed, it has been estimated, perhaps as many as two million Jews perished.

And still, the mythification of Masada notwithstanding, it is no simple position to take that the Jews must have stood uniformly in closed ranks alongside every one of their brethren who was nailed to the cross. While death and suffering were widespread and indiscriminate under the Romans, crucifixion was reserved for political revolutionaries. Throughout human history, even under the worst of circumstances, the majority of any society prefers to be left alone: to endure current hardships rather than trade them for horrors they know not of. The anger with which a crowd might have watched a crucifixion was undoubtedly a mixture of loathing and hatred for the Roman oppressor, along with a dose of anger at the political insurgent for endangering the innocent by creating an unstable situation in an already unstable society. This, mixed with a large dose of relief that the spectator was not the person being nailed to the cross. In a world with neither television nor radio, neither CDs nor cinema, any excitement served at the very least to break up the monotony of the banausic, the daily routine.

Readers who take exception to this are urged to read descriptions of the public tortures and executions in Shakespeare's day (not to mention the equivalent of the sports-bar Monday Night Football scene: bear baiting). The public confession and execution of Dr. Lopez, for example, was a *cause célèbre* in the England of its time, and occasioned not merely parlor talk but successful revivals of Marlowe's play *The Jew of Malta*, a rip-roaring tale of a Jew who does not get put on trial because he so palpably deserves his ultimate destruction.

As a sidebar we should observe that the discussion of whether the Jews killed Jesus is chilling in its simple-mindedness. Jesus was a Jew. He was a Jew living in a society where nearly everyone else was Jewish. He was a political rabble-rouser, or revolutionary, or Zealot, or a babbling madman who attracted people with danger-ous ideas. Or the son of God, a notion so extremely radical that any normal society would have rejected him outright.

The Jewish view of Jesus in his own time must be seen in the proper light. He not only affronted the Romans – which was something that people did from time to time. He also affronted his Jewish compatriots by breaking with established rabbinic norms, as promulgated by the Pharisees, the forerunners of modern main-stream Judaism. In later years, to the extent that claims were made, for or about him, that he was divine, the rabbinic view was one of outrage at so preposterous a notion, and the Talmud contains fanciful insults as rabbis seek to outdo one another in making up punishments for the upstart Yeshu.

Jesus' political message of overthrow of Rome may have been ideally suited to his audience; at the point at which divinity was claimed for him, though, it should come as no surprise to anyone that his fellow Jews rejected him. For at that point, Jesus suddenly ceased to be One of Us.

Shylock is another story. To the extent that popular images of subcultures are established in the general mind of society by the entertainment available to people, it is troubling to contem-plate that the English-speaking world's view image of the Jew is dominated by Shylock and Tevye. They are attended, of course, by the array of characters who have trotted onto the global stage with the existence of the State of Israel, but I would argue that no Israeli political figure is seen as lovable in the way Tevye is lovable.

This leaves us with an image in the arena of global opinion much closer to the apparently unreasonable greed and vengefulness of Shylock than to acceptance of the sweet, bumbling Tevye.

The Dark Night of the Channel Surfer

The theme of Shakespeare's *Merchant of Venice* is the theme of contemporary life: that of deadly ennui, and of the alienation experienced in a society which caters to every whim. The play speaks to many of our most up-to-date issues. Shakespeare's Venice is a society created for commerce. It is a successful Republic, a nation-state in which adherence to the principles of the Republic is meant to transcend every other form of allegiance, giving rise to a nation founded on a belief in principles rather than on any social grouping based on a false distinction – or rather, on a false similarity. It is as false to state that all French speakers are fundamentally alike as it is to state that all black people, white people, Fiji Islanders, or Roman Catholics are alike – alike especially to the extent that they require an independent state in which to practice their alikeness unfettered, unopposed by the Great Outside who, by their very un-alikeness, threaten the artificial community and its members. The notion of the Republic is meant to transcend this, and there appears to be a very real sense in which Shakespeare's audience would have accepted this setting as fundamentally different from all other societies of their time, which were based primarily on distinctions of religion, language, and social class. The Republic was a society in which there were no distinctions; where men – and perhaps women – were free to exercise the basic function of the society: the transacting of business.

Shakespeare set two plays in Venice, both of them about outsiders, and both about outsiders in whom the Otherness ultimately gives the lie to the notion of the Republic as a society without distinctions. Or rather, a society whose measuring-sticks are wealth and achievement. In the society of Shakespeare's Venice, the wealthy and the accomplished lord it over the less successful and the unattained. And attainment is, as the core story of *The*

Merchant of Venice makes clear, a socially acceptable proxy for romantic love.

Romantic love...The play opens with its title character – Antonio, the Merchant himself – sighing, "In sooth I know not why I am so sad," a sentiment echoed precisely by the heroine, Portia, on her first appearance: "By my troth, Nerissa, my little body is aweary of this great world."[1] Antonio and Portia are, re-spectively, the wealthiest man and the wealthiest woman in Venice. They are also, by the way, both destined to fall uncontrollably in love with Bassanio, the rogue who is the only character willing to call the Venetian spade a spade. He discloses to Antonio, without dissembling, his own intention to marry Portia for her money, a goal Antonio agrees is worthy of attaining, and a gambit that Antonio is pleased to finance for his beloved friend. When the game goes awry, Antonio falls into the trap. The whole of the fourth act of the play is given over to the trial of Antonio – which magically transforms *in medias res* into the trial of Shylock.

To the modern reader of the play, it may seem that there is dramatic tension in not knowing how the trial scene will play out. Will Antonio die? Will the Jew turn merciful, as he is being urged to do? This enlightened perspective is probably dead wrong. To our modern Western sensibility (especially when we are educated Jews, living in the freedom afforded us in twenty-first-century America), it appears that only two people know what the actual outcome of the trial is to be: Shakespeare and Portia. Shakespeare in the real world, the omniscient puppeteer who guides the trial to its stunning reversal; Portia in the world of the play, whose disguise miraculously escapes detection by the Duke and his en-tire court even though she is praised from the outset as the most famous woman in Venice – not to mention remaining undetected by her own husband; what more proof do we require that he had his eye on the gold, not the girl?

This is most assuredly not the perspective of the original au-dience of the play, however. The English of Shakespeare's day had set certain historical precedents: The first recorded case of a blood libel against the Jews was in the town of Norwich in the year 1144. Throughout the Middle Ages, starting with their arrival in 1066, the Jews of England had been exempt from taxation – viewed, wrongly, as a privilege by their non-Jewish neighbors. Instead, they were attached directly to the king's household, through an officer bearing the title of exchequer of the Jews. This official was charged with extracting extraordinary levies from the Jews to finance special projects as the king saw fit. The Jews of England, far from enjoying any special privilege or status, were drained drier, and swifter, than the general population, as these levies were not intended to be repaid. Ironically, it was probably the levies extracted from the Jews of England to finance the Crusades that finally bankrupted them. Having had the poor fortune to run out of money entirely, the Jews were formally expelled from England in the year 1290, at the order of Edward 1. This was largely because English landowners, nobles, and merchants were clamoring for the opportunity to make financial deals with the royal household. As they were Christians, they would be permitted to raise funds from their own serfs, and thus would not be subject to the ruinous fate that had befallen the Jews.

Thus, in Shakespeare's day, there were officially no Jews in England. There were known to be perhaps one hundred or two hundred individuals, mostly in London, living as Conversos, Jews who had converted to Christianity, and who openly conformed to the practices, rites, and beliefs of the Roman Catholic Church. In 1594, two years before *The Merchant of Venice* was first performed, in 1596, the most notorious Converso in England, Roderigo Lopez, had been noisily and elaborately and quite publicly tortured and executed on suspicion of having plotted to murder the queen. Lopez, who was serving at the time as one of Her Majesty's personal physicians, had means and opportunity. Motive, however, appears to have been falsely supplied by the earl of Leicester, who needed a credible means to escape from the scrutiny that he was under for his own treasonous activities. What better exculpatory goat to offer up than a fall-Jew?

What I mean is this: in the year of 1596 – less than two years after the public entertainment afforded by the Lopez execution, and the successful string of performances of Marlowe's *Jew of Malta* that it unleashed – Shakespeare's audience never for a moment doubted the outcome of the trial. The Jew would get his comeuppance, his fall would be abrupt and swift and hard. They did not wonder what Shakespeare was going to do; rather, they were fascinated to see how he was going to do it. They were like the audience of any action movie, all of whom know full well that the heroine *must* survive the gunshot wound, the fall into the ravine, the parachute that fails to open, the shark attack, and the martial arts extravaganza across the rooftops, complete with whirling *katana* blades and a hail of bullets. And yet, the action is nonetheless thrilling because of our inability to extricate ourselves from our emotional state.

Finally – and this is perhaps the cruel fulcrum of the argument – there is one more person who knows, in advance, the outcome of the trial, and that is Shylock himself. At the end of the trial, in Shylock's final moments on stage, we have the following exchange:

> PORTIA. Art thou contented, Jew? What dost thou
>   say?
> SHYLOCK. I am content.
> PORTIA. Clerk, draw a deed of gift.
> SHYLOCK. I pray you give me leave to go from hence,
>   I am not well, – send the deed after me,
>   And I will sign it.

It has been observed more than once that this appears to be a particularly unsatisfying close to the Shylock portion of the play. As Harold Bloom observes in his *Shakespeare: The Invention of the Human*,[2] if Shylock is not an evil clown, an oaf and a buffoon, it is also true that Portia is no moral heroine. Portia is, indeed, conniving and dishonest. But this essay is not about her. Suffice it to say that the profound sympathy with which Shakespeare draws the character of Shylock places every other character in the play at a moral disadvantage. Indeed, the romantic subplot of the exchange of rings brings out the real truth of Shylock: he alone understands the nature of love; he alone has experienced true love, and, as he carries it yet in his bosom, he is perhaps the only person in all Venice who has an honest relationship to money and commerce.

A brief digression is well worth the ink: the first fairy-tale element in the play, as observed by the great Shakespearean actor, director, and commentator Hartley Granville-Barker, is the tale of the caskets. The final, and parallel, one is the tale of the exchange of rings. In between, the following exchange in Act III, scene I between Shylock and his coreligionist Tubal goes all but unnoticed by audiences, actor, directors, and literary deep thinkers:

TUBAL. Your daughter spent in Genoa, as I heard, one night, fourscore ducats.

SHYLOCK. Thou stick'st a dagger in me, – I shall never see my gold again, – fourscore ducats at a sitting, fourscore ducats!

TUBAL. There came divers of Antonio's creditors in my company to Venice, that swear, he cannot choose but break.

SHYLOCK. I am very glad of it, – I'll plague him, I'll torture him, – I am glad of it.

TUBAL. One of them showed me a ring he had of your daughter for a monkey.

SHYLOCK: Out upon her! – thou torturest me, Tubal, – it was my turquoise, I had it of Leah when I was a bachelor: I would not have given it for a wilderness of monkeys.

Shakespeare often uses code words or phrases that crop up as *Leitmotifs* in his work. A noted authority on poetry, Helen Vendler, turned out a scholarly work that became a bestseller, *The Art of*

Shakespeare's Sonnets.[3] This is a complex analysis of the sonnets from the perspective of key words and phrases, and while the analysis breaks down on occasion, her approach gives rise to some stunning insights. The plays often benefit from the same structural and literary referential artistry, although on a larger scale it is not so easy to pick them out. A second characteristic of Shakespeare's writing is the dropping of tiny hints that expand in the listener's mind to create an entire offstage life for his characters. The most famous of these tidbits, perhaps, is Othello's death-speech, where he reminds us:

> OTHELLO. ... that in Aleppo once,
> Where a malignant and a turbaned Turk
> Beat a Venetian and traduced the state,
> I took by th' throat the circumcised dog
> And smote him – thus!
> *He stabs himself.* [4]

No mention is made anywhere else in the play of Aleppo, of circumcised Turks or traduced states. Yet at the moment of his death, Othello, with a single sentence, conjures up an epic vision on the scale of Lawrence of Arabia. Now *that's* writing!

Similarly, Shylock makes an offhand reference to Leah – obviously the mother of Jessica, his wanton and wayward daughter. Leah is obviously no longer alive – we neither see nor hear her, nor hear of her. In Act II, scene IV, when Jessica is eloping under cover of darkness with her Christian beloved, Lorenzo, she first despoils her father of all the money he has entrusted to her for safekeeping. She locks ducats and jewelry in a large box which she hands down from the window to the waiting Lorenzo with the instruction, "Here, catch this casket. It is worth the pains."

The use of the word "casket" is no coincidence. As Bassanio must choose his casket in order to win Portia – and with her the untold wealth that had belonged to her father – so Jessica conveys her own father's wealth to her betrothed. Portia cheats by singing a clever song whose rhyme scheme indicates to Bassanio which casket to choose. Jessica, who is less polished than Portia, but who is eager to learn the ways of the non-Jewish world of Venice and Belmont, Portia's fairy-tale castle, tosses the casket containing her father's wealth into Lorenzo's waiting hands. The technique is far inferior to Portia's in both love and money, but the parallel is unmistakable.

The exchange between Shylock and Tubal comes to close the loop on the metaphor: Jessica takes money and love by means of a casket; she then gives away the ring, just as Bassanio and his sidekick, Gratiano, will break faithfulness with their wives by giving their rings to the supposed Doctor of Laws (Portia in disguise) and his serving-boy (Nerissa in disguise).

Reading this text from the perspective of upper-middle-class, twenty-first-century America, it is easy to imagine Antonio sitting before his huge flat-screen television at midnight, a glass of scotch or a half-smoked reefer at his side, as he surfs the endless channels available on his top-of-the-range cable service. Antonio is exactly the type of man who complains that the more channels are made available, the less there is to watch. He is a victim of the boredom inherent in the Venetian social and economic system: when money becomes the end, and no longer a means, the soul of a society starts to wither. When money replaces romantic love – or, which is perhaps worse, when the participants in a society can no longer untangle money from love, so that they are not clear what the difference is, or whether there is a difference at all, the soul dies, never to be reborn.

In contrast to all the other characters in this sorry little circle, we see Shylock as a man of the world, a man who has had true love in his life; a widower who so cherishes the memory of his departed wife that he needs no replacement for her. He probably dotes sadly on his daughter, realizing that for her the draw of the non-Jewish world – the make-believe world of Venice, where there appears to be no distinction – is overwhelming. For Jessica does not have Shylock's deep well of experience to draw on. She is not a Jew in her innermost identity, but just a girl who wants to be accepted, who wants to have fun, who wants to be loved. She is the kind of child who will reject her father's way of life, and the millennia of truth that underlie it, so that she can have a Christmas tree. Jessica's superficiality is pathetic, but understandable. For where, in the financial wasteland that is the Republic, is she to obtain the deep background that makes her father so imposing a figure? In contrast to the power, the dynamic complexity, of the language Shakespeare puts in Shylock's mouth – the galaxy of insights, of emotions and sensibilities that Shylock is endowed with – in comparison to her father, Jessica is a tragedy. A lost soul. Unredeemable.

And Shylock knows this, too. The disaster that befalls him when she elopes is one that he has known all his life would sooner or later strike, and one, he knows with equal certainty, that he will be powerless to prevent. All life ends in death. This insight comes to us from the great rabbis, from the Buddha, from Socrates and Plato and Aristotle, from Freud and, of course, from Shakespeare himself. Should we not imagine that Shakespeare has endowed the Old Testament firebrand who is the focal character of this problematic play with the same insight? The fleeting nature of happiness, of attachment...? And yet, in Shylock's own world, as we have now seen, the one thing that lasts forever is true love. Lasts, indeed, beyond the grave. As Shakespeare has it in the sonnets, love that "bears it out, even to the edge of doom."[5]

The Trial's the Thing

How does Shakespeare do it? What are the mechanics, the legalities, and the sophistries that Portia uses to lay low the Jew and carry the day for the home team? – Because, let's face it, in Shakespeare's England, the Jews are definitely the out-of-towners.

If the audience needs additional reassurance that this Jew is going down, they are given it in a grand dollop at the opening of the trial scene. The Duke of Venice appears and immediately falls to commiserating with Antonio. This is behavior that in a modern American courtroom would lead to the judge's being removed from the bench. In the legal system of the historical Venice, with which Shakespeare appears to have had a more than passing familiarity, such behavior would likewise probably not have been acceptable. But no sooner is the brief exchange of mutual comforts between judge and accused over, than the Duke orders, "Go one and bring the Jew into the court." Antonio, you see, has a name; Shylock no longer does. The trial has not even opened and already the destruction has begun.

To our eyes, Shylock's case is correct, but perhaps only in the most literal terms. A degree of literalness, in fact, that we find intellectually jarring: will a man make a bargain for a pound of his neighbor's flesh? Will he go so far as to enforce the bargain? Even the most ardent supporter of Shylock must agree with the Duke's opening speech to the claimant: the joke has gone far enough.

> DUKE. Shylock, the world thinks, and I think so too,
>   That thou but leadest this fashion of thy malice
>   To the last hour of act, and then 'tis thought
>   Thou'lt show thy mercy and remorse more strange
>   Than is thy strange apparent cruelty;
>   And where thou now exact the penalty,
>   Which is a pound of this poor merchant's flesh,
>   Thou wilt not only loose the forfeiture,
>   But touch'd with human gentleness and love,
>   Forgive a moiety of the principal,
>   Glancing an eye of pity on his losses
>   That have of late so huddled on his back,
>   Enow to press a royal merchant down,
>   And pluck commiseration of his state
>   From brassy bosoms and rough hearts of flint,
>   From stubborn Turks and Tartars never train'd
>   To offices of tender courtesy:
>   We all expect a gentle answer, Jew!

Shylock's answer contains key elements. He begins by stating "by our holy Sabbath have I sworn / To have the due and forfeit of my bond." He then challenges the Duke, Venice, and all the Republic stands for:

> SHYLOCK. If you deny it, let the danger light
> Upon your charter and your city's freedom!

It is a singular quality of the character of Shylock that there is no wrong way to play him. He comes off equally successfully whether presented as a buffoon or as a hero, as tragic, courageous, cowardly, crafty, foolish, virtuous, or wicked. In Shakespeare's original production, the star player of the troupe, Richard Burbage, is said to have played him in an orange wig and beard, and with a grand pointy shovel of a false nose. Shakespeare's Shylock was a child's bogeyman turned into a full-scale stage punching bag. For the regular audience at the Globe – called the Groundlings, because they stood on the ground right up to the edges of the stage; also called the Penny Stinkards, for reasons which, on brief reflection, should be obvious – this was exactly the Jew they wished to see: an incompetent buffoon of a villain, too bumbling to get his wickedness quite right, too Jewish to deserve anything but contempt.

There is in this portrayal something of the subservience of a non-person who exists only at the whim of the ruling classes. Wealthy and successful in business though he may be, Shylock ultimately must grovel for permission to remain within the society whose very existence depends fundamentally on his business dealings. Although the audience of 1596 would not have been expected to remember the exchequer of the Jews (prior to the expulsion order of 1290), it is readily understood that Shylock, by making capital available, greases the wheels of the Venetian economy. And he does this by engaging in what the Elizabethans called "usury," defined as lending money at interest. In emulation of the biblical commandment, Christians were prohibited from making a living by lending money. The Aristotelian concept, which informed the Christian view of usury, was that interest is an unnatural parody of sexual reproduction. In the natural world, one's wealth grew by the reproduction of one's flocks, crops, and family. In the unnatural world of commerce, one's wealth grows improperly. Two sheep get together and make a third sheep. The notion of two ducats lying together and producing a third was, to the Elizabethan world view, a form of heresy. It should be noted that the ducat was a uniquely Italian form of currency. The gold coins were introduced in Genoa and Florence in 1252, and in Venice in 1284, another argument in favor of Shakespeare's choice of setting for a play about the moral complexities of money.

The Elizabethan writer and philosopher Francis Bacon (1561–1626), writing in his 1625 essay "Of Usury," gives a quick and telling glimpse of current thinking on the subject:

> Many have made witty invectives against usury. They say it is a pity the devil should have God's part, which is the tithe [one-tenth of one's goods; this biblical standard, first quoted in relation to Abraham and Jacob, remains Christianity's standard measure of financial obligation]. That the usurer is the greatest Sabbath-breaker, because his plough goeth every Sunday [i.e., Sundays too are reckoned in the calculation of the time value of interest].... That the usurer breaketh the first law that was made for mankind after the fall, which was, *in sudore vultus tui comedes panem tuum* ["By the sweat of thy brow shalt thou eat thy bread"]; not *in sudore vultus alieni.* ["By the sweat of the brows of others"]. That usurers should have orange-tawny bonnets, because they do judaize [referring to the outlandish headgear Jews were forced to wear in parts of Europe]. That it is against nature for money to beget money; and the like.[6]

Bacon, in fact, comes down in favor of permitting usury, for "men are so hard of heart as they will not lend freely." Bacon – and

Venice, and Shakespeare too – recognize that cash is a lubricant to the world of business. The easy hypocrisy of Shakespeare's society was enabled by the existence of a class of people not fully human, and whom the audience could excoriate for their own sins: a scapegoat. Jews, who officially did not exist in Shakespeare's England, were the perfect target: they were known for this repulsive economic behavior; they were rumored to be possessed of other horrifying traits, including a bizarre and particularly foul odor of the body, not to mention remarkable sexual traits and practices (Jewish women were sexually insatiable; Jewish men had multiple sex organs; one particularly inventive belief was that Jewish men menstruated). In short, you definitely would not want your sister to marry one.

The Jew, then, was good for one thing in particular: for doing the dirty work that greased the cogs, that turned the wheel, that drove the economy, that floated the wealth that supported good and proud and virtuous Christian Europe. As Caliban can curse, the Jew can lend money.

It is not the place, in the context of the trial scene, to discuss the extensive metaphors and parallels that Shakespeare gives, both to the Old Testament – specifically the Jacob narrative – and perhaps to his own family story. Let us merely tease the reader with the observation that Jacob is famous for causing Laban's flocks to reproduce wildly. Let us also observe that Shakespeare, coming from a Papist family, but growing up in Protestant England, had probably personally witnessed the public execution of his wife's close kinsman, convicted of sedition for the crime of being a Jesuit. Finally, it is no stretch to imagine that Shakespeare had some contact with some of the Jews residing in London in his day. The section of London where the Globe Theatre was re-established, Southwark, was a bohemian milieu, home to artists, and to outcast intellectuals, "strangers" (as people from other countries and ethnicities were called), and to a ragtag parallel economy in which these other groups had opportunity to participate.

Enter Shylock, then, with a bag full of ducats. It is all he has. And before the play has ended, the justice of the Republic shall do him out of it.

But stay... Are we being unnecessarily harsh on Venice? Portia, it is true, is a dishonest conniver, a racist, a closed-minded bitch who manipulates every situation to her own advantage. In short, she's just a young woman trying to survive and make some breathing space for herself in a man's world. She has been saddled with a ridiculous bond – the promise embedded in her dead father's will, according to which she must marry any man who chooses the correct casket. The ludicrousness of the will is underscored by the corollary: any man who attempts to choose, and fails, must swear never to wed. The great Shakespearean, Hartley Granville-Barker, compares the bond of the caskets to the tale of Jack and the Beanstalk. Both, he says, are pretty little fairy tales.

Just as Portia manipulates the bond of the caskets, and ends by marrying Bassanio, her own choice, after all, she will also manipulate the bond of the rings. In their twinned nuptials, Bassanio and Gratiano are given rings by their new wives, Portia and her serving-lady, Nerissa. Grand promises are exacted never to part ring from flesh, and oaths of eternal love and faithfulness are sworn, the which being no sooner accomplished, than Bassanio and Gratiano are off to Venice to ransom Antonio's flesh with Portia's ducats. The play will end with Portia emerging the clear winner: indeed, she establishes eternal control over Bassanio and will clearly call the shots throughout their marriage. Bassanio has won the lady, and with her the estate. But Portia leads him into her (now his) mansion with a clear hint that it is she who will control the sexual relationship. In winning, Bassanio has become her utter slave.

But in between Portia's triumphant manipulations of the caskets and of the rings, we have the somewhat more troubling confrontation with Shylock, a scene which Portia likewise manipulates, and likewise dominates.

Shylock, his reason somewhat unhinged by the defection of his daughter Jessica, seeks to use the court as a forum for airing his grief; the legalized murder of Antonio will be his recompense, and all Venice will be forced to be on his side, even as he slays their wealthiest and most successful businessman, the very symbol of all that Venice stands for.

Immediately on the heels of Portia's most famous speech ("The quality of mercy is not strain'd") Shylock spits back his response: "My deeds upon my head! I crave the law, / The penalty and forfeit of my bond."

One need not be an Elizabethan churchgoer to hear the parallel to the cries of the bloodthirsty Jews at the trial of Christ: "Let his blood be upon us, and upon our children, and upon our children's children!" But Shylock's downfall is precisely that he goes for the ultimate measure of the written law rather than the socially acceptable substitute. After all, at Shylock's entrance, the Duke addresses him with kind words and says that all the world expects him to relent, "touch'd with human gentleness and love.... We all expect a gentle answer, Jew!"

Shylock, then, has fallen into the same trap that has victimized the other men in this play: he takes the business of the contract seriously. And it is Portia's special gift to be able to see when men have trapped themselves in an earnest corner. Indeed, even though she was supposedly unrecognizable to her own husband, the trial scene should have served as a warning to Bassanio not to part with his ring. If he had learned nothing from watching bonds and contracts in action, he should have known this much.

Further, once Shylock transcends the merciful outcome being urged on him, there is no going back: the Doctor of Laws (Portia in disguise) will not permit him to recoup his cash, but insists that he shall have his bond. The technicalities she poses are: he must not spill a drop of Antonio's blood, nor shall he take one jot more, or less, than a pound of flesh. Under these impossible circumstances, Shylock realizes that he has lost utterly. As we observed earlier, it is only the modern reader who is surprised at this outcome. Shakespeare's audience would certainly have known that the Jew could not come away a winner, and it is likely that Shylock himself knows that his own downfall has come. In forcing the issue to the extreme, in invoking the strict letter of the law of the Republic of Venice, Shylock has risked everything. If he wins his suit, he gains the horrid and pitiful victory of murdering a fellow human being who, if an unpleasant anti-Semite, is still not responsible for the death of Shylock's wife, nor for the elopement of his daughter. If he loses, he is forced to assimilate into Venetian society.

One facet of the trial that is never commented upon is its aspect of *auto da fé*. Shylock is served up as a tremendous entertainment. Portia, with her mastery of dramatic timing, milks the scene for all it is worth; read the scene closely, watch the cadences of her speech, the swells and the releases of tension as she urges Shylock over and over again to take up the knife and do the deed. Like the trial and execution of Lopez – and certainly like the public trial and execution of Jesus – this is high entertainment. For a society that does not have the modern benefit of remote control, that is forced to take in its stories whole, either hearing them read aloud in church or seeing them played out on the boards, this is a real break in the monotony. Antonio and Portia both make their first appearance suffering from deadly ennui. Antonio is probably a lost cause – he has, after all, lost the company of the object of his own fixation, Bassanio. Portia, though, is all revved up and proceeds to switch channels and go after her own husband.

A Jew destroyed publicly! The Law of the Republic stood on its head! The laws of nature themselves turned inside out, as both Portia and Nerissa pass themselves off as men right under the noses of their husbands – and remember that in Shakespeare's day these were boy actors playing the part of women disguising themselves as men. Portia appears *ex machina* and down goes all before her! *That's* entertainment!

One final note on the outcome of the hearing: The Duke decrees that half of Shylock's wealth shall be paid to the state in the form of a fine; the other half shall go to Antonio. Antonio, for his part, argues that the fine, representing half of Shylock's wealth, should not be imposed. As for the half accorded to himself, Antonio proposes to administer it during Shylock's lifetime – and possibly, although nothing is quite clear from the text, to continue to pay Shylock the profits – and only to turn over the principal amount to Jessica and her husband, Lorenzo, after Shylock's death. The lone condition imposed by Antonio is, of course, that Shylock must convert to Christianity. Shylock, feeling suddenly unwell – and who would not? – shuffles off the stage and is heard from no more. It is, perhaps, an ignominious fall for one who laid such store by the law. But in the world as Shakespeare sees it, there are no stark whites and blacks, but only shadowy ambiguities. Those sworn to uphold the law play fast and loose with it. Those bound by oaths and promises, by troth of marriage or by the written testament of a dead father, all seek ways to escape their obligations. The great, such as Portia, rise to the occasion and take control of their environment. Those who, like Bassanio, are blinded by society's standards believe all that glisters to be gold. They are the poorest fools of all. They will have their gold, for all the good it will do them.

Finis: Test Pattern – At the Edge of Night

Finally, then, there is Shylock. As a literary character, he is one of the most complex in world literature. While he can be, and has been, successfully portrayed in any character or style, running the range from hero to villain, from tragic to slapstick hilarity, the arc of the part itself goes through an incredible emotional range as the story unfolds. He goes through a transformation, from petulant businessman, through moments of social sycophancy, to a descent into wrathful unreason – or perhaps a bizarre excess of reason – which proves his undoing.

Shylock is one of a dying breed. There appears to be no thriving Jewish community in Venice. Perhaps we are meant to presuppose it, as all the world knew of the Ghetto and its inhabitants. Perhaps we are meant to view Shylock as anomalous, as an accidental survivor. But as it is inevitable that he will convert to Christianity, it is possible that the greatest tragedy, for Shylock personally, is not his forced conversion but the loss of his daughter. Remember, Shylock is the only character in this play for whom love has eternal meaning. Shylock is the only one who keeps the ring his beloved gives to him. The tragedy of Shylock's downfall comes from expecting too much of the world. The Old Testament is the book of laws. In it, God lays down checklists to guide the righteous. Those who fail to complete the checklist must suffer. In the New Testament, those who cannot themselves complete the checklist are permitted to seek out a miracle, the intervention of the Redeemer. And in order to be redeemed, they gladly give up something of who they are.

Shylock, even after he walks off the stage, remains the throbbing presence of this play long after the curtain has been rung down. Shylock, the man who stands on principle. Shylock, the man who hews faithfully to his tradition. Shylock, who has a clear vision of both love and law and will not yield an inch in either.

Truly, no society can accommodate such a man as this.

Further Reading

The definitive work on the overall question of Jews in Elizabethan society remains James Shapiro's *Shakespeare and the Jews* (New York: Columbia University Press, 1996). Readers interested in the play itself, and in the history of the character of Shylock, are referred to John Gross's excellent book *Shylock: A Legend and Its Legacy* (New York: Simon & Schuster, 1992). An insight into the political and moral setting of the play is offered in *Shakespeare's Politics*, by Allan Bloom, with Harry V. Jaffa (New York: Basic Books, 1964). As always, the insights of Harold Goddard are fascinating and far-ranging; see, for instance, *The Meaning of Shakespeare* (Chicago: University of Chicago Press, 1960). Finally, readers who wish an in-depth approach to the play should consult the Arden edition, with an extensive introduction which, while thorough and scholarly, is quite accessible to the general reader.

Notes

1. *Arden Shakespeare: The Merchant of Venice*, 2nd Series, 2nd edition, © 1964 by SHAKESPEARE/BROWN. Reprinted with permission of Global Rights Group, a division of Thomson Learning (www.thomsonrights.com).
2. New York: Riverhead Books, 1998
3. Cambridge, MA: Harvard University Press, 1997
4. *Arden Shakespeare: Othello*, 3rd Series, 2nd edition. © 1996 by SHAKE-SPEARE/HONIGMANN. Reprinted with permission of Global Rights Group, a division of Thomson Learning (www.thomsonrights.com).
5. Sonnet 116
6. www.authorama.com (Authorama: Public Domain Books).

The Case of Alfred Dreyfus

ROBERT A. GARBER

I.

The morning of Saturday, January 5, 1895, was overcast in Paris. At the École Militaire, within view of the tower recently erected by Alexandre Gustave Eiffel, thirty-five-year-old Alfred Dreyfus of the General Staff, convicted of treason, was paraded into the courtyard to be formally degraded and drummed out of his country's service. There the majestic sergeant major of the Republican Guard, who appeared, in his plumed helmet, to be over seven feet tall, ripped the emblematic buttons and braiding from the officer's uniform. (They had been lightly basted in place for the solemn ceremony.) Then the sergeant major broke the captain's sword over his knee. (The weapon had been scored beforehand for the purpose.)

Thus degraded, Dreyfus was marched around the quad by four regal escorts. He loudly proclaimed his innocence to the assembled troops. "Soldiers, they are degrading an innocent man. Soldiers, they are dishonoring an innocent man. Long live France! Long live the army!" The vast mob on the other side of the courtyard fence responded. "Down with the Jew! Death to the traitor! Kill all the Jews!"[1]

II.

In 1791 France was the first nation in Europe to grant civil equality to all its Jewish residents.[2] A century later, in the Third Republic,

27

there was a high degree of Jewish assimilation in French civil life. How, then, did the remarkable scene at the École Militaire come to pass?

There was open populist anti-Semitism in the republic, it should be noted, well before the degradation of Alfred Dreyfus. The endemic anti-Semitism, always present to a degree, increased considerably in the spring of 1886 with the publication of *La France juive*, a two-volume, 1200-page screed by the notorious Edouard Drumont. His text blamed the Jews for all of France's troubles. According to Drumont and his adherents, Christian Aryans alone were possessed of decency, while Semites were naturally spies and traitors. *La France juive* initiated a flood tide of similar sentiments in newspapers and books. and Drumont's success allowed him to establish the anti-Semitic daily newspaper *Libre Parole* in April 1892, just in time for it to take a commanding place in the campaign against Dreyfus.

In 1889, an artistic candidate for municipal office issued a campaign poster (which he illustrated himself) with the inscription: "The Jews are great only because we are on our knees.... This is not a religious question. The Jew is of a different race and the enemy of our race. Judaism, that is our enemy!"[3]

And there was the Panama scandal. Only a few years before the courtyard degradation, the French company organized to build the Panama Canal had become bankrupt. Shareholders, mostly small investors, lost hundreds of thousands of dollars. Before the bankruptcy, many legislators, cabinet officials, and newspaper publishers were bribed by the company in an effort to forestall its collapse. It happened that Jewish corporate representatives handed over the actual bribes. Their activities also engendered significant anti-Semitism in France.

The fact that Dreyfus was a Jew from Alsace had particular significance for the French. As a result of the Franco-Prussian War of 1870, the provinces of Alsace and Lorraine had been ceded to the Prussian victors. Residents of the provinces were obliged to decide whether they were henceforth to be French citizens or

Prussians, whether they were to emigrate to the French hexagon or stay at home. The Dreyfus family, in the textile business in the Alsatian city of Mulhouse and, it was said, speaking French with a decidedly Teutonic accent, opted for French nationality.[4] The national shame of 1870, however, and the need for *revanche* caused many nativists to nurture suspicions about residents of the ceded regions. Alsatians may have thought of themselves as French, but somehow they were considered as German by much of the rest of France. This did not auger well for Alfred Dreyfus.

Dreyfus was the rare Jewish officer on the General Staff.[5] That, too, was significant in the events that led to his degradation.

III.

The Dreyfus case, which was quickly to grow into the international "Dreyfus Affair," began in the offices of the Statistical Section of the French army. This unit had little to do with statistics; it was the army's counterintelligence agency. In the last decade of the nineteenth century, the section, with five officers assigned to it, was under the command of Colonel Jean Sandherr, an outspoken anti-Semite. The colonel was mortally ill and not an especially effective commander. Second to him was Major Hubert Henry, who managed the section's paid informants, including Madame Bastian, the wife of a noncommissioned officer. Madame Bastian worked as a cleaning woman in the German embassy. She would retrieve scraps from the embassy's wastebaskets and pass them on, in what became known as "the ordinary way," to the Statistical Section.

In the last week of September 1894, apparently by "the ordinary way," an extraordinary document arrived.[6] Madame Bastian had retrieved from the wastebasket of the German military attaché, Lieutenant Colonel Maximilian von Schwartzkoppen, a handwritten document that came to be known as "the *bordereau*." The *bordereau* (a cover note or memorandum) startled Henry, who was the first to see it, and the officers to whom he showed it. The note read, in part:

Although I have no news that you wish to see me, nevertheless I am sending you, Monsieur, some interesting information:

1. A note on the hydraulic brake of the 120 mm. gun and the way this gun has behaved;
2. A note on the covering troops (some modifications will be made under the new plan);
3. A note on a modification in artillery formations;
4. A note concerning Madagascar;
5. The projected Field Artillery Firing Manual (14 March, 1894).

The last document is extremely difficult to obtain.... I am just about to leave for maneuvers.

The document was, of course, unsigned, and a search for the identity of the writer began. Alfred Dreyfus was quickly nominated. Clearly, the author of the *bordereau* was an artillery officer assigned to the General Staff. That fit Dreyfus. He was not well liked anyway. Senior officers were informed and a secret dossier on Dreyfus was established. Handwriting experts, including the erratic Alphonse Bertillion, could not agree on whose hand had produced the *bordereau*.

Within three weeks after the incriminating message arrived at the Statistical Section, orders were delivered to Dreyfus at home to appear at the office of the Chief of the General Staff for "an examination of probationary officers." Oddly, the last words of the order were "civilian dress." (It was easier to arrest a man who was not in uniform).

The scene at staff headquarters was melodramatic. Dreyfus was received by Commandant du Paty de Clam, a well-connected anti-Semite. One observer characterized du Paty as "pretentious, monocle in eye...a disturbing character, with a morbid mentality, a shadowy and unhinged imagination, a strange mixture of fanaticism, extravagance, and folly."[7] (Not always in uniform, he was a transvestite as well as a soldier).[8] Du Paty had bandaged his right hand, and he asked Dreyfus, while he waited for the general, to write a letter for him. He dictated a text that incorporated passages recalling the *bordereau.* He accused Dreyfus of trembling as he wrote. When the dictation was over, du Paty startled him by shouting, "In the name of the law, I arrest you; you are accused of the crime of high treason!"

Dreyfus, distressed and confused, was left alone with a pistol, so that he might avail himself of a stroke the army deemed honorable. He was not inclined to oblige. Major Henry of the Statistical Section, hidden like Polonius, had secretly witnessed the dramatic interrogation. He escorted Dreyfus to a prison cell, where he was held for several days before being examined further. Then Henry leaked the story of the Jew's arrest to Drumont's anti-Semitic *Libre Parole.* Its story of espionage was picked up by all the papers in Paris.

Du Paty paid a call on Alfred's wife, Lucie, instructing her to be silent about her husband's condition lest there be unnamed grave international consequences. In December, the accused man was finally allowed to contact his family, and it was then that he was first shown a copy of the *bordereau.*

That month, in a room dominated by a huge painting of Jesus crucified,[9] the army conducted its court-martial of Dreyfus in secret. The prisoner, his brother, Mathieu Dreyfus, and his lawyer, Demange, were the only defense representatives present. None of them ever saw the confidential file prepared by the prosecution for the eyes of the seven military judges alone and presented to them by du Paty before the verdict. Handwriting experts were called, but could not agree. The putative expert, Bertillion, offered a detailed and complex theory that Dreyfus had forged his own handwriting to disguise authorship of the *bordereau.* The trial judges could not understand his convoluted reasoning. To clarify matters, Major Henry pointed dramatically to Dreyfus. He declared "As to the traitor, there he is!" Swearing to it as an honorable person, he would not say how he knew.

The verdict, after a four-day trial, was "guilty." Dreyfus was sentenced to perpetual incarceration.

IV.

Devil's Island lies eight miles off the coast of French Guiana, very near the Equator, the smallest of the Îles du Salut, a three-island group. Just off the shoulder of South America, it is a narrow strip in the Atlantic, less than three-quarters of a mile by a quarter of a mile. Previously a leper colony, Devil's Island was outfitted with a small hut as the new home of former captain Alfred Dreyfus, its sole prisoner. A guardhouse was topped by a watchtower. Dreyfus was transported there in February 1895, a few weeks after the drama in the courtyard of the École Militaire. He was to remain there for more than four years, alone except for his warders, who were ordered not to speak to him. He was allotted a soldier's food rations, *sans* wine. Bread, lard, dry vegetables were the staples, though sometimes there would be pork, green vegetables, or some raw meat that Dreyfus could roast for himself. Paper was provided for correspondence and a journal (which he decorated with compulsively symmetrical doodles); the sheets were counted. Sleep in his barred hut was difficult because of the heat, the crawling bugs, the flying insects attracted by the permanent night light, and the activities of the noisy guards. During his stay on the island, his brother Mathieu Dreyfus consulted a forerunner of today's public relations experts to revive interest in the case. The adviser planted a story that the prisoner had somehow escaped. The result was construction of a palisade fence around Alfred's hut and an order for the prisoner to be shackled in bed every night, unable to turn. Weather permitting, exercise was confined to chopping wood or a stroll in his small compound, accompanied by a guard. Headaches were the norm and fever visited the prisoner often.[10]

Mid-summer of that year, the debilitated Sandherr retired from service, soon to carry secrets of the Statistical Section with him to the grave. Hubert Henry did not, as he expected, succeed Sandherr. Command of the Statistical Section was given to Colonel Georges Piquart. And that was to make all the difference in the Dreyfus Affair.

Piquart, age forty-one, was, like Dreyfus, from Alsace. He

was regarded as a superior military officer. Possessed of language skills, he was intelligent, alert, and reliable. He had been an official witness at the degradation and the court-martial of Dreyfus and had escorted him to the histrionic interview with du Paty. He knew Dreyfus slightly and didn't like him. Indeed, Piquart had no particular liking for Jews in general.

As Piquart settled into command of the Statistical Section, it became increasingly clear that leaks of military information continued. Was there another spy in addition to Dreyfus?

If there was a spy, Mathieu Dreyfus knew, it was never his brother. Throughout 1895, he led the prisoner's family in the effort to enlist adherents to their cause, though in a circumspect way. Declaring open war on the army did not seem a promising course. It was a difficult year for Mathieu and for Alfred's wife, Lucie. The president of the Republic, Félix Faure, was an anti-Dreyfussard. More promising contacts, like Senator Sheurer-Kestner of Alsace and the Jewish writer Bernard Lazare listened politely, but were not yet persuaded to speak out for the Dreyfussard cause.

Then, in March of the following year, a strange document found its way to the Statistical Section and Piquart's desk. In 1896, the telephone, patented scarcely two decades earlier, was not in common use for quick communication. Instead, Paris had a system of pneumatic tubes. A Parisian could take a message to the nearest post office and have it whisked to a central office, from where it continued, by tube, to the post office nearest the addressee. A bicyclist would deliver the message within minutes after it was first posted. A special blue post card, known as a *petit bleu*, was used for the purpose. It was a *petit bleu* that Piquart examined. It read:

Major Esterhazy,
27, rue de la Bienfaisance,
Paris

Sir: What I want particularly is a more detailed explanation than the one you gave me the other day on the matter in question. I would ask you, therefore, to be good enough to give it to me in writing, so that I may be able to decide whether or not I can continue my relations with the firm of R.

[signed] C.

The document was addressed to a Major Esterhazy. Was there another traitor?

Major Marie Charles Ferdinand Walsin-Esterhazy, then forty-eight, was an adventurer. The dissolute scion of an illegitimate branch of a noble Hungarian family, he fancied himself a count and bitterly resented his diminished circumstances. He felt persecuted and despised virtually everyone. It was this French officer who had called on Schwartzkoppen months before the *bordereau* was written to offer his services as an agent for Germany.

Years before he involved Dreyfus in his affairs, Esterhazy wrote to his mistress that if he were told that he would be transformed "tomorrow as a Uhlan [Prussian cavalry] captain running through Frenchmen with my saber, I would certainly be perfectly happy.... I would not hurt a dog, but I would have a hundred thousand Frenchmen killed with pleasure." He reviled Jews no more than any others and he maintained Jewish connections, notably with his fellow officer Maurice Weil. He acted as second for a Jewish duelist.[11] A gambler perpetually in debt, Esterhazy borrowed widely, especially from his Jewish acquaintances, and repaid his debts rarely.

The *petit bleu* had come from the German military attaché. Colonel von Schwartzkoppen had apparently dictated it – it was not in his hand, as Piquart noted. The document was torn into several pieces and then reassembled. It bore no stamp and obviously was never sent to the named recipient, Major Esterhazy.

Piquart informed his superior officer, General Boisdeffre, and Minister of War Billot that Esterhazy was implicated by the *petit bleu*. Boisdeffre, fearful of "another Dreyfus Affair," instructed the colonel to proceed with caution. If Esterhazy proved guilty, he could be cashiered quietly.

Alone, Piquart pondered the *petit bleu* and its addressee. Inquiry of fellow staff officers revealed that Esterhazy was a difficult man. He had poor work habits and often asked about military matters that were beyond his purview. Piquart obtained copies of Esterhazy's handwriting. They seemed familiar. He placed them side by side with his copy of the *bordereau*. The identity of the script was obvious and disquieting. The samples of Esterhazy's writing, with identifying markers hidden, were confirmed by handwriting consultants (including Bertillion) to match the *bordereau*. The possibility that Dreyfus had been wrongly convicted "terrified" Piquart, as he later recalled.

He reviewed the secret file that had been shown to the judges of the Dreyfus court-martial. Contrary to orders, it had not been destroyed. In it was a letter referring to "the scoundrel D –," but in the world of clandestine operations, initials meant little.[12] There was, in fact, nothing of substance to convict the man on Devil's Island. The Germans had denied any connection with Dreyfus and the denial carried credence because a French agent reported that the Germans had only one French army informant at the time, an infantry officer who had been on maneuvers in the fall of the year of the *bordereau*. That described Esterhazy, not Dreyfus.

Piquart returned to Boisdeffre and Billot. He was told to consult with General Gonse, deputy to the chief of staff. Gonse responded, "So, we made a mistake" as Piquart later recalled. He told Piquart to "keep the two affairs separate." When the colonel pursued the matter with Gonse, the general asked why Piquart was concerned if "that Jew remains on Devil's Island."

"But Dreyfus is innocent," Piquart answered.

Saying that the case could not be reopened, Gonse told him, "If you say nothing, no one will ever know."

"What you say is abominable, General. I do not know what I shall do, but in any event, I shall not carry this secret with me to the grave." And he did not.

Piquart soon received orders. He was to conduct an inspection tour that would take him out of Paris – the center of Dreyfussard activity – and eventually to North Africa. In his absence Major Henry would act as chief of military counterintelligence.

Henry had noted his chief's concerns about the Dreyfus case. For the honor of the army and unknown to Piquart, he undertook to "sweeten" the file. On one letter from Schwartzkoppen, he scratched out the initial *P* and inserted a *D*. A letter to Piquart from a female friend, signed "Speranza," was doctored to indicate that a fictitious "Jewish syndicate" worked for Dreyfus. Henry's *tour de force* was the fabrication of a letter from the Italian military attaché in Paris to Schwartzkoppen in which "this Jew" was mentioned. It was constructed of two torn sheets of paper reassembled as if it had arrived from Madam Bastian in "the ordinary way." A glance at the sweetened file was convincing to the generals.

On leave in Paris in June 1897, Piquart called on his lawyer, Louis Leblois. In Tunisia, the troubled soldier had fallen from his horse and had come to a new realization of the temporal nature of life. A codicil to his will was prepared. He discussed the Dreyfus Affair with Leblois, and in a sealed envelope he placed a narrative of his part in the Affair. He wrote without equivocation that Esterhazy was guilty and Dreyfus was innocent. In the event of his death, the envelope was to be forwarded to the president of the Republic, "who alone should be made cognizant of its contents."

Not long after meeting with his client, Leblois met a nephew of the senator from Alsace, Auguste Sheurer-Kestner, who happened to mention that his uncle had an interest in the Dreyfus Affair. Leblois arranged a meeting with Sheurer-Kestner, the senior vice-president of the Senate. Sworn to confidentiality, the Alsatian senator, now convinced of the identity of the sole traitor, spoke to diverse politicians and army officers, without revealing names or the source of his knowledge. The anti-Dreyfus regime was thus alerted, and protecting Esterhazy became the order of the day. He was warned that he was about to be named. The warning was given in a bizarre nighttime scene in a park, delivered by members of the Statistical Section and du Paty, who affected a disguise of dark glasses. On the way to the park, fearing arrest rather than a warning from the army, Esterhazy had stopped by Schwartzkoppen's office to demand cover. He was ordered to leave. So he needed protection, if not by the Germans, then from the French. To his relief, the army stood ready to oblige.

Before he received his travel orders, Piquart had been suspected of disclosing a copy of the *bordereau* to the press when a copy of it appeared in a newspaper, *Le Matin*. It was, in fact, supplied to the paper by Mathieu Dreyfus,[13] and by the end of 1897 copies of the traitor's handwriting along with that of Alfred Dreyfus appeared all through the country. A Parisian stock broker named Castro recognized the handwriting of his sometime client Walsin-Esterhazy and so informed Mathieu. Mathieu accused Esterhazy to Sheurer-Kestner, who, now relieved of his secret burden, agreed. The earnest brother publicly denounced the putative count. "I have the honor to make it known to you," he wrote to Minister of War Billot, "that the author...is Count Walsin Esterhazy." He sent a copy of his letter to the press. A copy of Esterhazy's "Uhlan letter" found its way to the newspapers. Now that Esterhazy was publicly accused, Sheurer-Kestner brought the matter to the floor of the Senate. "There is no Dreyfus Affair," declared the prime minister.

Assured of the army's support, Esterhazy reacted to the damning publicity by insisting on an inquiry that would establish his innocence and restore what he imagined was his good name. Because of the secrets he knew and the damage they feared he could wreak, the concerned generals and his friends in the Statistical Section were bound to support his histrionic protestations. They did so promptly. In January 1898, a two-day pro forma court-martial resulted in an acquittal. There were cries of "Long live the army!" and "Down with the Jews!" from apprehensive citizens.

The acquittal was handed down on January 11, 1898. Within

two days, a remarkable thing happened. Emile Zola, in a blazing fury, wrote and published one of the most celebrated open letters in all literary history. It covered the front page of *L'Aurore*, a daily newspaper whose editor, Georges Clemenceau, probably provided the title for Zola. *J'accuse!* it was called, and it moved the world.

Zola, then fifty-seven, the author of well-regarded works of naturalism like *Nana* and *Germinal*, was at the height of his powers as the leading novelist of France. An ardent campaigner for social justice, he had recently written exhortations to the youth of France and the people of France imploring them to fight "for Humanity, for Justice, and for Truth!"

Now, in *J'accuse!*, Zola addressed Félix Faure, the president of the Republic, advising him to have a care for his reputation. Beware, he warned, of a "mud stain on your name – I was going to say your reign...this abominable Dreyfus affair!" He accused du Paty of duplicity, describing him with sharp accuracy. He reviewed the known facts of the case and the activities of Sandherr, the generals, and Esterhazy. He recalled the doubts of Sheurer-Kestner, which had grown to convictions, and Piquart's performance of his duty as an honest man. On and on he vented indignation. Finally, he accused five generals of iniquity. He accused three handwriting experts of lies and fraud "unless a medical examination should declare them afflicted with diseases of the eye and of the mind" (Bertillion was not named). He accused the War Office of an "abominable campaign" to spin the story (as we would now say), and he accused the panel in the court-martial of Dreyfus of violating the law. He was intentionally laying himself open to punishment for defamation. He invited the charge.

J'accuse! caused a sensation. In a city besotted by newspapers, the issue of *L'Aurore* sold 300,000 copies as soon as it left the presses. Messages of support from around the globe were conveyed to the writer, but in Paris, police were posted at his home to prevent attacks from the mob, who added cries of "Death to Zola!" to "Death to the Jews!" and "Long live the army!" Within the week, as Zola had invited, he was charged (along with *L'Aurore's* publisher) with criminal libel and summoned to appear for trial on February 7, less than a month after publication.

When the trial began, there were demonstrations in support of the army outside the courtroom. Inside, the crowd was also agitated. The prosecution had artfully framed the indictment as narrowly as possible. Only Zola's claim that the officers of the Esterhazy court-martial had acted on specific orders was used as the basis of the criminal libel charge. Zola's wider accusations were ignored.

For many days the awed jury heard testimony from all the major figures in the Affair, save Dreyfus. There were the generals and the handwriting experts, du Paty and Henry, Piquart and Zola and Clemenceau, all in the courtroom with the lawyers and reporters. At one point, Henry accused Piquart, his former commanding officer, of indiscretion. He declared that everything he had said was "correct in every detail and I even say that Col. Piquart is lying." Piquart addressed the jury, describing his course to "truth and justice." His response concluded, "As a decent human being I had to fulfill my duty." Bertillion confused everyone with his testimony. Esterhazy, on the stand, refused to speak. Zola proclaimed the innocence of Dreyfus.

After two weeks of trial, the jury took about half an hour to return its guilty verdict, to the vocal exultation of the crowd. Zola's sentence was a fine of 3,000 francs and a year in prison. After retrial and a fruitless appeal, the novelist took refuge in England before the sentence could be imposed.

The verdict unleashed Gallic malice against Dreyfus in particular, and against Jews in general. Anti-Semitic demonstrations erupted throughout France and its colonies. From Bourges and Berry to Lyon and Avignon, there were anti-Semitic posters, threats to Jewish merchants, rallies, and cries of "Death to the Jews!," "Long live the army!," and "Long live Drumont!"[14] More than ever, newspapers and journals reveled in the unfolding story.

But if it stirred France, the verdict aroused worldwide interest, and the world, on the whole, was sympathetic to Dreyfus and the essential message of *J'accuse!*

Within a few days of the verdict, Piquart, as he foretold in his testimony, was cashiered from the service of his country. He was now free to speak his mind, and he did so. By midsummer of 1898, Esterhazy was arrested by order of Cavaignac, the new minister of war. Piquart was arrested on the charge of revealing secrets to his lawyer and spent two months in prison.

A month after the verdict against Zola, an officer in the Statistical Section reviewed the Dreyfus file. He held up the document – in which Dreyfus was named – that was supposed to have been sent to Schwartzkoppen from his Italian counterpart. The pieces of paper did not match. Henry's fabrication was obvious. Interrogated, he confessed to the counterfeit. It was done "solely in the interest of my country," he asserted. He was duly arrested on August 30, 1898, and confined in a fortress. The next morning he was dead.

Henry, in a feverish night of heavy drinking, had slit his throat with a straight razor that somehow had been left in his cell. A political cartoonist portrayed the specter of Dreyfus wielding the weapon.[15] Drumont's *Libre Parole* sponsored a fund, the "Henry Monument," for the benefit of the suicide's widow. Money poured in. Henry was extolled as a martyr, his forgery as a patriotic and noble act.[16]

The next day Esterhazy, dismissed for misconduct, fled to Belgium and then to England, where he spent the rest of his life. From England, he confessed to writing the *bordereau* – as a ruse ordered by Sandherr.

The case against Dreyfus was in the process of unraveling. There were warring camps throughout French society. Writers, artists, politicians, notables, shopkeepers, everyone had opinions, forceful and certain. In the political turmoil, a new cabinet was formed, the minister of war was replaced, and the new minister, before *he* resigned, charged Piquart again. Du Paty was retired from active service. In February 1899, President Faure died and was succeeded by Emile Loubet, who was not an anti-Dreyfussard like his predecessor.[17] In June, after yet another minister of war quit, the Court of Cassation, a united appeals bench, "in solemn conclave" set aside the 1894 conviction of Dreyfus and ordered a new trial to take place at Rennes, the historic capital of Brittany. Piquart was freed. Zola returned from England. And Alfred Dreyfus, the prisoner of Devil's Island, was on his way back to France. Revision was at hand. The efforts of Mathieu and Lucie Dreyfus, of Zola and Piquart and the loyal Dreyfussards appeared to be succeeding at last. But, of course, the struggle was not quite over.

V.

That August, Rennes was the scene of a media event covered by reporters from all over the globe. For a month, three hundred sweltering reporters gleaned every scrap of information, real or imagined, and swamped the telegraph facilities with their stories. They reported on the physical appearance of the central figure. After four and a half years on Devil's Island, Dreyfus was back in uniform. He was stooped and gaunt; his hair was thin and gray. He appeared to all to be "a little old man." He was thirty-nine. His daily entrances and exits from the courtroom were through a cordon of soldiers with their backs turned to him. Though some said it was for security, most understood the formation to be a sign of dishonor.

Ninety witnesses testified, mostly for the prosecution. The traditional Anglo-American standards of evidence did not apply under the French system. Opinion, hearsay, passion – all were admissible. Some sessions were held in secret, other in open court. Generals offered their views. Piquart told his story with dignity. The prisoner, at one point, assisted the court by translating some material in German. Bertillion once again confused all with unintelligible theory supported by undecipherable charts. Once again Dreyfus proclaimed his innocence.

One morning in Rennes, Piquart and his cousin walked to court with the lawyer Fernand Labori, who had represented Zola and now was on the Dreyfus defense team with Demange. A shot was fired from behind them, and Labori, "uttering the familiar French ejaculation 'Oh, la, la!' tottered and fell."[18] His wound took him away from the court for a week (and legal challenges to the testimony of the generals suffered thereby).

On Saturday, September 9, 1899, after summations and a final plea from Dreyfus, the seven judges retired to deliberate. An hour and a half later, they returned. The verdict was extraordinary. "In the name of the French people, by a majority of five votes to two, yes, the accused is guilty. By a majority, there are extenuating circumstances." No one had ever heard of treason with extenuating circumstances! It was the one crime that never, until that day, conceded extenuating circumstances.

Reporters rushed out to file their stories. The offices of Drumont's *Libre Parole* were decorated with flags, but overseas the reaction was different. Newspapers around the world were shocked and indignant. There were suggestions that the anticipated Paris Exposition of 1900 should be boycotted.[19]

The disconsolate defense was not sure how to proceed at first. The new punishment would be just ten years' imprisonment and surely not on Devil's Island. Should the verdict be accepted? An appeal was drafted and signed while an arrangement was being formulated. On September 19, 1899, the Council of Ministers in Paris announced that Dreyfus would drop his appeal and would be pardoned "in principle." The deal was encouraged by Mathieu and the family in view of Alfred's delicate health, but it was agreed that he would be able to continue to proclaim his innocence and name the guilty man and his military associates. The minister of war issued orders that declared, "The incident is closed." But the bitter fight to reclaim the name of Dreyfus could continue. And he would be free.

VI.

On the same day that Dreyfus was pardoned, his staunch advocate, Senator Sheurer-Kestner, died at sixty-six.

From Rennes, Dreyfus traveled to his sister's home in Carpentras to be reunited with his family and to recuperate. After a time, to elude reporters and admirers, he took his family to Switzerland. They returned to Paris at the end of 1900. On Christmas Eve of that year, a bill of general amnesty was passed. It discharged all, over objections by Dreyfus and by Piquart, who would not speak to the man whose freedom he, more than anyone else, had secured. There would be no prosecution of any of the generals, not of du Paty or of Esterhazy and not of Piquart or anyone else according to the terms of the amnesty. The verdict of 1899 was not reversed.[20]

Zola had first taken to writing about the Affair in 1897 upon his return to Paris from his summer home. At the end of September 1902, the writer and his wife again returned from the country to their Paris apartment. The first night home, fumes from a blocked flue overcame Madame Zola and killed her husband.[21]

In 1906, the government reinstated Piquart and Dreyfus and promoted both of them. Dreyfus had his insignia restored in a formal rehabilitation ceremony. It was held in a courtyard at the École Militaire, where he had been degraded nearly twelve years before. He was awarded the Legion of Honor. From that day on, photographs of the aging Dreyfus consistently revealed the rosette of the Legion in his lapel. On Bastille Day the next year he retired from the army, rejecting any pension. By then, Clemenceau was prime minister. He had named General Piquart as minister of war.

In 1908, the ashes of Zola were installed in the Pantheon, the final home of the immortals of France. At the end of the ceremonies, two shots were fired and Dreyfus was slightly injured. It was just a "demonstration," the shooter asserted. He aimed "not at Dreyfus, but at Dreyfusism." No one was sure what he meant. A verdict of "temporary insanity" freed him.[22]

Early in 1914 Piquart died as result of a fall from his horse. The Great War came that summer, and Dreyfus, a reserve officer, was mobilized for service. By war's end, he had attained the rank of lieutenant colonel (and his Legion of Honor was upgraded).

Esterhazy died, in England, in 1923. Mathieu died, in France, in 1930. That year, publication of Schwartzkoppen's papers affirmed his brother's innocence.

In 1935, at the age of seventy-six, Alfred Dreyfus died in Paris. Before the next decade passed, a second world war had been waged. Madeleine Lévy, a resistance fighter and a grandchild of Alfred, was caught by the Nazis. She died in Auschwitz-Birkenau in January 1944. That same year, in Nazi-controlled Vichy France, there was a new head of the Commissariat Général aux Questions Juives – "the virtual ministry of state anti-Semitism."[23] The new arbiter of "Jewish questions" was Charles du Paty de Clam, son of Commandant du Paty de Clam, who first interrogated Alfred Dreyfus.[24]

A year later, soon after the liberation, the infamous collaborator and lifelong anti-Semite Charles Maurras was tried for providing aid to the German enemies of France.[25] Upon receiving his sentence of life behind bars (and degradation!), he cried out, "It's the revenge of Dreyfus!" Fifty years after the drama at the École Militaire, there were still obsessions with the notion of settling scores.

In 1994, in Paris, a centenary exposition of "*un tragédie de la belle époque*" was held in a building on Place Léon Blum (named for the Dreyfussard who later became premier). After a hundred years, arguments about the case of Alfred Dreyfus echoed in the halls. They still resound.

Further Reading

The available material on the Dreyfus Affair is vast. Among the recommended one-volume texts available in English are

Birnbaum, Pierre. *The Anti-Semitic Moment: A Tour of France in 1898.* New York: Hill & Wang, 2003.

Bredin, Jean-Denis. *The Affair: The Case of Alfred Dreyfus.* New York: George Braziller, 1986.

Burns, Michael. *Dreyfus: A Family Affair, 1789–1945.* New York: HarperCollins, 1991.

Chapman, Guy. *The Dreyfus Case: A Reassessment.* New York: Reynal, 1955.

Halasz, Nicholas. *Captain Dreyfus: History of a Mass Hysteria.* New York: Simon & Schuster, 1955.

Hoffman, Robert L. *More than a Trial: The Struggle over Captain Dreyfus.* New York: Free Press, 1980.

Johnson, Douglas. *France and the Dreyfus Affair.* New York: Walker, 1966.

Lewis, David L. *Prisoners of Honor: The Dreyfus Affair.* New York: William Morrow, 1973.

Snyder, Louis L. *The Dreyfus Case: A Documentary History.* New Brunswick, N.J.: Rutgers University Press, 1973.

Notes

1. In the group of foreign reporters that Dreyfus passed was Theodor Herzl, on assignment for the Vienna *Neue Freie Presse.* Herzl had once believed that assimilation was the answer to anti-Semitism, but after witnessing the events of that day and the mob's hatred, he pressed the cause of a Jewish homeland. In February of the following year, he published his seminal Zionist work, *Der Judenstaat.*

2. For earlier anti-Semitism in France, see Arthur Hertzberg, *The French Enlightenment and the Jews* (New York: Columbia University Press, 1968),

3. Léon-Adolphe Willette, *Anti-Semitic Candidate* 1889, 53" × 39" lithograph poster. (Willette lost the election.)

4. One badge of the Dreyfus family's assimilation may be noted in the given names of Alfred's brothers and sisters. His great-grandfather was Abraham, his grandparents were Jacob and Rachel, and their children bore

the equally Hebraic names of Jacob, Joseph, and Raphael. Alfred's father, Raphael, however, chose to have his children bear more secular forenames. Alfred's siblings were Jacques, Henriette, Berthe, Louise, Ernestine, Léon, and Mathieu, as well as the traditional Rachel. For a history of the family generally, see M. Burns, *Dreyfus: A Family Affair, 1789–1945* (New York: HarperCollins, 1991).

5. Jewish officers and enlisted men were proportionally well represented in the military. The General Staff, however, was particularly wary of Jews.

6. The document was in unusually good condition to have arrived in "the ordinary way," according to some commentators, and not the sort of material to be lightly tossed in a wastebasket, but the consensus is still with Madame Bastian.

7. M. Paléologue, *An Intimate Journal of The Dreyfus Case*, trans. Eric Mosbacher (New York: Criterion Books 1957), p. 134.

8. Eugen Weber, *France: Fin de Siècle* (Cambridge, Mass., and London, Belknap Press, Harvard Univ. Press, 1986) 37

9. Roman Catholicism was the official state religion. The church was disestablished in France in 1905, in great measure as a result of the political turmoil following the Dreyfus Affair. The separation of church and state did not apply to Alsace-Lorraine, then under German control.

10. Vacationers can now book sailing tours to the islands.

11. Duels were not uncommon in this era. Esterhazy took part in the duel of his Jewish colleague Captain Crémieux-Foa, who challenged Drumont for his blanket accusation of Jewish officers of treason. Before the Affair's passions abated, Georges Clemenceau, then a newspaper editor, faced his fellow editor Drumont with pistols, and Piquart met Henry with swords.

12. As in the *petit bleu*, Schwartzkoppen was known by the Statistical Section to use the initial "C," for example.

13. Mathieu probably bought it from one of the handwriting consultants.

14. For a detailed survey of French anti-Semitism at the time, see P. Birnbaum, *The Anti-Semitic Moment: A Tour of France in 1898*, trans. Jane Marie Todd (New York: Hill & Wang, 2003).

15. In an unfinished letter to his wife, Henry said he was going to "take a swim in the Seine." Most commentators accept the suicide theory. But on forensic grounds, some question how the fatal stroke could have been accomplished. There was no autopsy.

16. Charles Maurras, who was later convicted of treason in World War II, initiated his long, dishonorable career as a leading promoter of the notion of the suicide as an act of martyrdom.

17. "Ministers rose and fell," wrote one reporter, "but the men of the General Staff went on forever, and each successive government underwent their pertinacious action." M. de Blowitz, "The Dreyfus Case," *Harper's Weekly*, August 19, 1899, p. 827.

18. W. Harding *Dreyfus: The Prisoner of Devil's Island* (New York: Associated Publishing Co., 1899), p. 133.

19. The fair, which bore the slogan "*Paris – Capitale du Monde Civilisé*," broke all prior attendance records.

20. The French army is stubborn in some ways. In 1994 its historian, Colonel Paul Gaujac, was summarily dismissed for his centennial study of the Affair. Concentrating on the damage to the army caused by the Affair, he wrote merely that "Dreyfus' innocence is the thesis now generally accepted by historians." *New York Times*, February 9, 1994, p. A10. He could not concede innocence, but left room for doubt with the grudging words "now generally accepted."

21. Apparently it was a simple accident, but there have been sinister suspicions. The writer Henri Troyat maintained that it was a crime, and an American reporter who was on the scene agreed with the police – "accidental death," he said; "But I've always wondered how that flue came to be stuffed up." *New York Times*, August 6, 1961, p. 70.

22. The vaunted eleventh edition of the *Encyclopædia Britannica* (1910) contained an unsigned one-paragraph entry under "Dreyfus, Alfred" which alluded to the shooting. It also had a substantial entry under "Anti-Semitism" that more fully discussed the Affair. It was written by a Jewish Briton, Lucien Wolf, a distinguished historian. By 1950, the fourteenth edition's much-enlarged entry under "Dreyfus, Alfred" never used the words "Jew" and "Jewish" – although the last paragraph retained the mention that Gregori, who fired at Dreyfus in 1908, was "an anti-Semite journalist." The endemic anti-Semitism, patent throughout the Affair, was not considered. The entry was written by a Paris-based journalist, Pierre Bernus. The current fifteenth edition includes the words omitted by Bernus. The Wolf essay survives in revised and expanded form.

23. Michael Curtis, *Verdict on Vichy* (New York: Arcade Publishing, 2002), p. 116.

24. Ibid., p. 46.

25. As the British historian Denis W. Brogan noted, Maurras was "condemned in a French court at Lyon for treason, on a charge that might, in fact, be summed up in 'the maintenance of hatred of Frenchmen for Frenchmen.'" Brogan, *French Personalities and Problems* (New York: Alfred A. Knopf, 1947), p. 117.

The Hilsner Case and Ritual Murder

MICHAEL CURTIS

On April 1, 1899, the day before Easter, the body of Anezka Hruzova, also named Agnes Hruza in some sources, a nineteen-year-old Christian seamstress who had disappeared on her way home on March 29, Ash Wednesday, was found in the Brezina Forest near Polna. This city was a German-speaking town of about 5,000 people including 212 Jews, in eastern Bohemia about 60 miles from Prague, and close to the Bohemian-Moravian border in the Austro-Hungarian Empire. Hruza's throat appeared to have been cut and her head partially severed. A small pool of blood and some stained stones were found, as were torn clothes and a rope near the body.

At once the rumor spread among the general public, fostered by the anti-Semitic press, that the victim had been murdered by Jews, raising the age-old blood libel, the accusation that the Jews murdered Christians in order to obtain their blood for ritual purposes, the baking of unleavened bread or Passover matzos. Articles in the press and in pamphlets repeated the occurrence and denunciation of ritual murder. Within a few days, on April 5, the day after the girl was given a martyr's funeral, a twenty-two-year-old Jew, Leopold Hilsner, a weak-minded, lazy, unemployed shoemaker who lived with his mother and often walked in the area where the body was found, was arrested. A witness had told the committee set up by the local authorities to investigate the crime, and which paid for testimonies, that she had seen Hilsner and two other Jews at the scene of the crime on the day of the murder, March 29. When later confronted with Hilsner at his trial, she conceded that she could not be certain he was the same man she had seen. Two other persons asserted that they had seen Hilsner and the two other men running toward the murder scene on the afternoon of March 29 and then walking away from it. Hilsner was charged with Hruza's murder; his arrest and the charge triggered anti-Semitic riots and the destruction of property in the Jewish part of town.

The original examination of the body stated that Hruza had sustained a number of wounds on the head, which was covered with blood, through the use of stones or sticks, her skin was lacerated, and she had suffered bruises on her arms. Her clothes had been violently torn off, and she had been dragged a distance into the hollow. A tremendous wound was found on her throat, which had been cut by a long, sharp instrument struck with great force. In the center of the throat was a strangulation mark. The throat wound was fatal, the strangulation mark dangerous. It suggested that a noose, part of which was found on the crime scene, had been thrown over the head of the victim, and that she had been dragged from the place of the murder into the forest. To do this several people must have participated in the crime.[1] The post-mortem examination reported that no signs of indecent assault or traces of a sexual crime were found. Its crucial point was that only an insignificant amount of blood was found in the body and only a few blood spots nearby, far less than might be expected after a murder of this kind. No other bloodstains or caked blood were found.

The police and judicial investigations outlined a series of allegations about Hilsner's character and behavior. He often carried a large, sharp knife; he never held a job for long and evidently disliked work; he lived off his poor mother; he had loose morals; he had threatened to kill a former girlfriend; he was mentally below normal; he had followed Hruza in the past and knew her daily routine; he had changed his clothes several times on the day of the crime; he had no alibi for the time the crime was committed; he had a shabby past. In contrast to the conclusions of the post-mortem examination, the assizes judge, Dr. Baudys, who in April 1899 investigated the crime, thought it had been committed by a sex maniac and recommended that the police act on this assumption, but the trial turned out otherwise.[2] Though the crime was not legally treated as a ritual murder, and official documents did not use the term, in effect the arguments of the prosecutors and outside pressure suggested that it was.

Blood-libel accusations had a long history in Central and Southern Europe, dating back to Fulda, Germany, in 1235 and Trent, Italy, in 1475, and continuing through the twentieth century, but none had ever been proved. In the years before Hilsner, there were a number of other cases of supposed ritual murder in Europe: the most famous of them took place in Tisza-Eszlar in Hungary in 1882; in Corfu in 1891, which resulted in the anti-Semitic editor of a Prague paper, Jaromir Husek, being charged with "incitement against a religious community"; in Xanten in the Rhineland in 1891–92; in Novy-Benatach in 1892; in the Moravian town of Kojetin in 1892; and in Kolin in Bohemia in 1893–94. Some of these allegations, many of which concerned Christian servant girls employed by Jewish families, were provoked by the rhetoric of a Viennese priest, Joseph Deckert, whose 1893 pamphlet *Ein Ritualmord* was widely distributed and influential in Bohemia and who claimed that irrefutable evidence existed of ritual murder crimes, going back to Simon of Trent, murdered in 1475.[3] Between 1864 and 1914, twelve ritual murder trials were held in Germany and German Austria; all except that of Hilsner collapsed.[4]

This increase in anti-Semitic ritual murder accusations coincided with an upsurge in the expression of Czech nationalism in the 1890s. Most Czechs saw the Jews as Germans rather than as Czechs. The period was marked by anti-German and mainly anti-Jewish boycotts, by political activity to obtain linguistic parity with German for the Czech language in Bohemia, and by pressure by Czech nationalists to close the province's Jewish schools because they used German as the language of instruction. Economic nationalism interacted with provincial interests.[5] Anti-Semitic sentiment and utterances were manifested by diverse groups and individuals: the populist politics of the Young Czech Party in 1897; the violent diatribes of August Rohling, an exponent of religious and racial anti-Semitism; the economic arguments of the National Liberal Party, secular and national, for whom Jaroslava Prochazkova wrote, which saw Jews as controlling the banks and the economy; liberals like Karel Adamek, who saw the Jews as spreading German culture in the Czech regions of the country.[6]

The Hilsner trial for willful murder took place in the district court in Kuttenberg (Kutna Hora), about 35 miles east of Prague.[7] The twelve members of the jury heard thirty-two witnesses. Lasting five days, September 12–16, 1899, the trial ended with Hilsner being sentenced to death for complicity in the murder of Hruza, and ordered to pay court fees and funeral expenses. In his own testimony at the trial, Hilsner pointed out that the chief witness against him, a man named Pesak, claimed to have seen him at a distance that turned out to be 890 paces (676 meters). He denied having a knife other than a penknife.

The official prosecutor, Dr. Schneider-Svoboda, supreme counselor of the provincial court, noting the great press and public interest in the case, alluded to it as the Austrian Dreyfus Affair. Presenting the evidence of the self-declared witnesses and the conclusions of the medical group, he argued that Hilsner had approached the scene of the murder, committed the crime, and left the area immediately. He acknowledged that Hilsner had no criminal record, but held that he was an unsavory individual who had been on the verge of crime on a number of occasions and who had threatened a girlfriend with death. The prosecutor thought that establishing a motive was of minor importance, but he acknowledged that the press had discussed this at length.

A more aggressive approach was taken by Dr. Karel Baxa, a

Prague attorney and nationalist politician who in 1923 became mayor of Prague, who was financed by a German-Czech committee and was acting on behalf of the victim's family. It was Baxa who, in stressing the importance of the motivation for the crime, made ritual murder central to the trial. He maintained that Hruza, the virtuous Christian virgin, had no enemies and could not have been killed out of revenge, or jealousy, or for sexual reasons. The murderers were not concerned simply with her death but with other factors. Since there were people who desired to kill their neighbors in order to get hold of their blood, the real motive in the Hilsner case was clear. Like the first murder in the world, Cain's slaying of his brother Abel, the blood of the victim cried out aloud for revenge.

No blood, Baxa argued, had been found in the victim's body, and little was found near it. She had been slaughtered with a large, sharp knife. This sacrificial lamb was a martyr, a Christian innocent murdered by attackers of a different race, eager to get her blood. Hilsner had acted with other Galician Jews living around Polna to collect as much blood as possible. Though the words "ritual murder" were not uttered by Baxa or by the official prosecutor, they nonetheless made the argument that the crime was committed for religious reasons. Hruza was a martyr in the true sense of the word. The purpose of the murder was to get her blood.

It was the defense counsel, Dr. Zdenmko Aurednicek, a local Kuttenberg lawyer, who openly related the history of ritual murder accusations starting with the twelfth century. He reminded the court that Popes Gregory x in 1272, Innocent iv, Martin v, Paul vii, and Clemens xiv had all condemned such accusations as stemming from Christian enmity toward Jews. The Hilsner case, he argued, was perhaps an instance of sadism or sexual perversity satisfied by the sight of the blood, but not one of ritual murder as the anti-Semitic press had declared and Baxa had implied.

By implying that Hilsner as a Jew had committed a murder for religious purposes, Baxa was accusing not only the defendant but the whole people of which Hilsner was a member, of ritual murder. Baxa's citing religious fanaticism as the motive for the crime was applauded by the anti-Semitic press, which was inciting race hatred.

Aurednicek sought to discredit Dr. August Rohling, professor of theology at the German University in Prague, on whose work Baxa had relied for theological arguments, and whose fanatical hatred of all religions other than his own Catholic religion, especially Judaism, had influenced many anti-Semitic writers. Rohling had plagiarized much of his diatribe from Johann Andreas Eisenmenger (1654–1704), whose 2,100-page *Entdecktes Judenthum*, published in 1710, had presented an immensely influential negative picture of Judaism.[8]

Eisenmenger, professor of Oriental languages at Heidelberg, an erudite and polyglot scholar who had explored the literature on Jews and aimed to expose its supposedly hidden secrets in the Talmud and in Jewish traditions and legends, had condemned the Jews for adhering to foolish beliefs and wicked laws, for mocking the Christian religion, and for blasphemously dishonoring of it. He asserted that Jews continually robbed and murdered Christians, including ritual murder, and that many Christian children had died to satisfy ritual needs.

Rohling's work *Der Talmudjude*, published in Munster in 1871, became the accepted text of anti-Semitism even though its author could not read either Hebrew or Aramaic. In it Rohling claimed that the Talmud ordered Jews to practice deceit and fraud and to show contempt for gentiles. He was challenged by knowledgeable theologians, Christian as well as Jewish. Dr. Theodor Kroner, principal of the Jewish Teachers Seminary in Munster, argued that he had misrepresented the sources of the Jewish religion. Hermann L. Strack, a prominent Protestant theologian at Berlin University, in his *The Jew and Human Sacrifice* (1892), accused Rohling of perjury and gross forgeries.[9] When Rabbi Josef Bloch accused Rohling of fabricating data and called him a liar for stating that Jews require Christian blood for the Passover ritual, Rohling brought a suit against him, but he was compelled to withdraw the complaint after the Tisza-Eszler trial in 1882 revealed his ignorance of Hebrew.

Emotions stirred by the Hilsner trial led to riots and destruction of Jewish property as well as to anti-Semitic expressions in newspaper articles, pamphlets, cartoons, picture postcards, letters, and songs. Sometimes these expressions were seen as excessive: August Schreiber, an editor of the *Deutsches Volksblatt*, was sentenced to four months in prison for libeling Jews. The reaction to events was not wholly one-sided. Jewish organizations and other groups protested to the prime minister and other officials about the injustice of the trial and the verdict. A Prague physician, Dr. J.A. Bulova pointed out a number of mistakes in the inquiry and in the post-mortem examination, and in 1900 published a pamphlet criticizing the trial, and the later second trial.[10]

The trial and consequent developments became a significant historical event with the emergence of Thomas Garrigue Masaryk, a distinguished academic and rising politician, as the most prominent and unexpected of the non-Jewish critics of the trial and of ritual murder accusations. Born in 1850 of humble origin, with a Slavic coachman father and a Czech domestic servant mother, Masaryk had studied in Vienna. He became an instructor in the university there, was appointed in 1882 as a lecturer in philosophy at the Czech University in Prague, and in 1896 became a full professor. As a politician, he co-founded the Realist faction of the Young Czech Party in 1889, and in 1891, representing a small Bohemian district, he was elected to the Reichsrat, the imperial parliament in Vienna. The following year he was also elected to the Czech Diet. Masayrk resigned from his parliamentary posts in 1893.[11] In 1900 he established the Popular (Progressive) Party. He was returned to parliament in 1907 and became president of the newly established country of Czechoslovakia in 1918.

Long before the Hilsner case, Masaryk had shown his courage, dedication to the truth, and sense of moral justice by his stand in the celebrated case of the disputed Königinhofer manuscripts in 1886. These documents purported to be historical manuscripts, poems, and stories about a legendary founder of the Czech Kingdom and other early Czech rulers. Some of them were said to be from the ninth or tenth century, thus indicating that Czech culture and political institutions had existed considerably earlier than previously believed, a fact that propelled Czech pride and national consciousness. Masaryk supported the philologist who questioned the authenticity of the manuscripts, which after heated dispute were seen to be forgeries. Czech nationalists attacked Masaryk as unpatriotic and a national traitor. For his part Masaryk held that the matter was mainly a moral one: Czech pride and culture must not be based on a lie – forgeries ought to be admitted, and the manuscripts could not have originated in the Middle Ages. The dispute about the manuscripts gave him an insight into Czech political problems.

Masaryk had at first paid little attention to the Hilsner case and apparently did not even know where Polna was. He read nothing about it. He was drawn after being approached by a former student, Siegmund Muenz, editor of the *Neue Freie Presse*, who informed him that all the Czech newspapers were running stories about the blood libel. Masaryk's response was a letter published in the paper on September 29, 1899, for which the clerical press bitterly attacked him, in which he referred to the significance of the anti-Semitic superstition of ritual murder, which was becoming an international and widespread phenomenon, as shown by the Hilsner and Dreyfus trials occurring in different countries at almost the same time. The Hilsner trial, he said, was a travesty, a miscarriage of justice, and later explained his views in the Austrian parliament on December 5, 1907. Masayrk saw immediately that this was not case of ritual murder. Quite apart from any other consideration, the murder had been committed after, not before, the Jewish festival of Passover, which meant that ritual murder, even if there was such a thing, was irrelevant. Equally significant for Masayrk was his certainty that no one who believed in Jesus could be anti-Semitic.

Aware of the discrepancies in the testimony of witnesses and in the medical post-mortem report, which he regarded as inadequate, and conscious of the undercurrents of anti-Semitism and ritual murder in the case, Masaryk wrote a pamphlet, *The Necessity of Reviewing the Polna Trial*, published on November 6, 1899, and written not to defend Hilsner, for whom he had no personal sympathy, but to defend the country against superstition. The pamphlet was immediately confiscated on the grounds that criticism of the trial proceedings was not permissible for technical reasons. However it was made public by special permission of the minister of justice after members of parliament raised the issue.

Masaryk's criticism was both general and detailed. The trial had taken place under the pressure of anti-Semitism and the superstition of ritual murder. The anti-Semitic superstition of ritual murder was gaining acceptance, and there was a growing danger of "spiritual and physical" violence against the Jewish people. In addition to the misrepresentations and untruths in the case, the lack of judgment and the inhumanity displayed made it comparable to the Dreyfus Affair.[12] Not surprisingly, Masaryk was seen by sympathetic admirers as the Zola of the Hilsner case, defending the truth and seeking justice, acting as a private citizen with no ties to the defense, expending time and energy and provoking political enemies, as the French writer had done in the Dreyfus Affair. He was caustic about the attitude of the press of the political parties, and their anti-Semitic expressions, and also about his fellow academics and professionals who remained silent and who had not condemned the student demonstrations against him.

Masaryk objected to the slipshod police investigation, the failure to perform a complete autopsy, the refusal to follow up certain clues. He discussed some of the technical details, on which he would later elaborate, concerning the condition of the body; the bent legs resulting from rigor mortis; his belief was that the body had been moved from the place of the murder to where it was found in a more conspicuous place. Bloodstains, he thought, must have been present where the murder was committed. The throat of the victim was not cut; she was stabbed. Referring to Baxa, Masaryk said it was blasphemy for a Christian to state that ritual murder comes from the spirit of the Jewish religion. No statement in the Talmud could serve as a basis for the idea of ritual murder.

The response to Masaryk's pamphlet was immediate. He was subjected to criticisms in the papers of the nationalist and clerical press in Prague and Vienna, and from other elements in the political world from which he suffered to some extent in his career. Czech university students prevented him from lecturing on November 13 and joined with clerical students, radicals, and the National Labor Party in demonstrations that led to the cancellation of his lectures for about two weeks. A hostile pamphlet attempting to refute Masaryk's detailed arguments ended with an allusion to rumors that he had been paid by Jews to defend Hilsner, but other critics argued that megalomania or inflated ego explained his behavior.

Undeterred by these hostile responses, Masaryk continued his criticism of the case in political and literary forums. In the Reichsrat (parliament) in Vienna on November 10, 1899, a Christian-Socialist deputy, Ernst Schneider, defended the ritual murder accusation, relying to a large extent on the supposed expertise of August Rohling, who had been appointed a canon by church authorities. Masaryk responded to Schneider and also to Baxa's role in the Hilsner case by pointing out the inaccuracies in Rohling's work which had fostered belief in ritual murder accusations as well as expounding extreme forms of anti-Jewish prejudice.[13] Generalizing from Rohling's work, and his influence, and specifically criticizing Baxa, Masaryk reproached people who pretended to be saving the Czech nation from the Jewish threat, and especially from supposed Jewish control of industry, banks, and the press, whereas they actually were poisoning the nation with base incongruent lies and ignorance. Anti-Semites regarded every murder committed by a Jew as a ritual murder, and this was fraud, deceit, dishonesty, and superstition in the worst or fullest sense of the word.[14]

Masaryk repeated some of this in literary form. After an article, "The Nature and Origin of the Ritual Superstition," in *Die Zeit* on March 24, 1900, he issued a second pamphlet, *The Significance of the Polna Crime to the Ritual Murder Libel*, arguing that this crime was not one of ritual murder, but perhaps one of passion. Many details of the case had not been solved and a new examination was needed. To write the pamphlet and provide a detailed analysis of the case, Masaryk studied medical and legal literature, criminology, and physiology, consulted experts, and even employed a detective agency. In a severe indictment of the trial and the evidence provided, he was critical of both the prosecution and the post-mortem examination. He disputed the prosecution's conclusions about the time and place of the murder, giving detailed reasons for his analysis, including the time of day, the technique of strangulation, the numerous head wounds, the rainy state of the ground, and the openness of the spot where the body was found. Some of the points in his detailed analysis were telling. The body of the victim was not hidden; it had been moved to the spot where it was found, several hours after death. Bloodstains must have been present where the murder had been committed. The small amount of blood found in the body was explained by the removal of the body from the place of the crime. The throat of the victim had not been cut by a slashing horizontal incision by a butchering knife; she had died because she was stabbed. The case therefore could not be one of ritual murder; in any event Hilsner's knife, mentioned in the trial, was rounded and did not have a point. Moreover, by March 29 the Jewish festival of Passover had ended.

For Masaryk, the motive for the crime was of primary importance. On the basis of the scientific findings alone, no composite psychological picture of the motivation could be found, but on the basis of the evidence there was no case for ritual murder. Masayrk cautiously suggested that the mother and younger brother of the victim had not been adequately considered, since the inquiry about the latter had stopped in 1899. Masaryk was possibly right on this point. According to one analyst, although this is not legally accepted or generally agreed on, Hruza's dying brother confessed in 1969 that he had murdered his sister.[15] However, while Jan Hruza was regarded by some as a suspect, no conclusive evidence was ever presented. Irrespective of conjecture about the identity of the true murderer, the main point for Masaryk was that suggestions of the ritual murder legends "are the disgrace of our times; a fiery accusation against official Christianity." The legend, which had to be refuted, was false, a superstition that abused both religion and nationality. It had been fostered by clericalism, his main enemy, consisting of priests, the Catholic press, and people like Rohling, but also by nationalists, including professionals and university people.

Masaryk challenged the validity of the testimony of the witnesses and castigated the prosecuting lawyers and medical experts for their incompetence, inexact observations, and wrong conclusions. Only an objective review of the trial could overcome the mistakes – religious, medical, and judicial – of the Kuttenberg trial. The Polna case was "a horrible symbol of decay of our Bohemian and Austrian culture," and was a disgrace for the Bohemian people. He saw the Jews of Bohemia as belonging to the elite of Jews, not only of Austrian Jewry but also of Jewry as a whole. How could they be accused of barbaric ritual murder? Because of the inexact observations, premature conclusions, and discriminatory behavior shown during the case, he suggested, the Dreyfus trial "has found a psychological sequel in the Polna case.[16]

Masaryk's intervention in the case and criticism of the proceedings and of the legal and medical authorities was courageous not only in itself but also in light of his own past beliefs and prejudices. In an autobiographical memoir of February 1914, he confessed that, coming from a poor peasant family in the city of Hodonin, in southern Moravia near the Slovak border, he had been infected in his youth in the 1850s by the virus of anti-Semitism in his environment and in his family, especially from his mother, school, parish priest, and society in general. He told the writer Karel Capek that in his youth he had been afraid of Jews.[17] The mistreatment of a Jewish boy in his school had shocked him but did not end his anti-Semitic prejudice.

These prejudices, and to some extent the ritual murder myth, remained until Masaryk attended the university, when he met Jewish boys of his own age and tutored the sons of a Jewish bank director in Vienna. He maintained cordial relations with Jewish colleagues at the Czech University in Prague. In 1883 Masaryk referred to anti-Semitism as a "hateful disease which has put our organism in a fever," and suggested that Jews and non-Jews should get to know each other better.[18] Yet he confessed later that he had never got over the folk anti-Semitism of his youth on an emotional as distinct from a rational level.[19]

Masaryk spoke out against all discrimination based on religious, ethnic, or racial grounds. Anti-Semitism, as he explained in a speech in the Vienna Parliament in 1907, was immoral, crude, and vulgar: a Christian could not be an anti-Semite. The program of his People's Party in 1900 condemned anti-Semitism of every kind, demanding tolerance toward Jews and decisively rejecting the ritual murder superstition exploited for their own means by clericalism and then by radicals. As for himself personally, Masaryk explained in March 1914 that of all his struggles, that against anti-Semitism cost him the greatest amount of effort and time, of intellectual concentration and emotional strain.

Masaryk also acknowledged that if in adult life he was not anti-Semitic, he was also not philo-Semitic. He had acted in the Hilsner case not out of love for Jews but because he regarded the ritual murder accusation as a disgrace and because the issue was one of human rights. He recognized that if he had suffered a brief professional check to his career, he had won the praise of Jews, particularly in the United States. Among the Orthodox and Zionist Jews who befriended him were Justice Brandeis, himself of Bohemian descent, Julian Mack, and Nahum Sokolow. Acknowledgment of Masaryk's helpful role was shown by the dedication in 1930 of the planting of the Masaryk Forest of 12,000 trees in the valley of Emek Jezreel in Palestine with money raised by the Jewish National Fund.

At the Kuttenberg trial, Hilsner was sentenced to death but, thanks to the efforts of Masaryk and others, the Supreme Court in Vienna ordered a new trial by jury in Pisek in southern Bohemia, which would provide a more neutral and less passionate setting than Polna vicinity. The Supreme Court also called for experts on the medical faculty of the Czech University in Prague to examine the report of the medical officials in the first trial. These new experts found that report contained substantial errors: it was not true that insufficient blood was found in the body, nor was there any evidence that blood had been removed from it. They suggested that the crime was sexual in character.

For a time the legal proceedings were slightly confused. Hilsner, fearful about his fate on the gallows, and promised immunity if he did so, "confessed" that he had carried out the crime and was helped by two Jews whose names he mentioned. After it became clear that one of these men was in prison on the day of the murder and the other was miles away in Moravia, Hilsner recanted the confession. The implication of ritual murder was absent at the Pisek trial in October–November 1900, though a continuing undercurrent remained.[20] This became evident when the prosecution held that the knife mentioned in the first trial as being in Hilsner's possession was the kind of knife used for ritual slaughter. Hilsner was now charged with a second murder, that of Maria Klima or Klimova, a servant girl who had disappeared on July 17, 1898. A body had been found on October 27, 1898, in the same forest where Hruza had been discovered, but it was severely decomposed. Nevertheless, it was assumed to be that of the servant girl, and Hilsner was charged with her murder as well as that of Hruza.

In spite of the new medical report and the absence of any new evidence, Hilsner was again found guilty of complicity in murder and sentenced to death. This was commuted to life imprisonment in July 1901. After nineteen years in prison he was pardoned by Emperor Charles I in March 1918. He changed his name and spent the rest of his life in poverty until his death in Vienna in January 1928 at the age of fifty-two. By this time Masaryk was president of the new Czechoslovakia. Hilsner's lawyer, Dr. Aurednicek, was less successful. He lost his clients in Kuttenberg as a result of his acting for the defense and was obliged to move to Vienna to practice.

The Hilsner case and the responses to it, which included heightened anti-Semitism displayed in pamphlets, cartoons, picture postcards, leaflets, letters, songs, and parliamentary speeches, has to be put in the context of the position of the Jews in the Czech territories of the Austro-Hungarian Empire. Various forces contributed to anti-Semitic beliefs and behavior: the influence of clericalism and nationalism in Austria; the pan-German nationalists led by Georg Schönerer and the Christian Socialists led by Karl Lueger, who was elected mayor of Vienna in 1895 and assumed the position in 1897; the struggle between Czechs and Germans over linguistic and cultural equality in the Austro-Hungarian Empire, especially in Bohemia, with demagogues trying to influence people on this question by resorting to anti-Semitic rhetoric. The Czech political parties, despite their theoretical belief in racial equality, displayed intolerance, prejudice, and anti-Semitism; extremists of the Young Czechs and of the Nationalist Socialist party expressed these prejudicial views as the rise of radical nationalism was accompanied by anti-Semitism.

Czech nationalists saw the fact that most Jews, though often speaking Czech as their language of daily life, attended German-language schools, as pro-German behavior. Czech business people, especially in small trade, saw Jews as economic rivals. These linguistic and economic concerns occasioned demonstrations, riots, destruction of Jewish property, economic boycott against Germans and Jews, as well as the rumors of ritual murder.

In the Austro-Hungarian Empire the position of Jews was

complicated, especially in areas where the Czechs claimed recognition and implementation of the historic identity and rights of Bohemia. Though many Jews tried to be neutral between Czechs and Germans, and though Jews in rural areas of Bohemia were more likely than those in urban areas to be bilingual, in general Jews living in Czech areas were part of the Germanic world from a linguistic and cultural point of view.[21] Those in Prague were essentially loyal to Emperor Franz Josef in Vienna.

According to the Austrian census of 1900, the Jewish population of Bohemia was 92,746: of this number 50,080, or 53.9 percent, declared Czech as their language of daily use, 43.6 percent declared German, and 2,145 spoke other languages.[22] However, these figures must be treated with caution. In a similar census in 1890 about two-thirds of Bohemian Jewry, and three-quarters of the Jews in Prague said their daily language was German. The apparent shift to Czech may have resulted from Jewish caution and political expediency and reluctance to offend Czech nationalism. Yet if some Jews showed an increasing interest in Czech culture, most recognized that advancement lay through mastery of the German language and culture. Only a very small number of Jewish children attended Czech schools in Prague. Most Jews in higher education chose German rather than Czech institutions, and Jews, in the main, continued their cultural assimilation with German culture.[23]

Fourteen years after the Hilsner case another ritual murder trial, notorious and well known, took place in Kiev in October 1913. Lasting three weeks it ended with the Jewish bricklayer Mendel Beilis being found innocent. Again Masaryk disputed the testimony of the expert witnesses at the trial and the prosecution's indirect reliance on the discredited August Rohling. Masaryk took the opportunity to call for a reexamination of the Hilsner case but was unsuccessful. Others were also conscious of the possible connection of the two cases. On the arrest of Beilis, the Association of Progressive Czech Jews, protesting against the superstition of ritual murder, proclaimed on September 26, 1913, that "The Polna affair, which evoked such great excitement among the Czech people, is still a fresh memory."

The Hilsner case still arouses emotion on both sides. During the Nazi occupation of Czechoslovakia in World War II, memories of the case were revived by the Nazi-sponsored Czech Fascist organization, which opened an appeal for funds to erect a monument on the site where Hruza was found, while a Czech anti-Semitic paper published a history of ritual murder cases.

In 1999 commemoration ceremonies took place in Polna, remembering Hilsner with a declaration criticizing the behavior of the authorities in the town a century earlier, and the Jewish museum in Prague organized a special exhibition and conference about him. At the same time, however, a pamphlet was published proclaiming the guilt of Hilsner with a photo of Masaryk wearing a yellow star of David on which were the words "Perish, deport, shame."

In 1999 and 2001 President Thomas Klestil of Austria and President Vaclav Havel of the Czech Republic were urged to condemn what happened to Hilsner and thus perform a symbolic act that would not only commemorate the victim of Czech nationalism and Austrian anti-Semitism but would also celebrate President Masaryk, who was engaged in the case and symbolized the link between Prague and Vienna. In June 2000 a number of Austrian citizens attended the unveiling in a cemetery in Vienna of a tombstone for Hilsner that proclaimed his innocence. Since problems still remain regarding a judicial approach to the case, this was a fitting tribute. Hilsner was not a heroic or even an admirable figure, but he was certainly innocent of the charge of ritual murder.

Further Reading

Epstein, Benjamin R., ed. *Thomas G. Masaryk and the Jews.* New York: Pollak, 1941.

Hajek, Hanus J.T.G. *Masaryk Revisited: A Critical Assessment.* New York: Columbia University Press, 1983.

Newman, Edward P. *Masaryk* London: Camion, 1960.

Pynsent, Robert B., ed. *T.G. Masaryk (1850–1937).* Vol. 2: *Thinker and Critic.* New York: Macmillan, 1989.

Winters, Stanley B., ed. *T.G. Masaryk (1850–1937).* Vol. 1: *Thinker and Politician.* New York: Macmillan, 1989.

Notes

1. Ernest Rychnowsky, "The Struggle Against the Ritual Murder Superstition," in *Thomas G. Masaryk and the Jews,* ed. Benjamin R. Epstein (New York: Pollak, 1941), pp. 154–155.

2. Paul Selver, *Masaryk* (Westport, Conn.: Greenwood, 1975), p. 175.

3. Hillel J. Kieval, *The Making of Czech Jewry: National Conflict and Jewish Society in Bohemia, 1870–1918* (New York: Oxford University Press, 1988); idem, "Death and the Nation: Ritual Murder as Political Discourse in the Czech Lands," *Jewish History,* 10, no. 1 (1996): 75–91.

4. Peter Pulzer, *The Rise of Political Antisemitism in Germany and Austria* (London: Halban, 1988), p.69.

5. Kieval, "Death and the Nation," p. 77.

6. Steven Beller,"The Hilsner Affair: Nationalism, anti-Semitism, and the Individual at the Turn of the Century," in *T.G. Masaryk* vol. 2: *Thinker and Critic,* ed. Robert B. Pynsent (New York: MacMillan, 1989) pp. 52-76.

7. Arthur Nussbaum, "The 'Ritual Murder' Trial of Polna," *Historia Judaica,* 9, no. 1 (April 1947); Nussbaum, *Der Polnaer Ritualmordprocess: Eine Kriminal-psychologische Untersuchung* (Berlin, 1906); Frantisek Cervinka, "The Hilsner Affair," *Leo Baeck Institute Year Book,* vol. 13 (1968), pp. 145–148.

8. Jacob Katz, *From Prejudice to Destruction: Antisemitism, 1700–1933* (Cambridge, Mass.: Harvard University Press, 1980), p. 15.

9. Frantisek Cervinka "The Hilsner Affair," in *The Blood Libel Legend: A Casebook in Anti-Semitic Folklore,* ed. Alan Dundes (Madison: University of Wisconsin Press, 1991), pp. 135–161.

10. Cervinka, p. 148.

11. Z.A.B. Zeman, *The Masaryks: The Making of Czechoslovakia* (London: Weidenfeld & Nicholson, 1976), p. 49.

12. H. Gordon Skilling, *T.G. Masaryk, Against the Current, 1882–1914* (University Park: Penn State University Press, 1994), p. 146; idem, "Masaryk: Permanent Dissenter – the Hilsner Case and Antisemitism," *Cross Currents* 8 (1989): 243–260.

13. Kieval, *Jewish History,* p. 69.

14. Selver, p. 180.

15. Roman Szporluk, *The Political Thought of Thomas G. Masaryk* (New York: Columbia University Press, 1981), p. 204.

16. Rychnowsky, p. 233.

17. Karel Capek, *Talks with T.G. Masaryk*, trans. Michael H. Heim (North Haven, Conn.: Catbird Press, 1995), p. 49.

18. Skilling, "Masaryk: Permanent Dissenter," p. 252.

19. Capek, p. 49; idem, *President Masaryk Tells His Story* (New York: Putnam, 1935), p. 29.

20. Skilling, *op. cit.*, p. 246

21. Szporluk, p. 120.

22. Michael A. Riff, "Czech Antisemitism and the Jewish Response Before 1914" *Wiener Library Bulletin*, 29, no. 39–40, pp. 17–18.

23. Gary B. Cohen, *op. cit.*, "Jews in German Society: Prague,1860–1914," *Central_European History*, 10, no. 1 (March 1977): 33–34; idem, *The Politics of Ethnic Survival: Germans in Prague, 1861–1914* (Princeton, N.J.: Princeton University Press, 1981); Skilling, *op cit.* p. 91.

Mendel Beilis and the Blood Libel

REBEKAH MARKS COSTIN

The verdict was handed down in October of 1913. A jury of semi-literate peasants had found no validity to the government's case against Menachem Mendel Beilis. He was acquitted of all charges against him.

Of what was he charged? Of a murder, more horrible than can ever be imagined. The body of thirteen-year-old Andrei Yushchinsky was found dead, stabbed repeatedly, and drained completely of blood. The allegations were of a ritual murder: a killing by Jews in which they used the blood of innocent Christian children to make their bread – their strange matzah – for Passover. The tsar's minister of justice went to work to create a case against a Jew named Beilis.

This all sounds so simple. In some regards it is, and yet it is also much more complex. This is not a straightforward case of murder. This is the case of a dying regime grasping for hope on the wings of an age-old vehicle: the blood libel. Ah, the blood libel! Terrifying if you don't know the recipe and history of the unleavened matzah – and totally ridiculous and improbable if you do.

Unfortunately for Beilis, there were not many peasants in Russian who had any idea – or any interest – in the ingredients of matzah. Nearly all of them hated Jews. There were not many who made a point of getting close enough to them to learn that matzah is made exclusively with flour and water – no blood.

This was good news for imperial Russia, which quickly seized upon the murder as an opportunity to deflect challenges to its sovereignty and whip some anger toward an already despised minority. And so the stage for the Beilis trial was set.

The Start

On March 12, 1911, a thirteen-year-old boy named Andrei Yushchinsky left his home for school. On this day, though, he did not arrive at school, and was seen, by a disputed number of people, crossing the bridge over the Dneiper River in Kiev, Ukraine. Eight days later his body was found in the Lukyanovka caves in an outlying district of Kiev.

Andrei was found half dressed, stabbed nearly fifty times. The child had lost most of his blood. His clothes were soaked in it, and there was a blood-saturated remnant of a pillowcase that also showed traces of semen. Missing were his trousers, overcoat, and schoolbooks, which were never recovered.

Andrei, fondly referred to as Andryusha, was buried in fine attire on Sunday, March 27, 1911. At the funeral, leaflets were distributed that read:

ORTHODOX CHRISTIANS!

The Yids have tortured Andryusha Yushchinsky to death! Every year, before their Passover, they torture to death several dozen Christian children in order to get their blood to mix with their matzos. They do this in commemoration of our Savior, whom they tortured to death on the cross. The official doctors found that before the Yids tortured Yushchinsky they stripped him naked and tied him up, stabbing him in the principal veins so as to get as much blood as possible. They pierced him in fifty places. Russians! If your children are dear to you, beat up the Yids! Beat them up until there is not a single Yid left in Russia. Have pity on your children! Avenge the unhappy martyr! It is time![1]

And so we're off, right? Well, no, not really. The message of the leaflets went largely unheeded. The Jews had seen it all too often, and their level of anxiety, which was already high, was unaffected by yet another threat to their existence. For their part, the Russian people were tired of the pogroms and the concomitant violence. They preferred a more subtle anti-Semitism: one-third killed, one-third emigrated, and one-third converted.

Nevertheless, the leaflets were the first salvo in what was to become The Beilis Case and an introduction to a most extraordinary cast of characters. We will spend a fair amount of time on the development of the case, for the competing facts and conflicting personalities reveal much about the time and place. Of necessity, we will leave much of the detail unsaid, due to the enormity of the case.

The Case Against Beilis

The investigation started as most murder investigations would. While the city coroner performed an autopsy on the body, the head of Kiev's secret police, Detective Mishchuk, began his investigation. Mishchuk had two lines of investigation: the first was the child's immediate family, and the second was a possible connection to a family named Cheberyak whom Andryusha had allegedly visited the morning of his disappearance.

Mishchuk began by arresting members of Andryusha's family – his mother, his stepfather, his grandmother, and a number of relatives. He suspected that if there was any connection to the Cheberyak family, known common criminals, then Andryusha's family must also have criminal connections. He also followed a rumor that there was a trust fund in Andryusha's name that would revert to the parents if the boy died. Although Mishchuk pursued this line of questioning vigorously, to the extent that he even held the poor mother in custody for weeks and refused her request to attend her son's funeral, the family was found unblemished and was released.

He also questioned, but not completely, a woman named Vera Cheberyak. Cheberyak's son, Zhenya, was Andryusha's friend and allegedly the person he had gone to visit on his last morning. Cheberyak's apartment was well known throughout the neighborhood and in the police community as the headquarters of a large gang of criminals, drunkards, thieves, gangsters, and prostitutes. During the Kiev pogrom of 1905, for example, Cheberyak and her gang brought in so much loot that she had had to burn bundles of silk in the stove that she couldn't sell and was afraid to keep.

Yet despite this notoriety, she seemed to enjoy almost unbridled immunity from law enforcement authorities. As will be revealed later, the single exception in this unchecked immunity occurred only two days before Andryusha's murder, when the police finally raided Cheberyak's apartment. She had somehow been warned, and the police found no stolen goods there that day. Although the importance of this would be revealed later, Mishchuk found no connection between the raid and the murder, and he was prevented from conducting any further investigations against Cheberyak.

Nevertheless, Mishchuk concluded that the murder was committed by a gang of criminals that most likely originated from Vera Cheberyak's apartment. Although he had been prevented from thoroughly interviewing her, he had enough of a sense about her and her actions to assume her culpability. He also concluded that the motive for the murder was to provoke a pogrom so that Cheberyak's gang could benefit once again from the mass looting.

Mishchuk found no indication of a ritual murder, notwithstanding the assertion in the leaflets, for the autopsy report from the city coroner, issued shortly after the discovery of the body, had found no evidence of ritual murder, but only confirmation that the body had been stabbed numerous times and that the blood had been drained from it. There was no evidence that any instrument was used to suction blood out of the body and no indication that vital organs had been pierced during the life of the victim, which would have facilitated the gathering of blood.

It was clear to Mishchuk, and to anyone else who paid the slightest attention to the details of the investigation, that this was purely a criminal murder. Common sense would preclude as ridiculous any indication of a ritual murder. Yet common sense was in short supply in Kiev in those dark days. The attempt to stir up passion for a pogrom had failed, but the insidious damage had only just begun.

Within days of the funeral, Nikoli Pavlovich, a member of both the Union of the Russian People and the Double-Headed Eagle, the groups which had distributed the inflammatory leaflets, had been arrested for disorderly conduct, and the offices of his virulently anti-Semitic organizations were raided. This inflamed a certain nineteen-year-old student leader at Kiev University named Vladimir Golubev. Despite his young age, Golubev had vital connections with the hierarchy of these anti-Semitic monarchist organizations, all the way to the Ministry of Justice in St. Petersburg, and with these connections he succeeded in getting the case against Pavlovich dropped.

Emboldened by his success and assisted by State Prosecutor Chaplinsky, who would ultimately prosecute the murder, young Golubev continued to press for an accusation of ritual murder. Prosecutor Chaplinsky walked a delicate line. The weight of the evidence pointing to an obviously criminal murder masquerading as a ritual murder (the leaflet and the bloodless body) pulled hard against the desire to blame the murder on a despised minority and return glory to true Russians. Chaplinsky needed local police to develop the criminal case, in order to have something ready should the ritual murder case fail, but he needed someone who could keep it under wraps until Golubev and Chaplinsky could garner support for a ritual murder. A leak of any of the evidence against common criminals might compromise a potential ritual murder case.

Mishchuk, who wanted to do a straight job and whose conclusions were in fact right on the mark, was exactly the wrong kind of police investigator for Chaplinsky and his growing group of conspirators. He did not believe the allegation of ritual murder and would not cooperate with the conspirators' agenda. Eliminated from further participation, he was framed by a petty thief named Kushnir who had been assigned to help him. Kushnir informed Mishchuk of evidence that would allegedly solve the case, which Mishchuk pursued to his detriment. Mishchuk found and submitted the evidence, declared the case solved, and demanded the 500-ruble reward.

Unfortunately for Mishchuk, the evidence proved to be false, and he was arrested and charged with obstructing justice and forging material evidence. He was dismissed from the case, sentenced to three months imprisonment, and barred from appearing at the trial two years later.

After Mishchuk was banished from the Beilis case, a nationally famous detective, Nikolai Krasovsky, was brought to Kiev to investigate the crime quickly and quietly. It was hoped that this new detective would be a better fit than the first.

As the support for the ritual murder charge among the conspirators strengthened, the need for an actual Jew increased. In fact, there was no evidence whatsoever that would lead them to a Jew. But that was soon to change. Their chance came from some very odd and unreliable depositions.

Statements made in July 1911 supplied the prosecution with its first reference to a Jew in the case. Four months after the murder, a lamplighter and his wife – known but not well-respected figures in the Lukyanovka neighborhood – stated that they had seen Andryusha and Zhenya on the morning of the murder. Kazimir Shakhovsky stated under oath that he remembered the day because his employer had advanced him a ruble, and he remembered the time, eight in the morning, because he had just finished extinguishing the oil lamps.

He said he had spied Andryusha with his friend up the street and a third lad about fifty yards off, but he did not know where they went. "I advise you check with Vera Cheberyak," he volunteered, "the neighbors will tell you what kind of woman she is."[2]

But this was not the end to Shakhovsky's testimony, which came in bits and pieces throughout the warm months of July 1911. In a second deposition, Shakhovsky testified that –

> The place where Cheberyak lives is separated from Zaitsev's factory by a fence. On March 12, you could pass from one place to the other because the fence was damaged. Work at the factory usually started Easter [i.e., after the date of the murder], and on the day of the murder the factory was empty and no workmen were there.... Going from the Cheberyak place, you could see a large number of kilns for making bricks.... In charge of the whole grounds was the clerk Mendel Beilis, who lived at the other end of the grounds. He was a very good friend of Vera Cheberyak and used to visit her.[3]

Thus the name of Mendel Beilis first appears in the record. Menachem Mendel Beilis, thirty-nine, worked at the Zaitsev brick factory. He also lived on the premises with his wife and five children. Both the brickyard and a Jewish surgical hospital nearby had been built by a wealthy and learned Jewish gentleman named Jonas Zaitsev, who was a friend of Beilis's father, through whom Mendel got his job. Beilis himself was not a learned man, although his father had studied with Zaitsev and his eldest son attended gymnasium. Nor was he a religious man, for he worked on the Jewish Sabbath. He had, it should be noted, a healthy black beard. After Zaitsev died, Mendel Beilis remained a clerk and dispatcher at the brickyard. It was in this brickyard, mentioned by Shakhovsky and his wife, that neighborhood children came to ride the brick-making clay mixer.

Yuliana Shakhovsky swore, on July 20, that her husband had told her that he seen Beilis taking the victim toward the kilns. Now, in his third deposition, her husband swore that he had forgotten something. He just remembered, he said, that Zhenya told him that he and Andryusha had been chased away from the kiln by a man with a black beard. The man, in his opinion, was Beilis, who, again in his opinion, was responsible for the murder.[4]

Young Vladimir Golubev, the instigator of the case against Beilis, and Prosecutor Chaplinsky were delighted with the introduction of a Jew into the story, and Chaplinsky moved immediately to have Beilis arrested on July 22, 1911. This was no ordinary seizure. Chaplinsky invoked a legal device known as Article 21, which allowed for the suspension of a number of civil rights, including the protection afforded by a search warrant. At three o'clock in the morning of the 22nd, fifteen policemen, led by the local chief, roused the seven members of the Beilis family from their beds. The family stood outside in their nightclothes, bewildered, as the police ransacked their unremarkable home. To be sure, they found no evidence of bloody rites or ritual murder. Yet this did not stop the police from arresting Beilis and his eldest son and placing them in the secret police lockup.

"About four in the afternoon" of the first day, Beilis later recalled, "I heard the weeping of a child; it sounded like my own. I finally recognized the voice of one my children. Out of sheer horror, I began to knock my head against the wall."[5]

After two days, his son was released. Beilis himself was transferred to the city jail, where he languished for twenty-six more months.

Detective Krasovsky was suspicious of the lamplighter's story. He was not alone. Outraged by the lies told by Shakhovsky, a courageous shoemaker named Nakonechny, who lived in the neighborhood and knew Vera, the lamplighter, and Beilis, came forward to dispute Shakhovsky's testimony. Nakonechny explained to Krasovsky that Shakhovsky often stole wooden planks and boards from the Zaitsev yard, and that Beilis had once caught him. Since that time, Shakhovsky had hated Beilis, and the shoemaker suspected that his testimony was probably made in retaliation.

In fact, when Shakhovsky saw Nakonechny giving testimony

at the police station, he retracted the part of his story about the man with the black beard. He left, however, his testimony about seeing the boys on the morning of Andryusha's disappearance. During this deposition, his fourth, he did add a new fact: he and his wife had been coached and pestered by some detectives to give their testimony. Unknown to Krasovsky, a secret police agent named Polishchuk had been working over the lamplighter and his wife, filling them with vodka and, by turns, pleading with and threatening the couple to get them to implicate the Jew.

Not only did the Shakhovskys give testimony about Beilis, but Yuliana Shakhovsky, the lamplighter's wife, brought in her friend Anna Volkivna, commonly known as Anna the Wolf-Woman. Anna got her name because she would sleep out of doors in the summer near some caves known as Wolf's Ravine. Anna's testimony was essentially the same Yuliana's: that she had seen Andryusha and Zhenya and another boy playing in the factory yard and a man with a black beard had seized Andryusha and carried him off to the kiln while the other boys ran away.

With no additional evidence against him, Beilis was charged with the murder of Andryusha on August 3, 1911, twelve days after his arrest.

By December, nearly nine months after the murder, the only evidence in the case was a mass of confused depositions by the lamplighters and the Wolf-Woman of alleged final sightings of Andryusha. In December 1911, Vasily Cheberyak, Vera's husband, added his own testimony, which echoed that of the lamplighter: Zenya had reported to him, a few days before the murder, that Beilis had chased him and Andryusha from the brickyard. All pointed to the Zaitsev brickyard and to the Jew Beilis as the last person to be seen with young Andryusha. It was almost a year before any new evidence was added.

Detective Krasovsky, however, was not finished with Vera Cheberyak and her gang. Over the course of the summer of 1911, he heard a number of stories that convinced him more and more that she was somehow involved in Andryusha's murder. Krasovsky was more tenacious than Mishchuk: he revisited the story of the raid at Vera's apartment two days before Andryusha disappeared. For many years, notwithstanding her notoriety as a hostess to all manner of riffraff and criminals, Cheberyak had managed to avoid any kind of prosecution by the police. Yet that spring there had been a rash of robberies in Kiev, and the good people of the city had pressed for a response from the police. The police finally acted. After the raid, the robberies ceased, and so did the steady flow of the underworld to Cheberyak's apartment. How was one to interpret this? Was it purely fortuitous, or had someone squealed? For a criminal mind, the latter is always easier to believe, although the former is more likely to have been the truth.

Krasovsky heard a story circulating in the Lukyanovka neighborhood that seemed to offer some sort of an answer. The lamplighter had testified earlier that there was a third boy with Zhenya and Andryusha that morning – it is believed that the unidentified boy started the tale. The boy's story was that he was playing with Zhenya and Andryusha in the Lukyanovka woods when his two friends started to argue over a switch – a whittled tree branch. Zhenya asked Andryusha for his branch, and when Andryusha refused, he threatened to expose his truancy of that morning. Andryusha retorted that he would tell about the stolen goods in Zhenya's home. Immediately, Zhenya ran home, followed by the unidentified boy, and told his mother about his quarrel with Andryusha. Standing unseen at the door, the boy heard one of Vera's gang say of Andryusha that, "he must be put away at once." With that, the unknown boy ran away, terrified. He was never identified, but his story was well known throughout the neighborhood.

Detective Kirichenko, Krasovsky's assistant, took note of this interaction, which took place on May 10, 1911 during the course of the investigation. It was recorded thus during the trial:

> While Krasovsky and the others were searching the shed, I struck up a conversation with Zhenya Cheberyak and asked

him about the murder of Yushchinsky. He wanted to tell me something but suddenly he stuttered and said he couldn't remember. I was sitting to the one side of the door and he to the other. Cheberyak was in the next room behind the wall where I sat and listened in on our conversations. When I asked Zhenya who killed Yushchinsky, I noticed that his face went into a nervous tick. I somehow glanced round into the neighboring room at the same time that he did, and when I leaned over in my chair, I saw that Cheberyak was behind the wall and with her hand and entire body was making threatening gestures. Both Zhenya and I caught the gestures.[6]

And finally, this story from the deathbed of young Zhenya, Andryusha's friend. During the summer of 1911, less than five months after the murder, all three of Vera Cheberyak's children became deathly ill. Zhenya and the youngest daughter faded rapidly. By August 8 Zhenya was dying at home. The house was filled with detectives, family, and a priest who was brought in to administer the last rites. The priest explained (both in deposition and later at the trial) that after the rites were administered the boy tried to speak to him but didn't because his mother was standing so close behind.

Polishchuk, the detective who had been enlisted to maneuver the lamplighters and the Wolf-Woman to incriminate Beilis, graphically described Zhenya's death. Vera, the boy's mother, stayed near her son and urged him, as he was dying, to "tell them I had nothing to do with it!" The boy said, "Leave me alone, mother." As the boy was questioned, his mother hovered over him and smothered him with kisses. Before he died, the boy cried out: "Don't scream, Andryusha! Don't scream!"

As one can see, a lot of circumstantial evidence pointed to Cheberyak, but no hard evidence had been discovered. By then the conspiracy to turn this crime into a charge of ritual murder was accepted at the highest reaches of the Russian Empire, all the way to Minister of Justice Shcheglovitov. In fact, by the spring of 1912, the emperor himself had been assured that Beilis was the murderer. According to the conspirators, given these new circumstances Krasovsky was spending far too much time investigating the Cheberyak gang, and they already had more evidence than they wanted on them. If Krasovsky continued at the rate he was going, they believed, it wouldn't be long before he found the evidence he was looking for against Cheberyak. He made it evident that he would not cooperate with the conspirators, and it was becoming hard to silence him. They needed to halt Krasovsky's investigation before it became evident that they were protecting the true murderers.

And so Detective Krasovsky, in a trumped-up accusation not unlike the ones against his predecessor Mishchuk, was accused of embezzling sixteen kopeks (the equivalent of eight cents) from a previous case dating from 1903. He spent six weeks in jail, but in the end was acquitted and exonerated. He was dismissed from the case and sent back to his rural post. His replacement, curiously, was Kirichenko, his former assistant and protégé.

Unfortunately, having committed itself to pressing the ritual murder, the conspiracy had no case. All it had were the weird depositions naming Beilis as the last person to see the boy alive, a deposition from a convicted spy who had lied about a conversation he had with Beilis in jail, and the last deposition from Vera's husband. They had to rely on the old blood-libel calumny, for otherwise the case against Beilis would simply collapse. But what to do? There was little against the Jew Beilis, and the medical evidence was weak, if not completely contradictory to a ritual murder.

The first thing to do was to shore up the medical evidence. The ritual murder part of the conspiracy rested on the autopsy reports. There were two of them. The first was made by Coroner Karpinsky, the city coroner, and was issued shortly after the discovery of the body in March 1911. Nothing in the report mentioned ritual murder, nor could any of its findings support such an event.

This was unsatisfactory to the conspirators, so they hired two more experts, Professor Obolonsky and Anatomist Tufanov, who were members of the Faculty of Medicine of the University of Kiev. They too examined the body, and after a full month finally issued their report on April 25, 1911. Again, there was no finding of ritual murder.

Since the prosecution did not have the medical evidence to support the claim of ritual murder, a dubious psychiatric expert was enlisted. I.A. Sikorsky, professor emeritus of the University of Kiev, a notorious anti-Semite, joined the prosecution. The professor declared, according to the indictment, that the murder was typical of the "racial revenge and vendetta of the Sons of Jacob."[7] The choice of victim and the blood-letting might have been significant as a religious act, according to the old charlatan.

To add medical weight to Sikorsky's psychiatric opinion, the prosecution found Dr. Kosorotov, professor of forensic medicine at St. Petersburg University. Of course, it took 4,000 rubles to attain his helpful testimony. This is what 4,000 rubles bought in 1912:

> The wounds were inflicted during the life of the victim. the arrangement of the wounds does not show that torture was the main purpose.... The body was left nearly bloodless.... All this makes one think that the wounds were inflicted with the purpose of obtaining the biggest quantity of blood, possibly for some special purpose.[8]

On December 23, 1911, nearly six month after their report was published, Professor Obolonsky and Anatomist Tufanov added a new statement to their autopsy report:

> We believe that A. Yushchinsky died of severe blood loss resulting from his wounds.... The blood loss was so severe that the body was almost completely drained of blood.... The last wounds were made in the area of the heart.... Inasmuch as the

most severe hemorrhaging was in the left temple region...we must assume that it would have been more convenient to collect blood from Yushchinsky's body from these wounds, if blood actually was collected.[9]

The conspirators also believed that it was necessary to press the religious aspect of the case. Since establishment of a ritual murder was paramount, no matter who had done it, they needed an "expert" on matters Jewish, one who would testify that ritual murder was an integral part of Jewish religious practice. Unfortunately for them, there was no true expert in all of Russia who could be paid to defend the blood-libel fable. What they needed was a theologian who was personally committed to the existence of this falsehood. They found their man in a hitherto unknown former Catholic priest named Father Justin Pranaitis. The following excerpt from the views of Pranaitis, as set forth in the indictment, gives the flavor of his scholarship:

All the rabbinical schools, notwithstanding their divergences on various questions, are united by their hatred of non-Jews, who according to the Talmud are not considered human beings but only "animals in human form." The hatred and the spite which the Jews, from the point of view of their religious law, feel toward people of a different nationality and religion, are especially strong towards Christians. Because of this feeling, the Talmud allows and even commands the killing of non-Jews.... The extermination of non-Jews is commanded as a religious act...[that] hastens the coming of the Messiah.[10]

And finally, in the nature of a good detective story, Detective Krasovsky was out, but not gone. He returned to Kiev in the spring of 1912 as a private investigator – to resume work on the Beilis case. He was aided by his former student, Kirichenko (the current investigator), who kept him abreast of every detail of the case. It was through Krasovsky's secret investigations that yet another part of the criminal puzzle was found.

Enter now a journalist named Brazul-Brushkovsky. Through Brazul, Krasovsky was able to meet two revolutionaries, Sergei Makhalin and Amzor Karayev, who were able to get a confession out of Pyotr Singayevsky, the half-brother of Vera Cheberyak. Singayevsky confessed to committing the murder with his friends Rudzinsky, who was serving time in Siberia for an armed robbery, and Latyshev, who had jumped out a window during an interrogation and died. Karayev also discovered the lie that had prevented the police from finding the real killers.

Detective Krasovsky now had the evidence against Cheberyak and her gang that he was looking for. But since he was no longer officially involved in the case, he could not use it. However, Brazul started to write and publish articles about the confession, which could not be ignored. The conspirators had to postpone the trial originally scheduled for May 25, 1912, and withdraw their indictment.

This should have been the end of the case: the true murderers had been discovered, and nothing could be found to support a case against Beilis. Unfortunately, it was not the end. Unfazed, the conspirators merely redoubled their efforts to find new and better ways to frame Beilis.

And so poor Beilis was left to rot for another year in prison while the prosecution came up with essentially nothing. By the eve of the trial, the only evidence against Beilis was the words of a few scoundrels, the purchased testimony of a medical expert, the eagerly proffered expertise of a marginalized and excommunicated priest, and "vague hints and background allegations." Stories of Beilis delivering matzah for old man Zaitsev, a single interaction between the dead child Andryusha and a Jew named Schneyerson, who shared a famous name and nothing else with a well-respected Jewish family, a saddle-maker's awl unconnected to Beilis or the murder, milk purchased from a cow Beilis had sold a year before, and sightings of strangely dressed Jewish men stood in as evidence in the feeble and pathetic case put forth by the prosecution and its desperate and paranoid supporters.

In the end, the case against Beilis stood largely on the testimony of Zhenya Cheberyak, the son of Vasily and Vera, who told of Andryusha being seized by a black-bearded man near the factory. Zhenya, of course, was the boy who had died soon after giving his deposition, smothered by his mother's kisses as he lay on his deathbed.

The Indictment

The long, rambling, and convoluted indictment was handed down in the fall of 1913. It described the discovery of Yushchinsky's corpse and gave a description of it. The medical evidence was partially recited, omitting the initial findings by City Coroner Karpinsky. The autopsy by Professor Obolonsky and Anatomist Tufanov was cited with particular emphasis on their conclusions, added six months after the initial dissection, which imagined a ritual murder. This was supported by the purchased expert opinion of Professor Kosorotov, which hinted at, but did not prove, a ritual murder.

The indictment depicted Andryusha's life and the arrests of his relatives. Then the indictment turned to Vera Cheberyak, boldly asserting that though she had "constant connections with the criminal world," there was no evidence to connect her to Andryusha's murder. The indictment then recounted the arrest of Beilis, devoting just a third of the space to his accusation, more than it did to Vera Cheberyak, who was not under investigation – though she surely should have been.

When the indictment finally gets to "the Jew Mendel Beilis," it reports that his arrest was based on "new circumstances [that] were considered...sufficient for suspecting him of the murder of Yushchinsky from motives of a religious character."[11] There is no mention of these "new circumstances," although the term most likely refers to the depositions of the lamplighters and the Wolf-Woman.

A description of the investigation performed by the first detective, Mishchuk, follows, although it omits his conclusion regarding Vera Cheberyak's probable involvement in the murder, and his disregard for the ritual murder charge. It also omits any mention of his subsequent dismissal, prosecution, and conviction.

The private investigations by the journalist Brazul were presented at length, but the summaries of the depositions of the revolutionaries Makhalin and Karayev, who had elicited confessions of the murder from the Cheberyak gang, diminished their value.

Detective Krasovsky's observations about the Cheberyak gang were described, but then instantly discounted by notice that he had been dismissed from the case. As with Mishchuk, no mention was made of the unsuccessful attempt to frame him with trumped-up charges of embezzlement.

The indictment concluded with a lengthy discussion of the supposed Jewish custom of ritual murder. The two experts on this topic were Professor Sikorsky and Father Pranaitis who affirmed its existence. Contrary opinions were offered by two of Russia's leading scholars – non-Jews – in the field of Jewish religion.

For a brief moment, common sense prevailed when the president and recorder of the Board of Judges, the committing authority, refused to accept the indictment. They were overruled, however, by their colleagues on the board. After all, they argued, didn't a man incarcerated and under accusation for such a long time deserve a trial? The president and the recorder answered with their feet. They resigned.

The Jury

V.G. Korolenko, a famous journalist of the day, put on paper what many thought when they saw the make-up of the Beilis jury. He observed "seven peasants, three townsmen, two government clerks.... For a university city the choice is certainly extraordinary." Of another trial going on at the same time in the same building, he wrote, "I was pleasantly (or unpleasantly) surprised. I learned that for a minor crime there were two or three professors, ten educated men and only two peasants."[12]

Was he only imagining it, or was the jury rigged? It was plain to all that the jury was rigged, but it was only after the Revolution of 1917, when documents from the archives of imperial Russia were declassified, that the full extent of this claim became apparent. A 1912 memo from Minister of Justice Shcheglovitov, addressed to all thirteen districts of the empire, directed prosecutors to watch for "persons otherwise eligible for jury duty, but belonging to that element which is most opposed to the Government and the Government courts." Persons who were "strangers to the high aims of justice are usually well engraved in the memory of the Prosecutors...and naturally, they ought not to be included in the lists at all."[13] There is further evidence that the chief of the Secret Police had the jury watched during the trial. And just to add good measure, the receipt for the amount of 4,000 rubles from the bribed professor of forensic medicine at the University of St. Petersburg was discovered among the declassified documents.

The Trial

The trial began in September 1913 and lasted for thirty-four days. All of the evidence outlined above, and a great deal more, was presented. The prosecution's case introduced three possible perpetrators: Andryusha's family, Cheberyak and her gang, and Beilis and unnamed conspirators.

Andryusha's family was dismissed easily, but the prosecution spent many more weeks of the trial disproving allegations of culpability against the Cheberyak gang. As it did in the indictment, the prosecution sought to defuse and deflect the overwhelming volume of evidence pointing to Cheberyak and her gang. That left them with the Jew Beilis and "unnamed conspirators."

There was virtually no testimony at the trial about Mendel Beilis himself. Everyone agreed that he was a kind, pleasant man of whom it would be unthinkable that he was able to commit such a crime. The testimony of the lamplighters and the Wolf-Woman regarding Beilis proved worthless.

The prosecution, nevertheless, sought to establish the existence of ritual murder as a true tenet of Judaism. For this, they spent a considerable amount of time promoting the blood libel. The prosecution allowed Father Justin Pranaitis to rant and rave for four days before the defense was permitted to present its five experts. Since Pranaitis's testimony was so dangerous, though, we will pause to listen to the cross-examination that demolished his virulent allegations.

Ben-Zion Katz, a Hebrew scholar at the trial to advise the defense committee, discredited Father Pranaitis's testimony with ease. If the non-Jewish defense counsel would ask a few questions, in all innocence, to "better understand" Pranaitis's testimony, the deceptiveness of the defrocked priest's expertise would be clear to all. And so it went:

Q: What is the meaning of the word *Hullin* [animals permissible as food]?
A: I don't know.
Q: What is the meaning of the word *Erubin* [Sabbath walking limits]?
A: I don't know.
Q: What is the meaning of the word *Yebamot* [family relationships]?
A: I don't know.
Q: When did *Baba Batra* live and what was her activity?
A: I don't know.[14]

The last question – akin to asking an alleged London native "Who was Victoria Station and what was her activity?" – was fatal once it was tactfully explained to the jury. Baba Batra is a tractate of the Talmud, quite well known to scholars, students, and many Jewish laymen. Clearly, Pranaitis had simply taken the Aramaic word *baba* ("gate") to be the Russian appellation for a grandmother or elderly woman. Katz had recognized Pranaitis as a quack who knew only the smallest amount of Hebrew and nothing at all of Aramaic, the language of the Zohar and most of the Talmud, about which he so confidently spoke. Katz knew Pranaitis would be hoodwinked by the word *baba*.

The exchange drew immediate laughter from the Jewish spectators. Ben-Zion Katz laughed so loud that he was obliged by the court to leave the room. No matter – he had destroyed Pranaitis's utility as an expert for the prosecution.

The trial concluded with the inconclusive medical evidence presented by all four witnesses, including the one bribed with 4,000 rubles, and the questionable physical evidence. A dizzying number of witnesses, both major and minor, were paraded into the court. And then it was finished and time for the summations.

Summations

Each of the four prosecutors and four defense counsels delivered summations. In this extraordinary case against a Jew accused of murdering a young boy, there was nothing against the man Mendel Beilis. The prosecution blamed an international Jewish cabal for impeding their access to better evidence and witnesses. The defense sought to expose the entire process. Finally, on October 28, 1913, the jury received its charge and the world was ready for the verdict.

The Verdict

Judge Feodor Boldyrev had two charges to the jury: Was a ritual murder committed? Did the accused commit it?

> Has it been proved that on March 12, 1911...Andrei Yushchinsky
> was gagged, and wounds inflicted on him...and that when

he had lost five glasses of blood...wounds were inflicted on him...and that these wounds, totaling forty-seven, caused Yushchinsky agonizing pain and led to almost total loss of blood and to his death?[15]

The verdict: "Yes, it has been proved."

Is the accused...guilty of having entered into collusion with others who have not been discovered in the investigations, in a premeditated plan prompted by religious fanaticism, to murder the boy Andrei Yushchinsky, and did the accused, in order to carry out his intentions, seize Yushchinsky, who happened to be there, and drag him off to one of the buildings of the brickworks?

The verdict: "No, not guilty."

Judge Boldyrev turned to Beilis with the formula for acquittal: "You are free. You may take your place with the public."

Russia at the Dawn of the Twentieth Century

How could this trial have even occurred? Violations of law were rampant, and the inclusion of "experts" and the lack of any checks on their abuse were criminal. Yet the time and place is everything in this story.

Russia in 1911 was a country divided between two diverse groups: the peasants, or serfs, and the landed gentry, royalty, and church. The peasants, the vast majority of the populace, lived in adverse poverty and deprivation, whereas the others lived in comfort and privilege. While the Enlightenment in the West was offering freedom and opportunity for all members of society, Russia continued to control and oppress its lower class without abatement. The ruling class was consumed not with redressing the real grievances of the peasants, but only with maintaining its own exalted position in the country. As these diametrically opposed positions battled, Russia was being torn apart.

For many who were oppressed, and to others who saw the danger in the situation, as peasant anger grew along with the determination of the monarchy to hold them down, the only solution in sight was the overthrow of the tsar and his government. Groups of socialists and communists, mixed with anarchists and terrorists, arose in a widespread movement of opposition against the ruling classes. Many Jews were attracted to these social reform movements, which appeared to hold out "glorious promise" of equal rights and social justice, both sorely missing from Mother Russia.

The tsar had no intention of offering equal rights to anyone, of course, for it would have compromised his own tight control of the country. One way for the tsar to undermine the growing social reform movement and deflect the explosive forces that threatened him was to create an environment of hate against the Jews, who were caught between the peasant class, who saw them as part of the ruling class, and the ruling class, who identified them as instigators of change. The tsar reasoned that if the revolution could be discredited as a sinister Jewish plot to tear and demolish the very fabric of Russian life and history, than the masses of Russian would turn to him, not as the persecutor he was, but as their protector against this common foe.

This plot was not conceived and carried out casually. In 1903, the tsar's secret police published a document called *The Protocols of the Elders of Zion*. According to historians, the tsar's propagandist concocted twenty-four fraudulent "protocols," or minutes, of an international meeting of Jewish bankers, journalists, and financiers outlining a purported Jewish-Masonic plot to dominate world affairs. In fact, it was later revealed that the *Protocols* were a forgery taken almost verbatim from an 1864 French political satire.

The *Protocols* were accepted as truth, though, and they did succeed, to some extent, in tarnishing the reputation of the Jewish community, but they could not stop the forces of revolution. In October of 1905, angry workers finally revolted and organized a nationwide strike. In response, tsarist troops gunned down thousands of protestors in a massacre that came to be known as Bloody Sunday. All-out civil war seemed imminent, and the frightened tsar was forced to yield to the demands of his opponents. He signed the October Manifesto and created an elected parliament, known as the Duma. He also granted the country a limited constitution.

The feeble concessions made by the tsar in the October Manifesto were barely enough for the liberals; for the tsar and his supporters, they were too much. The tsar and his followers found the Duma problematic, for they could not control its members or stem the changes and advancements they brought to the beleaguered nation.

In a further effort to deflect anger away from himself and keep whatever remaining control he had over his vast and restless people, the tsar continued to cultivate animosity and hate against the Jews. The years surrounding the Beilis trial were wracked by violence and bloodshed, with a state-sponsored campaign of pogroms throughout the country from 1903 to 1906, culminating in the infamous 1905 Kishinev pogrom.

The Beilis case fit neatly into the government's purposes. Such a legal case was easy to manage, since the tsar controlled the entire judiciary through what was derisively known as "Shcheglovitov Justice," named in honor of the imperial minister of justice, and enforced with violence, fear, and intimidation.

The Reaction

Was anyone persuaded by these tsarist tactics? The foreign press certainly was not. Journalists from all over the Western world went to Kiev to watch the debacle unfold. The Western press attended the entire trial. In fact, a number of Western countries produced petitions, signed by scores of their most famous and influential citizens, speaking out against the Beilis trial.

And so, too, the jury, even the rigged, uneducated one, could see through the farce that this trial was. Within four years, the travesty that was the Russian monarchy came to an end. And justice came at last to each of the characters in this bizarre theater of the absurd.

After the February 1917 revolution, an Extraordinary Commission of the Provisional Government was set up to look into the "derelictions and delinquencies of the overturned regime." (Its report was subsequently published in seven volumes).[16] In addition, the archives of imperial Russia were opened and the heretofore secret documents were declassified.

Any doubts of the veracity of the conspiracy and the desperate attempt to frame Beilis and stir up trouble with a trumped-up charge of ritual murder were laid to rest by the documents and testimony uncovered in these proceedings. Exposed for all to see was the full scope of the conspiracy.

Beilis safely left Russia for Palestine with his family shortly after the trial. In 1922, they moved to the United States, where, near New York, Beilis died a natural death in 1934 at the age of sixty. Vera and her gang, on the other hand, came quickly to violent ends – being shot to death in prison within a few short years of their farcical turn on the witness stand. The prosecution team saw the Beilis case as a victory and was rewarded richly for its part in it. Nevertheless, all their efforts were canceled out by the revolution four years later, and many of the team and its investigators shared the same fate at the hands of the revolutionaries as the tsar to whom they had so blindly pledged their allegiance.

But was it good for the Jews of Russia in 1911? The jury is still out.

The blood-libel accusation, with all its lurid iconography, seemed to die with Andryusha and lay quiescent for nearly a century until its recent resurrection at the hands of jihadi fundamentalists. What never died is the capacity to hate, and the ability to use hatred to the best political advantage. Thus the blood-libel falsehood continues to cause mischief.

The lies of the *Protocols* spread beyond the boundaries of Russia: they were published by Henry Ford in his *Dearborn*

Independent, they were read by British soldiers in Palestine before the creation of the State of Israel, and they have resurfaced again today in the Middle East. They did not die with the tsar.

Further Reading

Beilis, Mendel. *The Story of My Sufferings*. Trans. Harrison Goldberg. New York: Mendel Beilis Pub., 1926.

Leikin, Ezekiel. *The Beilis Transcripts: The Anti-Semitic Trial that Shook the World*. Northvale, N.J.: Jason Aronson, 1993.

Lindemann, Albert S. *The Jew Accused: Three Anti-Semitic Affairs*. Cambridge: Cambridge U. Press 1991.

Samuel, Maurice. *Blood Accusation: The Strange History of the Beiliss* [sic] *Case*. New York: Alfred A. Knopf, 1966.

Notes

1. Quoted in Maurice Samuel, *Blood Accusation: The Strange History of the Beiliss* [sic] *Case* (New York: Knopf, 1966), p. 17, from Kennan's account in The Outlook, November 8, 1913.
2. From the stenographic record of the trial, quoted in Samuel, p. 64
3. Stenographic record, quoted in Samuel, pp. 65–66.
4. Ezekiel Leikin, *The Beilis Transcripts: The Anti-Semitic Trial that Shook the World* (Northvale, N.J.: Jason Aronson, 1993), p. 41.
5. Mendel Beilis, *The Story of My Sufferings* (New York: Mendel Beilis Pub., Co. 1926), p. 40.
6. Trial transcript, quoted by Samuel, pp. 51–52
7. Indictment, quoted by Samuel, p. 82.
8. Ibid., p. 83.
9. Medical examiner's report, entered into evidence at trial, quoted in Samuel, p. 83.
10. Ibid.
11. Indictment, quoted by Samuel, p. 161.
12. Published by Korolenko in his newspaper *Russkoye bogatstvo*, quoted in Samuel, p. 169.
13. Documents submitted to the record of the Extraordinary Commission of the Provisional Government, *Padeniye Tzarskovo Rezhima*, quoted in Samuel, p. 170.
14. Stenographic record of trial, quoted by Samuel, p. 218.
15. Stenographic record, quoted by Samuel, pp. 229, 248–249.
16. *Padeniye Tsarskovo Rezhima* (Leningrad, 1924–26).

The Leo Frank Murder Case

SALLY STEINBERG-BRENT

The Murder of Mary Phagan

Leo Frank was the only Jew to be lynched in the United States of America.[1] In 1913 Leo Frank was accused of the murder of a thirteen-year-old Christian girl, Mary Phagan, who worked at the National Pencil Company in Atlanta, Georgia, where Frank was the superintendent. Most of the National Pencil Company's 170 employees were teenage girls.[2] Mary Phagan was found murdered, gashed, her body covered with sawdust, with her neck in a noose, in the basement of the pencil factory at three o'clock in the morning on Sunday, April 27, 1913.[3]

Leo M. Frank was born in Texas in 1884 to German-Jewish parents who moved to Brooklyn when he was three months old. He attended Pratt Institute and received a degree in mechanical engineering from Cornell University. After he worked as a draftsman and a test engineer, his uncle, Moses Frank, sent him to study production techniques with Eberhard Faber in Germany. Leo Frank moved to Atlanta at the age of twenty-four to become manager of the pencil factory in which his uncle was a principal stockholder and in which he also had stock. Production rose each year, thanks to Frank's industriousness.[4] Leo Frank married Lucille Selig, who was from an Atlanta Jewish manufacturing family, and the couple lived with her parents. Frank was elected president of the Atlanta B'nai B'rith chapter. In early 1913 he ap-

95

pointed a committee "to investigate the complaints against Jewish caricatures that are becoming so frequent on the local stage."[5]

An African-American night watchman, Newt Lee, who found Mary Phagan's body when he went to the Negro toilet in the basement, was the initial suspect.[6] The only evidence against him, other than his discovering the body and calling the police, was the assertion by a bank cashier, later repudiated, that the barely literate notes found near the body were in Lee's handwriting. The police were suspicious because Lee told them he had found the body of a white woman, whereas she was so covered with sawdust that they could not determine the girl's race until they rolled her stocking down. However, Lee said that he knew the woman was white because of her hair.[7] Lee maintained his innocence in the face of a grueling police interrogation.

The day of the murder was a Saturday and Confederate Memorial Day, a legal holiday in Georgia.[8] Thus, Leo Frank was one of the few people in the factory, where the body was found and where it was assumed that the murder had taken place. At first Frank did not recognize the body of Mary Phagan. Later, he admitted that he had given Mary her pay of two fifty-cent pieces and two dimes in his office on the day of the murder.

The police were under pressure to find the murderer. Notes found next to Mary Phagan's body read:

> mam that Negro
> hire down here did
> this I went to make
> water and he push me
> down that hole
> a long tall negro black
> that hoo it wase
> long sleam tall negro
> i wright while play with
> me

he said he wood love me
land down play like the
night witch did it
but that long tall black
negro did buy his slef

No one believed that Mary Phagan had written the notes; even if she had, it was assumed that she would have done so at the direction of the murderer. When a fingerprint expert finally dusted the notes, he said that they had been so manhandled by police and reporters that he could not find any prints.[9]

The Investigation

The police investigation was neither thorough nor professional.[10] When Hugh Mason Dorsey, the Fulton County solicitor general, notified all the pencil company employees that they would have to appear at the coroner's inquest, James Conley, a black factory sweeper, came to his attention. The day watchman reported that on May 1 he had seen Conley washing his shirt at a faucet in the factory basement. Although the watchman speculated that the stains on the shirt were blood, they turned out to be rust. The police asked Conley for a writing sample because of the notes left next to the murder victim. Conley claimed both that he was illiterate and that he had not been at the factory on April 26.

Detective John S. Starnes found what he thought were bloody fingerprints on the door to the basement, the door Conley had used on previous occasions to escape creditors. Although Starnes chipped two pieces from the door, no evidence in regard to these samples was presented at the trial.[11]

The press reported that hair and bloodstains believed to be Mary Phagan's had been found in the room next to Leo Frank's office. However, the stain only contained a few drops of blood and the hair was probably not Mary's, although this was not disclosed at the trial.[12] According to the defense, the police pursued only clues that appeared to implicate Frank; thus the blood and hair, which had been planted by an employee to collect a reward, misled them.[13] The sensational allegations made front-page headlines, while the qualifications and retractions were often relegated to the inner pages of the newspapers.[14]

After Solicitor General Dorsey took over the investigation, he had Mary Phagan's body exhumed twice. A reporter visiting Atlanta in 1922 became interested in the Frank case and read all the evidence in the record department of the courthouse. He discovered an envelope containing photographs showing teeth indentures. Mary Phagan had been bitten on her left shoulder and neck before being strangled. According to the reporter, the photographs did not correspond to the X-rays of Leo Frank's teeth, also contained in the envelope. This evidence was apparently known to the prosecution, but was not disclosed to the defense or to the public. The reporter proposed writing a series of articles about the case, but was discouraged by a prominent Jewish lawyer and local rabbis, who thought the series would have adverse repercussions on the Jewish community. Thereafter, the reporter received a printed warning that said, "Lay off the Frank case if you want to keep healthy." Subsequently his car was demolished when another automobile forced it onto the track of an approaching streetcar, but he escaped injury.[15]

At the coroner's inquest, two women testified about sexual harassment by Leo Frank. The sister-in-law of a girl who worked at the factory testified that Frank had told her when she came to the factory that she could not visit her sister unless she met with him. "He pulled a box from his desk. It had a lot of money in it. He looked at it significantly and then he looked at me . . . winked [and] said, 'How about it?'" A former employee testified that she had only worked at the pencil factory for three days because Frank's "actions didn't suit me. He'd come around and put his hands on me. . . . He barely touched my breast."[16]

Subsequently the two young women witnesses swore that they had been coached into making false accusations of sexual misconduct against Frank. Still later they repudiated their retractions.[17]

Another former employee, who had been working at the factory for six weeks at the time of the murder, testified that on perhaps six occasions he had seen Frank "feel the girls" or "rub up against" girls while pretending to instruct them in their work. He was able to name just one such girl.[18]

A young man named George Epps testified that Mary Phagan had been his "good friend," that she had complained to him that Frank had tried to flirt with her, and that she had asked him to escort her home as often as he could "and kinder protect her." Epps appeared in bare feet at the trial, where most of his inquest testimony was ruled impermissible, and Mary's mother testified that the boy was only a neighbor. "He wasn't no special friend of hers," she said.[19] Moreover, a reporter who testified for the defense stated that when he interviewed Epps and his sister, the boy had merely said he occasionally rode to the city with Mary.[20]

Mary Phagan's stepfather testified at the coroner's inquest, "Mary often said things went on in the factory that were not nice and some of the people there tried to get fresh. She told most of those stories to her mother."[21] Mary Phagan's mother told a Pinkerton detective that she had never heard Mary say anything bad about Superintendent Frank, but this statement was not made public.[22] Mary Phagan's stepfather cried as he shook hands with each of the coroner's jurymen after his testimony, and her seaman brother screamed and ran from the room.[23] Mary's stepfather would later shake hands with the jurors after they pronounced a guilty verdict.[24]

The coroner's jury recommended that Leo Frank and Newt Lee both be charged with murder pending further investigation.[25] The coroner himself later stated, "Personally, I have never made up my mind that Mr. Frank is guilty." He added that he had so strong a doubt that he would feel "very badly" if Frank were hanged.[26]

The police arrested and briefly held several other suspects. James Gantt, an employee who had been fired just prior to the murder, came under suspicion when his sister exploded his alibi. She then recanted, saying she had been drunk and that police and reporters had driven her to near-hysteria.[27] The day after telling a detective he did not know Mary Phagan, Leo Frank told another detective that Gantt was infatuated with Mary Phagan.[28]

An unemployed street car conductor named Arthur Mulliney, who had reportedly been seen near the pencil factory at 10:00 P.M., was under suspicion until it was determined that the murder had taken place in the afternoon. The factory's elevator operator was also arrested. A man named Paul Bowen was arrested in Houston because he had been heard to mutter "Why did I do it?" in an Atlanta hotel on the weekend of the murder. A Texas judge freed him.[29]

Both a self-appointed investigator and the chief of detectives were indicted for criminal libel because of their allegations against each other in the case, stemming from the fact that the Atlanta police safe contained a list of brothels and saloons that paid protection. The police released to the press an affidavit from a madam who claimed that Frank was a "pervert" and that on the day of the murder he had sought to bring a young girl to her "rooming house." The madam later retracted her statement, saying that she had been intimidated and plied with alcohol by the police, but her retraction received scant publicity.[30]

After being questioned, but before being charged, Leo Frank hired a detective agency. The detectives he hired publicly stated that Frank was guilty. Later they expressed doubts. Because the murder had occurred at the factory, Frank also hired a lawyer to protect its interests. When Frank was brought to police headquarters for questioning on the day after the murder, this lawyer was present. This sparked a rumor that Frank had engaged a lawyer before his arrest, which led some people to conclude that he was guilty of the crime.[31]

After Frank's arrest, his wife rushed to the police station, but was not permitted to see her husband.[32] When she eventually spoke with Leo at the police station, he told her not to return because she would be hounded unmercifully by reporters.[33] The prosecution subsequently argued that Mrs. Frank's failure to visit Leo for two weeks following his arrest was evidence that she knew Frank was guilty.

On the day that Leo Frank was indicted, Jim Conley admitted having written the murder notes, claiming that Frank had dictated them to him. The two notes contained 128 words, which Conley swore he had written in two and a half minutes. Detective Harry Scott testified that he dictated eight words to Conley and it took him about six minutes to write them.[34] William Schley Howard, one of Frank's attorneys, theorized that the experience of having the detectives dictate words for him to write inspired Conley's fabrication that Frank had dictated the murder notes to him.[35] The grand jury was not informed of Conley's admission when it deliberated the case against Frank. At the foreman's behest, the grand jury was reconvened. The solicitor general pleaded with the grand jurors for almost an hour and a half not to indict Conley, because doing so would damage the state's case against Frank. The grand jurors were finally persuaded to indict Leo Frank. They did not indict James Conley or Newt Lee.[36]

Conley's notarized statements to the police differed substantially. His first statement, dated May 18, 1913, detailed his visits to saloons on the day of the murder. In an affidavit dated May 24, 1913, Conley stated that Frank had asked him on the day before the homicide if he could write (a fact that Frank already knew) and told Conley to write the murder notes. At Leo Frank's trial, Pinkerton Detective Scott testified that he and Atlanta Chief Detective Newport Lanford "tried to impress [Conley] with the fact that Frank would not have written those notes on Friday, that was not a reasonable story. That it showed premeditation and that would not do. We pointed out to him why the first statement would not fit.... He said he told the truth."

In his "second and last" statement to the police, dated May 28, 1913, Conley said that he had denied being in the factory on the day of the murder because he did not want to be accused of "having a hand in it."[37] This affidavit stated that two women had come to Frank's office, and Frank had hidden Conley in the wardrobe. Thereafter, Frank asked Conley if he could write and thrice dictated a note for him to write that Frank said he was going to send to his people, commending Conley to them. Conley asserted that Frank said, "Why should I hang?" Frank then gave him a cigarette box containing two paper dollars and two quarters; Conley left the factory, visited a saloon, gave his "old woman" $3.50, and did not leave home until about noon on Sunday. Conley claimed not to have heard about the murder of "Mary Puckett" until he returned to work on Monday morning.[38]

"On May 28th, Chief Lanford and I grilled [Conley] for five or six hours," Detective Harry Scott testified at the trial. "On May 29th, we talked with Conley almost all day. We pointed out things in his story that were improbable and told him he must do better than that. Anything in his story that looked to be out of place, we told him would not do."[39] Conley's statement to the police dated May 29, 1913 was released to the papers in its entirety. Conley now quoted Frank as saying, "Why should I hang? I have wealthy people in Brooklyn."[40]

Jim Conley described Mary Phagan's mesh bag at the trial. The bag was lost, which gives credence to robbery as the motive, a much more likely motive for Conley than for Frank. Conley's May 29th statement was similar to his testimony at the trial, except, as Scott testified, Conley denied knowing anything about the matter in the elevator shaft, claimed he had never said anything about the little mesh bag, "he never said anything about Mr. Frank having hit her," and there was no thought of burning the body. To explain why his affidavits varied, Conley said that he had not wanted to mention that anyone had walked past him as he sat in the factory's dark hallway because he was afraid they would have accused him of the murder. A piece of a pay envelope with Mary Phagan's employee number on it was found near where Conley admitted sitting. The governor noted that Conley described the clothes and stockings of the women who went into the factory, implying that he had observed them carefully.[41] Conley repeated the story of having been in the wardrobe when two female employees came to Frank's office, but made no other accusations of sexual impropriety against Frank.[42] The affidavit stated that Frank gave him $200; it was typewritten, except for a handwritten addendum declaring that Frank took the money back and promised to return it on Monday. Governor Slaton surmised that the addition was written to account for the $200.[43]

The Atmosphere in Atlanta

According to Albert S. Lindemann, the case might not have attracted such widespread attention if Leo Frank had not been Jewish.[44] Before the Civil War there were about fifty Jews in Atlanta; by 1910 there were approximately four thousand. Most of them were merchants and business people and their families. By the beginning of World War I the majority of Atlanta's Jews were from Eastern Europe. Atlanta's Reform rabbi, David Marx, and others blamed the East European Jews for the change in the city's climate that made Leo Frank's arrest and conviction possible.[45]

In 1906 Atlanta suffered a race riot in which mobs of whites, enraged by reports that two white women had been murdered by blacks, randomly attacked African-American men, women, and children for over a week until the National Guard finally restored order. The allegedly murdered women were never found.[46] Ten blacks and two whites were killed and seventy people were injured.[47] Immediately thereafter, several saloon licenses belonging to Jews were revoked because public anger over the sale and consumption of alcohol, especially the sale of liquor to blacks, was directed at Russian-Jewish bar owners rather than against German-Jewish producers of alcohol.[48]

The class issue also played a role.[49] Tom Watson, the founder of the People's Party in Georgia, who had been the Populist candidate for vice president in 1896, wrote, "[The Frank case] has shown us how the capitalists of Big Money regard the poor man's daughter."[50] Frank earned $180 per week (plus profit-sharing) as superintendent of the factory, in contrast to Mary Phagan, who earned 12 cents per hour, and in contrast to Mary's father, who earned 20 cents per hour, or $12 for a typical work-week.[51] Watson's concerns focused on rich Jews, as when he commented, "Frank belongs to the Jewish aristocracy, and it was determined by the rich Jews that no aristocrat of their race should die for the death of a working-class" girl. Nonetheless, his vituperation affected all Jews.[52] The fact that Frank was perceived not only as a capitalist but also as a Northerner made him a target. "Our Little Girl – has been pursued to a hideous death...by this filthy perverted Jew of New York," wrote Watson.[53]

Rumors spread that Jews were trying to use bribery to fix the trial, despite the fact that Atlanta's Jewish community, apart from his family and friends, did not openly or actively support Frank, especially in the early stages. In fact, a few Atlanta Jews wrote Jewish organizations in the North, urging them to avoid public comment on the case for fear that it would antagonize non-Jews without increasing Frank's chances for acquittal.[54]

Mayor James Woodward declared, "I want to appeal to the people of Atlanta not to be misled by the sensational reports in the newspapers." Georgia's outgoing governor, Joseph Brown, worried about the possibility of a lynching, asked the people to let the law take its course and told his successor that he had had the military ready to protect the defendant.[55]

The autopsy concluded that Mary Phagan's hymen was not in place, but that she had not been raped. Nevertheless, the public perception of a sexual aspect to the murder persisted. At the trial Solicitor General Dorsey reduced Mary Phagan's mother to tears on the witness stand by asking whether Mary was pretty and had dimples and holding up her hat and dress for her mother to identify.[56] Three days after the murder the *Atlanta Constitution* had carried the headline, "Every Woman and Girl Should See Body of Victim and Learn Perils."[57] The *Georgian* featured a front-page picture of Frank, retouched to make his lips thicker, with a headline calling him a "monster." Tom Watson's *Jeffersonian* doubled its price, and its circulation grew from about 25,000 to 87,000 during its anti-Frank crusade.[58] After the trial, but during the appeal process, the *Jeffersonian* also used a retouched photograph of Frank above an editorial that read:

> You could tell that Frank is...guilty of the crime that caused the Almighty to blast the Cities of the Plain, by a study of the accompanying picture; look at those bulging, satyr eyes, the protruding, sensual lips and also the animal jaw.[59]

Watson called Frank "a typical young libertine Jew...dreaded and detested by the city authorities of the North" for their "utter contempt for law and ravenous appetite for...the girls of the uncircumcised."[60]

The Trial

Judge Leonard S. Roan, who conducted the trial, was widely respected. Frank's lawyers did not request a change of venue, despite the mob that lingered outside the courthouse and despite Georgia's liberal laws regarding change of venue.[61] When asked, members of the jury denied that they felt intimidated. On appeal the Georgia Supreme Court ruled that mob pressure had not affected the jurors,[62] despite the fact that Judge Roan had ordered the windows opened because of the oppressive Atlanta summer heat, and the police had not dispersed the mob, which cheered the prosecution and booed the defense.[63] At the point in the trial when one of Frank's attorneys was cross-examining the county physician, who admitted that there was no evidence that Mary Phagan had been raped, the judge inadvertently held up a newspaper with the headline in red "State Adding Links to Chain" facing outward. At the defense's request, Judge Roan instructed the jury:

> Gentlemen, it has been said...that you might have been able to see some...headlines...that might influence you. If you have

seen anything in the newspapers...I beg of you now to free
your mind of it, regardless of whether it be helpful to the State
or to the defense.[64]

Frank's lawyers did not use this opportunity to ask for a mistrial.[65]

According to the autopsy evidence, Mary Phagan was murdered between twelve noon and one in the afternoon. Frank told
the police that he had remained in the office for about an hour
after giving Mary her wages before he went home. Monteen Stover,
another employee, testified that as far as she could see, the office
was empty when she went up to the office window to get her pay
at 12:05. She waited for about five minutes and left. Putting Stover
on the stand implicated Frank by demonstrating that he was not in
the office when he had said he was. In addition, the pretty, blonde
fourteen-year-old girl served as a stand-in for the victim.[66] Frank
speculated that he might have heeded "a call of nature" during
the time Stover came to his office.[67] Stover testified that she had
been wearing tennis shoes. Thus, Frank might not have heard her
footsteps. Governor Slaton speculated that she might have arrived
before Mary Phagan, rather than afterwards.[68]

Because Frank initially denied knowing the murder victim's
identity, the prosecution introduced at his trial a former employee
who had been staying at a home for unwed mothers. She stated:

> I am now staying at the station house....I worked at the pencil
> company during February and March, 1913....I have seen Mr.
> Frank hold his hand on Mary's shoulder. He would stand pretty
> close to Mary when he talked to her. He would lean over in
> her face.[69]

The state's case against Leo Frank partly depended on the
timing of his leaving the factory and arriving home for dinner.
After being held overnight in jail and being coerced by her husband, Albert, as well as by the solicitor general and detectives, the

Franks' illiterate twenty-year-old cook, Minola McKnight, gave a statement contradicting the time Frank said he was home for dinner. She subsequently repudiated her affidavit. When a reporter asked why her lawyer had allowed her to sign such a statement, she replied, "Ain't got no lawyer 'cept God. He's my lawyer. I never had pen or pencil in my hand."[70] Lucille Frank wrote open letters to the citizens of Atlanta, published in the city newspapers, protesting McKnight's arrest and accusing Dorsey of torturing her cook. Dorsey responded, "I welcome all evidence from any source that will aid an impartial jury...in determining the guilt or innocence of the accused."[71] At the trial the hearsay testimony of Albert McKnight's bosses was permitted, stating that "Albert had said that Minola had said that she had overheard Mrs. Frank tell her mother that Mr. Frank had been drinking [because] he had murdered somebody; they testified that Minola had confirmed this."[72] Minola McKnight insisted that she had been kept "locked up" to get her "to tell a lie."[73] Mrs. McKnight's deposition was used in Frank's appeal, as was her husband's affidavit. His affidavit stated that at the behest of his employers, who were tempted by the reward money offered, he had made up a story about Frank's failing to eat lunch and leaving the house abruptly on the day of the murder. After being jailed, McKnight repudiated his retraction, saying that he had retracted his original statement because the detective who worked for the defense had promised him a job as a Pullman porter and threatened that if he didn't renounce his statement "the Jews" would get him.[74] The detective and two reporters affirmed McKnight's retraction, as did Mrs. McKnight, who said she had been present when her husband met the detective and that he had not given her husband a bribe.[75] Nine days after the judge's ruling in favor of the prosecution, Mrs. McKnight was slashed across the face. She refused to identify her attacker.[76] Her husband was also severely beaten.[77]

On the evening of the murder Leo Frank telephoned Newt Lee, the night watchman, and asked if everything was all right. This action was unprecedented. Frank explained that he had called because the night watchman was fairly new and Frank was worried about James Gantt, the firm's former bookkeeper, who had recently been discharged. According to Lee's trial testimony, Gantt and Frank had argued and Frank had intimated that Gantt had been discharged for stealing.[78] The day of the murder, Gantt had been drinking and had asked and been given permission to enter the factory to retrieve personal property he had left there.

Frank's lawyers had good reputations, but they made several miscalculations according to the Anti-Defamation League's analysis. The patrician attire of Leo Frank's relatives, lawyers, and witnesses contrasted with the plain and simple clothes of the solicitor and of Mary Phagan's mother. The cross-examination of Conley by Frank's lawyers was overly verbose.[79] Defense character witnesses had to admit that Frank looked into the women's dressing room, a point the prosecution emphasized in its closing argument.[80] The defense was forced to fall back on the argument that Frank merely peered into the dressing room to see whether the girls were loitering, that the dressing room had no lavatories, and that the girls only changed their top garments.[81] Moreover, introducing more than a hundred witnesses to testify to Leo Frank's good character made his character an issue. The burden then shifted from the prosecution's having to prove that Frank had committed the murder to the defense's trying to establish that Frank was of good moral character. Frank's character remained an issue despite the fact that his lawyers presented several witnesses who attested to Conley's lack of character and bad reputation, while the prosecution could produce no character witnesses in Conley's behalf. [82]

There were more than one hundred witnesses for the prosecution.[83] Frank's lawyers did not cross-examine the ten factory girls who said that Frank had a bad reputation for lasciviousness. (Half a dozen of the girls later repudiated their testimony and then retracted their renunciations.)[84] The defense asked the judge to charge the jury that no presumption should arise against the defendant because of a failure to cross-examine any witness. Judge

Roan denied this request, which the Georgia Supreme Court ruled was proper because it was the jury's province to decide the force and effect to be given to the defense's failure to cross-examine witnesses. The Georgia Supreme Court also ruled that it was not improper, therefore, for the solicitor general in his summation to comment on the defense's failure to cross-examine witnesses.[85]

At the trial Conley testified that Frank had used his office "several times" for "chatting" with a "lady," employing Conley as a lookout to lock and unlock the factory door. Moreover, he testified that on the day of the murder Mary "Perkins" had gone to Frank's office and that shortly thereafter Conley had heard a scream. Conley stated that Frank had called him to his office a while later, that Frank was "shivering and trembling and rubbing his hands" and that he was holding a rope similar to the one found around Mary's neck. Conley testified that Frank had told him that he wanted to "be with the little girl and she refused" and he had "struck her and I guess I struck her too hard and she fell and hit her head."[86]

Conley stated that he had found Mary's body in an adjoining room, that he wrapped the body in a cloth, that together he and Frank carried the body to the elevator, which Frank unlocked, that they took the body to the basement in the elevator and carried her out. Conley testified that he rolled her out of the cloth and then they went back upstairs.[87] Conley claimed that Frank gave him $200 and told him to burn the body in the furnace. When he refused, Frank took the money back, telling Conley to keep his mouth shut and asking him to come back later to burn the body. Although he had only a second-grade education, was an admitted liar and an alcoholic, and had a criminal record, Conley was cross-examined by Frank's lawyers for sixteen hours and did not change his story enough to discredit it. The most the lawyers could do was point out flaws in the timing in Conley's story.[88] For example, Conley's description of the time it took to move the body was so long that it did not fit the times at which witnesses said they had seen Frank.[89]

In his statement to the jury, Leo Frank explained his refusal to confront Jim Conley prior to the trial, saying that at the detectives' behest he had spoken to Newt Lee.

> What was the result?...they grilled that poor Negro and put words into his mouth that I never said and...distorted my meaning. I decided then and there that if that was the line of conduct they were going to pursue, I would wash my hands of them....On May 3rd Detectives Black and Scott came up to my cell; wanted to speak to me alone without any of my friends around...and it was for this reason that I didn't see Conley, surrounded by a bevy of city detectives and Mr. Scott, because I knew that...there was not a word that I could utter that they would not deform and twist and distort to be used against me, but I told them...that if they got the permission of Mr. Rosser [Frank's lawyer] to come, I would...speak to Conley and face him.[90]

There was also evidence that Frank had not known that Conley had been at the factory on the day of the murder and that once he learned that Conley admitted being there and Conley's literacy became material, Frank disclosed that Conley could write.[91]

The Franks had been married less than two years and were childless. Solicitor General Dorsey elicited the following testimony about Frank from Conley:

> After he said about how [Mary Phagan] got hurt, he said, "You know I ain't built like other men."...the reason he said he wasn't built like other men, I had seen him in a position I hadn't seen any other men that has got children....I have seen Mr. Frank in the office there about two or three times...and a lady was in the office, and she was sitting down in a chair and she had her skirt up to here [he demonstrated] and he was down on his knees.[92]

In its case the defense called two practicing physicians who testified that they had examined Leo Frank's private parts and had found them normal. In his presentation to the governor, Frank's new lawyer, William Schley Howard, theorized that Conley had invented a story of Frank's "perversion" based on myths about circumcised men.[93] During the cross-examination of Conley, the defense belatedly moved to have this testimony stricken because it was prejudicial and because oral sex was then a capital crime in the state of Georgia, an offense for which Frank was not being tried.[94] The prosecution argued that the testimony was admissible because the defense had not objected to it. Judge Roan ruled that, although the testimony would have been inadmissible had a timely objection been raised, the jury had already heard the testimony, and therefore it was admissible. Cheers erupted, and the defense moved for a mistrial, which the judge denied on the ground that the jury had been sequestered during the colloquy.[95]

Testimony disclosed that, for a fee, Conley allowed men to use the factory basement for immoral purposes.[96] A witness named C. Brutus Dalton corroborated Conley's account of Frank's assignations, but on cross-examination admitted that he had served time on a chain gang, had been fined for stealing, and was under indictment for bootlegging.[97] In the aftermath of the trial, Dalton retracted his testimony, saying that it had been fabricated in conjunction with the police from exploits of his life. Dalton now claimed that although he had used the factory basement for liaisons and had paid Conley a quarter to be a lookout for him, he knew "nothing about or against the defendant."[98] Subsequently Dalton repudiated his retraction, maintaining that he had been paid by the defense to retract his testimony and adding that he had witnessed Frank's hugging, kissing, and pinching girls and on more than one occasion taking a girl toward the dressing room.[99]

On cross-examination, Dorsey asked of Frank's insurance agent, who appeared as a character witness, "Didn't your investigators ever report Frank took girls on his lap and caressed them?" Frank's attorney's objection was overruled. The fact that the agent answered an emphatic "No, sir" hardly mattered once the jury heard the allegation. Dorsey continued, "You never heard of Frank kissing any girls and playing with the nipples on their breasts? . . . Didn't you hear that Frank played with little girls?" At this Frank's mother jumped up and screamed, "No, nor you either!" She was led moaning from the courtroom. The judge, who had excluded women and children from the courtroom when "the evidence was of such a nature as to be indecent to be heard by them," threatened to have Frank's wife and mother removed if there were any further outbursts.[100]

Solicitor General Dorsey threatened to use "a fearful mass of testimony" about Frank's sexual misconduct if Frank's lawyers forced the issue, and said he would indict Frank for other offenses if they successfully appealed his conviction. The defense did not force the issue, but stated that "we are not claiming perfection for this defendant any more than we claim it for ourselves or than you claim it for yourselves; and no more than Mr. Dorsey and his associates should claim it for themselves. Let him who is without sin cast the first stone. We are not trying this man on everything that may have been said about him. We are trying him for murder."[101] At the trial Dorsey insinuated that Frank had a "delicate relationship with an office boy." This had been reported in the press, along with allegations that he was a bigamist, a Mason, a Catholic, and a pervert.[102]

The state also called as a witness a factory employee who testified that he had seen Frank detain Mary Phagan to talk to her and had heard Mary protest that she had to get back to work. "He told her he was the superintendent of the factory and that he wanted to talk to her, and she said she had to go to work. She backed off, and he went on towards her, talking to her. The last thing I heard him say was that he wanted to talk to her. This is all I saw or heard." However, on cross-examination the witness could not describe Mary Phagan.[103]

In his closing argument, Solicitor General Hugh Dorsey accused the defense of abusing him and denied that as a sworn officer of the law he would hang Leo Frank on account of his race and religion.[104] He pointed out that the issue of Frank's being Jewish was first raised by the defense. Dorsey's summation to the jury appeared to denounce anti-Semitism.

> The word Jew never escaped our lips. I say that the race this man comes from is as good as ours; his forefathers were civilized and living in cities and following laws when ours were roaming at large in the forest and eating human flesh. I say his race is just as good as ours, but no better. I honor the race that has produced a Disraeli, the greatest Prime Minister that England has ever produced; that produced Judah P. Benjamin, as great a lawyer as England or America ever saw.... I roomed with one of his race at college; one of my partners is of his race... but when Lieutenant Becker wished to make away with his enemies, he sought men of this man's race. Then you will recall...Schwartz, who killed a little girl in New York: and scores of others, and you will find that this great race is as amenable to the same laws as any others of the white race or as the black race is. They rise to heights sublime, but they also sink to the lowest depths of degradation, too![105]

Solicitor General Dorsey also referred in his closing argument to the case of Oscar Wilde and other notorious criminal cases. Judge Roan did not instruct the jury that they should not be influenced by these other cases in deciding the Frank case. This omission constituted one ground of Frank's appeal, but because his lawyers had not asked the judge to make such an instruction, the Georgia Supreme Court held this ground to be without merit.[106] Solicitor General Dorsey also suggested that Frank's medical witnesses had been family physicians, and the judge did not rebuke Dorsey, as Frank's lawyer requested. The Georgia Supreme Court ruled that even if the prosecution's closing argument "may not have been thoroughly logical or well g[r]ounded," it was not so excessive or misleading as to warrant a new trial.[107]

Dorsey argued that the use of the word "did" proved that Leo Frank had dictated the murder notes. If Jim Conley had written the notes by himself, Dorsey maintained, he would have used the word "done" and not the word "did." The trial transcript showed that Conley correctly used the word "did" as many as fifty times.[108]

As soon as Dorsey finished his summation, Reuben Arnold, one of Frank's lawyers, asked that the jury be excused and moved for a mistrial on the basis of five incidents he believed "tended to coerce and intimidate" the jurors. "Your Honor, the behavior of the spectators throughout this trial has been disgraceful." The prosecution objected. The judge responded, "Of course I heard the cheers, but whether the jury was influenced, I don't know." The deputy sheriffs who had supervised the jurors during the course of the four-week trial were called to testify, but their testimony was inconclusive. Despite Arnold's reference to the atmosphere that still prevailed in the courtroom, "Your Honor, You can't keep them quiet now," the judge denied the motion.[109]

At the behest of Judge Roan, who feared a lynching if the jury found Frank innocent, neither Leo Frank nor his lawyers were present when the jury rendered its verdict. Their absence became the basis for an appeal. In finding Frank guilty, the jury disregarded defense counsel Arnold's explanation of the legal theory of "reasonable doubt" in circumstantial cases: that a conviction cannot be had against the accused so long as there is another possible theory for the crime.[110] In his charge to the jury, Judge Roan said that if they returned a guilty verdict without recommending mercy, he would have to sentence "the defendant to the extreme penalty."[111]

There was such a "wild" demonstration when the guilty verdict was announced that Judge Roan delayed sentencing.[112] One of the errors on which Frank's lawyers based his appeal was the fact that just after the polling of the jury had begun, loud cheering from the crowd in the streets adjacent to the courthouse was heard, which arguably intimidated members of the jury from answering freely.

The Appeals

Leo Frank's conviction became a cause célèbre, partly because of Tom Watson's anti-Semitic ranting in his newspaper, the *Jeffersonian*.[113] The editors of Atlanta's three daily newspapers asked if the case should be reconsidered, questioning Solicitor General Dorsey's methods and revealing some of the evidence that cast Frank's guilt in doubt. In contrast, the *Macon Daily Telegraph* editorialized, "If a mistake is made involving a single human life, it would be deplorable; but it is better such a mistake should be made than that our legal system should be brought into disrepute."[114] In March 1914 the *Atlanta Journal* demanded that Frank be given a new trial, stating that executing him would be "judicial murder."[115] However, Tom Watson attacked the *Journal*, which declined in circulation and stopped asking for a new trial.[116] The German-Jewish publisher of the *New York Times*, Adolph Ochs, was persuaded to publish articles supporting Frank. Influential Jews tried to win public opinion by contacting non-Jewish leaders. These efforts fed the Jewish-conspiracy theories of Watson and others. A majority of Christian ministers in Atlanta signed a petition asking for Frank's sentence to be commuted, but the Georgia public seemed convinced of his guilt.[117]

After the trial Leo Frank's lawyers petitioned the courts thirteen times.[118] First they made a motion for a new trial on more than a hundred grounds; the number of grounds may have been another tactical error on the part of his attorneys.

Before the motion for a new trial was to be heard, Judge Roan confided to two fellow judges that he was dissatisfied with the verdict because of the atmosphere surrounding the trial. Judge Roan was troubled by the fact that William Smith, the lawyer who represented Jim Conley, had come to see him because he was convinced that Conley, not Leo Frank, was Mary Phagan's murderer. Smith was in a difficult position. As a lawyer, his first duty was to his client. His revelation would have been a breach of prevailing legal ethics, except that Conley had already been convicted of being an accessory after the fact to Mary Phagan's murder, and therefore, according to Smith's interpretation of the double-jeopardy statute, could not be tried again for "the same transaction."[119] Roan reasoned that no United States court could receive confidential (and incriminating) statements between attorney and client even if the attorney was willing to reveal them.[120] However, Smith's conclusion as to who murdered Mary Phagan was apparently based on his study of the evidence, not on any confession from Conley. According to his son, Smith was moved to examine the evidence because he felt responsible for Frank's conviction.[121]

Judge Roan told his colleagues that he wanted to grant a new trial, but was afraid that there would be mob violence. His fellow judges advised him to deny the motion and let the case run its course through the courts.[122] Judge Roan denied the motion for a new trial, orally stating that he had thought about this case more than any other he had ever tried, was not certain of the defendant's guilt, and was not thoroughly convinced whether Frank was guilty or innocent, but that he did not have to be convinced, the jury was convinced, and he felt it his duty to overrule the motion.[123] However, according to a prior ruling by Georgia Chief Justice Thomas J. Simmons, "it took thirteen men to deprive any man of his life or property in Georgia," meaning that the judge had to concur with the verdict of the jury.[124]

With regard to the atmosphere in and around the courtroom, the Georgia Supreme Court held in *Frank v. State*, 80 S.E. 1016, 1033:

> The applause by the spectators, under the circumstances as described in the record is but an irregularity not calculated to be substantially harmful to the defendant, and... the action of the court, as a manifestation of the judicial disapproval, was

a sufficient cure for any possible harmful effect.... an outside disturbance or irregularity should never be cause to vitiate the trial, unless such irregularity, from its very nature, is of a character that will poison the fairness of the whole trial.

According to one report, every time a Jew testified in Leo Frank's behalf, the spectators interrupted the testimony with laughter.[125] Nevertheless, the court held, "The general rule is that the conduct of a spectator during a trial will not be ground for the reversal of the judgment, unless a ruling upon such conduct is invoked from the judge at the time it occurs."[126] When the testimony of Herbert Schiff, the factory's assistant superintendent, was interrupted by inappropriate laughter, defense attorney Reuben Arnold threatened to move that the courtroom be cleared, but he did not invoke a ruling from the trial judge.[127]

By a vote of four to two, the Georgia Supreme Court denied Leo Frank's appeal, dealing extensively with evidentiary questions. Justice Samuel C. Atkinson, writing for the majority, ruled that Jim Conley's testimony regarding Frank's conduct in sexual matters was material and relevant. The court specifically referred to Conley's testimony that the defendant had said, "I want you to watch for me like you have been doing the rest of the Saturdays."[128]

The Georgia evidentiary rule cited by the court gave vague guidance:

Evidence of prior attempts by the accused to commit the same crime upon the victim of the offense for which he stands charged is admissible; or where other offenses committed by the accused tend to prove malice or motive, or the like, evidence of other offenses is *sometimes* admitted" [emphasis added].[129]

Justice Atkinson stated in *Frank v. State*, 80 S.E. 1016, 1025–1027:

In the case before us, there was no eyewitness to the crime,

and the evidence under discussion tended to show a lascivious motive on the part of the accused which had several times
in the near past been exhibited at that place, and under like
circumstances of watching and signaling, and from the effort
to act upon which, at the same place, on this occasion, and
resistance thereto, the murder may have resulted.... There
was evidence from which the jury could find that the killing
occurred on the second floor, on which was located the office
where the accused admitted that he was when the girl entered
the building, went to the office and spoke to him. There was
also evidence from which it might be inferred that the person
who committed the crime sought to have some character of
sexual relation, natural or unnatural, with the girl. Practically
all other persons were eliminated from suspicion except the accused and Conley, the leading witness for the state. The accused
was a white man, married, and superintendent of the factory.
The witness was a negro employe, who admitted that he drank
intoxicating liquors. Naturally it would be urged...to the jury
that there could be no possible motive why the accused should
kill one of the employees of the factory, and that it would be
improbable that he would indulge in lechery in his office or
place of business, while the negro sweeper would be more likely
to do so. Thus the question...whether or not the accused had a
lecherous motive which might lead to the effort to accomplish
it upon the girl, and upon her resistance, then to murder, was
vitally involved.... The evidence tended to show a practice, plan,
system, or scheme on the part of the accused to have lascivious
or adulterous association with certain of his employes and other
women at his office or place of business, at which the homicide
occurred. Some of these acts were shown specifically to have
occurred not long before the homicide.... There was not only
evidence of the practice of the accused with other women, but
during the trial there was also introduced evidence tending
to show that in pursuance of his general practice he made
advances toward the deceased. We think that the evidence was

admissible, both on the subject of motive and of plan, scheme, or system, and as tending to show identity. If it is suggested that his conduct in regard to having lascivious relations with other women did not show any intent to violate the deceased, this would be to put too narrow a construction upon the subject of motive and plan.

In finding Dalton's testimony similarly admissible, the judge stated:

> The point that we are now dealing with is in regard to the admissibility of evidence and not its credibility. The latter question was passed upon by the jury, and the judge declined to set aside their verdict.[130]

The Georgia Supreme Court dissent disputed that a common motive of lechery pervaded the homicide and the other "transactions" or that there was some logical connection between the crimes other than the tendency to commit one crime as shown by the tendency to commit the other.[131] The dissent presented a more cogent rule:

> On a prosecution for a particular crime, evidence which in any manner shows or tends to show that the accused has committed another crime wholly independent from that for which he is on trial, even though it be a crime of the same sort, is irrelevant and inadmissible; but to this rule there are several exceptions.[132]

The dissenting opinion noted that the rule had been strictly applied by the court and discounted motive as a valid exception in the Frank trial. The dissent maintained that evidence that the deceased had been violated was admissible to support the theory that she was killed to prevent discovery of the assault, but evidence of prior lascivious transactions with other women was not relevant.[133] The dissent contended:

When one is on trial charged with the commission of a crime, proof of a distinct and independent offense is never admissible, unless there is some logical connection between the two, from which it can be said that proof of the one tends to establish the other.... In order to justify the admission of evidence relating to an independent crime committed by the accused, it is absolutely essential that there should be evidence establishing the fact that the independent crime was committed by the accused, and satisfactorily connecting that crime with the offense for which the accused is indicted.[134]

Actually, if true, such evidence would be relevant, but so prejudicial that it would, therefore, be inadmissible. More specifically, the dissent noted that "whenever motive is to be established, it must be the motive which underlies the crime charged."[135]

If the evidence be so dubious that the judge does not clearly perceive the connection, the benefit of the doubt should be given to the prisoner, instead of suffering the minds of the jurors to be prejudiced by an independent fact, carrying with it no proper evidence of the particular guilt.[136]

The dissent stated:

If the guilty cannot be convicted without breaking down the barriers which the law has erected for the protection of every person accused of crime, it is better that they should escape rather than that the life or liberty of an innocent person should be imperiled.[137]

The dissenting opinion maintained that intent was not an element of the homicide and, therefore, did not constitute an exception to the rule of evidence that renders evidence of other crimes inadmissible.[138] The dissent also dispensed with the "sexual offense" exception to the rule, stating that this exception was limited, except in rare cases, to offenses between the same parties.[139] The dissenting justices did not accept the argument that the murder formed a common plan or scheme with the alleged acts of lasciviousness.[140] For example, with respect to Conley's explanation of the statement that Frank was not built like other men, the dissenting opinion concluded, "It is not competent for a witness to explain the meaning of words used by another person, whose conversation or utterances he has recited before the jury."[141]

The majority opinion ruled relevant Frank's testimony that while in jail Frank had refused an interview with detectives accompanied by Conley. "The fear of bringing out damaging evidence...might have been the cause of declining the interview.... This would be a proper matter of inquiry by the jury."[142]

In ruling on the admissibility of character evidence, the court cited the Georgia Penal Code 1910, Section 1019, in which the exception seems to swallow the rule: "The general character of the parties, and especially their conduct in other transactions, are irrelevant matter, unless the nature of the action involves such character and renders necessary or proper the investigation of such conduct."[143]

The court cautioned that there is no presumption that a person accused of a crime is of bad character, nor does an inference of bad character arise from the failure to produce evidence of good character. "An accused may, however, elect to offer evidence of his good character, and its relevancy is to seek to create a doubt of his guilt in the minds of the jury."[144] Where the accused introduces evidence of good character, the court reasoned, the prosecution is permitted to introduce evidence of bad character. In the Frank case, the court ruled, the probative value of the defendant's evidence as to good character involved his character with regard to lasciviousness, and therefore it was not improper for the state to introduce character evidence with respect to lasciviousness.

The majority of the Georgia Supreme Court also found that "unless it appears there has been an abuse of discretion," the issue of jurors' putative prejudice was for the trial judge to decide.[145]

Leo Frank's lawyers filed another motion for a new trial based on new evidence, including affidavits from prosecution witnesses repudiating their testimony and from employees of the National Pencil Company stating that the police had tried to suborn perjury from them.

The new evidence Frank's lawyers produced in support of their motion for a new trial included letters written by Jim Conley to a fellow prison inmate named Annie Maude Carter. The salacious letters were similar in diction to the murder notes. The defense also produced forensic evidence and an affidavit indicating that the paper on which the murder notes were written was found in the basement of the factory, not on the second floor, where Frank's office was, as the prosecution had alleged. However, Georgia law provided that reversals by higher courts had to be based on errors of law, not errors of fact, and that for evidence of perjury to be used as the basis of an appeal, the perjurer had to be prosecuted.

> If Dorsey and his police suborned perjury from state witnesses as charged – and there seems little doubt that this was done... they could hardly have prosecuted the "turncoats" without risking exposure of the role they themselves played.[146]

When the subsequent motion for a new trial was denied and the case was remanded to the trial court for sentencing, Leo Frank did not make the usually futile request for clemency. Before being again sentenced to death, he said to the court:

> If the State and the law wills that my life be taken as a blood-atonement for the poor little child who was killed by another, then it remains for me only to die with whatever fortitude my manhood will allow. But I am innocent of this crime.[147]

Leo Frank's new lawyers filed a motion to set aside the verdict based on the fact that neither Frank nor his lawyers had been present in court when the verdict was rendered. The Georgia Supreme Court affirmed the denial of the motion. The court held that the issue of Frank's absence when the verdict was rendered, as well as the question of whether or not his attorneys had the right to waive his presence, should have been raised in the original motion for a new trial.

Frank's lawyers filed a motion for *habeas corpus* with the United States District Court for the Northern District of Georgia, alleging that Frank's imprisonment violated the Constitution by depriving him of liberty without due process of law.[148] The district court denied the motion. Frank's new lawyer, Louis Marshall, president of the American Jewish Committee, filed a petition for *habeas corpus* with the United States Supreme Court under the Federal Act of 1867, which gave federal courts jurisdiction over state prisoners who had not been granted relief by state courts. Supreme Court Justice Joseph R. Lamar denied the petition, as did Justice Oliver Wendell Holmes. However, Justice Holmes stated "I very seriously doubt if the petitioner [Frank] has had due process of law." On the third presentation to the Supreme Court on a petition for a writ of error, Justice Lamar granted the petition, ruling that precedental federal legal questions were involved.[149]

In its brief to the U.S. Supreme Court, the state cited fourteen Georgia cases where verdicts were set aside because they were influenced by hostile demonstrations to show that the Georgia courts were not averse to overturning guilty verdicts where a hostile environment rendered such action appropriate.[150]

The Supreme Court, in an opinion by Justice Mahlon Pitney, *Frank v. Mangum*, 237 U.S. 309, 59 L.Ed. 969 (1915), discussed five major issues:

(1) The disorder in the court and the question of whether not only the jury, but also the judge, succumbed to mob domination;

(2) The defendant's right to be present during the entire trial and at the rendering of the verdict and whether his presence was an essential part of the right to a trial which could not be waived by the defendant or his counsel;

(3) Whether the rendering of the verdict in the defendant's absence and the absence of counsel without the defendant's consent was a violation of due process guaranteed by the Fourteenth Amendment sufficient to render the verdict and judgment null;

(4) Whether the failure to allege Frank's absence at the reception of the verdict as a ground for a new trial in the first motion for a new trial deprived him of the right afterwards to attack the judgment on that ground; and

(5) Whether the Georgia Supreme Court decision, requiring the objection to the defendant's absence to have been made in the motion for a new trial and holding that it could not be relied on in the motion to set aside the verdict, was the equivalent of an *ex post facto* law and, therefore, unconstitutional because it departed from the prior practice of the court.

The Supreme Court delineated "the essential question" before it as "not the guilt or innocence of the prisoner, or the truth of any particular fact...but whether the state, taking into view the entire course of the procedure, has deprived him of due process of law."[151]

The Court held that:

a criminal prosecution in the courts of a state, based upon a law not in itself repugnant to the Federal Constitution, and conducted in accordance with the settled course of judicial proceedings as established by the law of the state, so long as it

includes notice and a hearing or an opportunity to be heard, before a court of competent jurisdiction, according to established
modes of procedure, is "due process."[152]

The Supreme Court stated that the petition for review contained a "narrative of disorder, hostile manifestations and uproar"
which, if true, showed "an environment inconsistent with a fair
trial and an impartial verdict. But... The narrative has no proper
place in a petition" addressed to the Supreme Court, except to
throw light on the state court proceedings. The narrative consisted
of mere allegation, which the defendant had the right to submit,
but the Court had considered the rebuttal affidavits and found the
allegations "groundless except in a few particulars" that the state
courts had ruled harmless errors. Moreover, the fact determina-
tions of the Georgia Supreme Court regarding the allegations were
entitled to comity, and therefore the United States Supreme Court
had to take them as truth.[153]

The majority of the Supreme Court held that the accused
had the right to be present during the entire trial, but could waive
the right. Where the defendant's counsel waived the defendant's
presence without his consent, the Court held that there was sufficient error to render the verdict null if a timely motion for a
new trial were filed. However, because Frank's lawyers' motion for
a new trial, which contained more than a hundred grounds, had
not included his right to be present, the Georgia Supreme Court
had ruled that Frank could not thereafter move to set aside the
verdict because of his absence when the verdict was rendered. The
Supreme Court concluded that the Georgia court's procedural
ruling was reasonable and not in violation of the Fourteenth
Amendment.[154] The Court agreed that the defendant had waived
his right to be present by failing to raise a timely objection.[155]

The Supreme Court dispensed with the defense's *ex post
facto* argument as applying only to legislative actions.[156] The
Court concluded that because Leo Frank was given an oppor-

tunity to be heard and was not deprived of any right guaranteed by the Constitution, he had been convicted under due process of law.[157]

Two justices of the Supreme Court, Justice Oliver Wendell Holmes and Justice (later Chief Justice) Charles Evans Hughes, rendered a minority opinion that the trial was unfair, although they did not concur that the presence of the defendant when the verdict was rendered was required by the Constitution of the United States.[158]

Justice Holmes wrote the dissenting opinion in which Justice Hughes concurred, *Frank v. Mangum*, 237 U.S. 309, 346–350, *dissent*:

> Mob law does not become due process of law by securing the assent of a terrorized jury.... The fact that the state court still has its general jurisdiction and is otherwise a competent court does not make it impossible to find that a jury has been subjected to intimidation in a particular case.... And notwithstanding the principle of comity and convenience (for in our opinion, it is nothing more...) that calls for a resort to the local appellate tribunal before coming to the court of the United States for a writ of habeas corpus, when, as here, that resort has been had in vain, the power to secure fundamental rights that had existed at every stage becomes a duty, and must be put forth.
>
> The single question in our minds is whether a petition alleging that the trial took place in the midst of a mob savagely and manifestly intent on a single result is shown on its face unwarranted.... This is not a matter for polite presumptions; we must look facts in the face. Any judge who has sat with juries knows that, in spite of forms, they are extremely likely to be impregnated by the environing atmosphere. And when we find the judgment of the expert on the spot, – of the judge whose business it was to preserve not only form, but substance – to have been that if one juryman yielded to the reasonable doubt that he himself later expressed in court as the result of most

anxious deliberation, neither prisoner or counsel would be safe from the rage of the crowd, we think the presumption overwhelming that the jury responded to the passions of the mob.... There is no reason to fear an impairment of the authority of the state to punish the guilty.... But supposing the alleged facts to be true, we are of opinion that if they were before the [Georgia] supreme court, it sanctioned a situation upon which the courts of the United States should act; and if, for any reason they were not before the [Georgia] supreme court, it is our duty to act upon them now, and to declare lynch law as little valid when practised by a regularly drawn jury as when administered by one elected by a mob intent on death.

Professor Leonard Dinnerstein points out that American standards of fairness and justice have evolved in the last century.[159] Justice Holmes's fame stemmed both from his eloquence and from his foresight. In 1923 Holmes cited his dissent in the Frank case in writing for the majority of the Court that a mob-dominated trial is no trial at all.[160] In the second half of the twentieth century the Supreme Court ruled that where a defendant has been exposed to extensive pre-trial publicity, "any subsequent court proceedings...could be but a hollow formality."[161]

The Commutation

More than 100,000 letters, including heartfelt letters from Frank's wife and from his mother, as well as chain letters, a letter from Vice President Thomas R. Marshall, and letters from senators, other Southern governors, university presidents, editors, and labor leaders, begged the Prison Commission and the governor of Georgia to commute Frank's sentence to life imprisonment. There were thousands of petitions with millions of signatures, including those of 10,000 Georgia residents. The since-deceased Judge Roan had written the State Prison Board saying that he recommended to the board and the governor that Frank's sentence be commuted to life imprisonment. Initially no one opposed the Prison Board's commuting Frank's sentence, but on the day after the hearing a delegation headed by former governor Joseph Brown asked the commission to reopen the hearing.[162] The commission thereafter voted two to one to decline Frank's petition for commutation.[163]

After John M. Slaton became governor of Georgia, his law firm (which continued to use his name) merged with the firm of Frank's attorney, Luther Rosser, creating a putative conflict of interest.[164] However, Governor Slaton declined to recuse himself, despite the fact that he received thousands, and his wife hundreds, of letters, including chain letters, saying that they would be killed and their home destroyed if he commuted the sentence.[165] Governor Slaton wrote, "I have been unable to even open a large proportion of the letters sent me, because of their number and because I could not through them gain any assistance in determining my duty."[166]

Governor John Slaton received Leo Frank's appeal for clemency some two weeks before his term was to expire. He stated, "I shall be guided solely by the merits of the case and my own conscience.... If Leo M. Frank is guilty, he ought to be hanged. If he is not guilty, then he ought to be saved."[167] His successor had indicated that he would not pardon Frank.[168]

The governor held a hearing. He had two private interviews with Jim Conley's lawyer, William Smith, whose report analyzing the murder notes and Conley's speech and writing patterns Frank's attorney William Schley Howard had submitted to the Prison Commission. Smith's study of the murder notes and the similarities in grammar and diction between the notes and Conley's other known writing and speech, including the trial transcript, was a factor in convincing Governor Slaton that Conley was not telling the truth. Smith had said publicly, "I have never ceased to be a student of the Frank case. Practically all my spare time has been devoted to a study of it. I have come to the conclusion – or at least this is my personal judgment – that Leo M. Frank is innocent."[169] Despite the ethical dilemma of his having been Conley's lawyer, he felt obliged to come forward in order to save an innocent man's life. Smith's own life was threatened after he made his statement to the press.[170] Because he had not made a statement earlier, Tom Watson accused Smith of accepting a bribe to say that Conley had committed the murder.[171] By the time of his death in 1949, William Smith's vocal cords were paralyzed, but he scrawled a deathbed note, "In articles of death, I believe in the innocence and good character of Leo M. Frank. Wm. Smith."[172]

In addition, Governor Slaton had received a letter from an African-American in the state penitentiary identified only as "Freeman," saying that he had been playing cards with Conley in the basement of the pencil factory on the day of the murder. Just before noon Conley had climbed a ladder to the first floor, and shortly thereafter, Freeman heard muffled screams and climbed to the first floor, where he saw Conley struggling with someone. Frightened, Freeman went back down to the basement and left through a rear door. This letter was not made public for eight years. A similar story had appeared in the *Atlanta Georgian* on June 6, 1913, but the newspaper dropped the story when it could not be verified.[173]

As was his custom in deciding pardon cases, Governor Slaton studied the trial transcript. He also visited the pencil factory, accompanied by Dorsey and Howard, as well as by the police department's lead investigator. The governor asked whether the elevator could be stopped before it hit the bottom of the shaft. Howard referred to the trial transcript and found Conley's testimony, as well as that of other employees, that the elevator stopped itself when it hit the ground. The governor went down in the elevator and found that it hit bottom.[174] Slaton noted, as had been pointed out in an article in *Collier's*,[175] that the detectives testified that when they went to the factory on the day after the murder, a pile of excrement, crushed by the elevator, produced a strong odor. At the trial Conley testified that he had defecated in the elevator shaft on the day of the murder, and that he and Frank had used the elevator to bring the body to the basement. However, the detectives had seen the excrement when searching the basement on the day of the murder and it had not yet been crushed. If the events had happened as Conley had testified they had, the feces would have already been crushed when the detectives arrived. Furthermore, the mechanic, who had been in the factory until about 3:00 in the afternoon on the day of the murder, stated that the elevator made a lot of noise, and if it had been used, he would have heard it.

On June 21, 1915, the formerly popular governor commuted Frank's sentence, thereby committing political suicide. When he came to bed at 2:00 A.M., Governor Slaton told his wife, Sarah, whom he called "Sallie," "It may mean my death or worse." Mrs. Slaton kissed her husband and said, "I would rather be the widow of a brave and honorable man than the wife of a coward!"[176] In his commutation decree, Governor Slaton cogently summarized the evidence, including the new evidence. He stated that he was not attacking the verdict, but carrying out the will of the judge, who would have made the penalty a life sentence had he realized it was in his power under Georgia law.[177]

Governor Slaton wrote:

This case has been marked by doubt. The trial judge doubted. Two judges of the Court of Georgia doubted. Two judges of the Supreme Court of the United States doubted. One of the three Prison Commissioners doubted.[178]

A few days after the commutation Governor Slaton stated:

Two thousand years ago another Governor washed his hands of a case and turned over a Jew to a mob. For two thousand years that Governor's name has been accursed. If today another Jew were lying in his grave because I had failed to do my duty I would all through life find his blood on my hands and would consider myself an assassin through cowardice.[179]

The Lynching of Leo Frank

Before announcing his decision, Governor Slaton had the Fulton County sheriff spirit Leo Frank away from the county jail to Milledgeville State Prison Farm. The warden was ordered to double the prison guard and to refuse Frank any visitors not authorized by the Prison Commission.[180]

Following the commutation, Tom Watson, editor of the *Jeffersonian,* wrote, "When John M. Slaton tosses on a sleepless bed, in the years to come, he will see a vivid picture of that little Georgia girl, decoyed to the metal room by this satyr-faced New York Jew." He also wrote provocatively, "We will make certain that no other Georgia girl, budding into womanhood, will die a horrible death defending her virtue against a rich depraved Sodomite Jew." If that was not sufficient to convey the message, he harangued, "Let no man reproach the South with Lynch law…let him say whether Lynch law *is not better than no law at all.*"[181]

Thousands of men arrived in Atlanta after they heard of the commutation. Atlanta's sheriff had warned Jewish leaders of a possible riot and authorized some to carry guns. The shouting mob marched on the governor's mansion. After a violent confrontation, state troopers dispersed the crowd. A boycott of Jewish merchants was largely unsuccessful,[182] although some Jewish families left the state, and one large Jewish-owned concern, the Empire Plow Company, abandoned its property in Georgia and, instead, built a new factory in Ohio.[183]

Seventy-five armed men and boys were arrested in the woods behind the governor's house six miles from the capital. The governor refused to swear out warrants against them. Demonstrations continued, and the governor remained under guard until his successor, Nathaniel Harris, was inaugurated on June 26. Governor Slaton immediately left the state for an extended trip.[184]

On July 17, 1915 at Milledgeville Prison Farm a convicted murderer, William Creen, slit Leo Frank's throat. A surgeon serving a sentence for murder and another prisoner saved Frank's life.

The new governor received many requests for Creen's pardon and release.

On the night of August 16–17 a group called the "Knights of Mary Phagan" broke into the prison farm. They overpowered the guards, seized Leo Frank, and drove him to Marietta, Georgia, Mary Phagan's hometown and burial place, where he was hanged from a tree outside the town, blood dripping from his neck wound. When Frank's body was cut down, it was stomped and kicked. Photographs of the hanging body became popular in Georgia. The grand jury that investigated the lynching could find neither evidence nor testimony against the Knights of Mary Phagan, despite the fact that their identities were widely known and included prominent men.[185]

Harold W. Ross, the founding editor of *The New Yorker*, who covered the Frank case for the *Atlanta Journal* as a reporter, watched Leo Frank when he was shown the body of Mary Phagan and spoke to him afterward. Ross observed Frank in detention and at the trial and listened to his statement to the jury. He concluded that Frank's conduct was that of an innocent man, that he did not have a fair trial, and that the evidence against him did not prove him guilty "beyond a reasonable doubt." Ross wrote:

> If juries convict men upon [such] evidence... and judges uphold them, no man is absolutely safe from paying the penalty for a crime he did not commit....

> ...the police did what they always do in Georgia – arrested a Negro...

> But this time the public – always excitable in the South – was not satisfied.... So they arrested more Negroes. But this did not stop the clamor....

> The murder of Mary Phagan must be paid for with blood. And a Negro's blood would not suffice.

... I was, I think, the first newspaperman to talk to [Conley] after his series of confessions.

"Is Frank a pervert?" I asked flatly.

"No," was the reply. Moreover the Negro exhibited surprise at the question....

Yet, a week later...he made still another confession in which he said Frank was a pervert and a month later at the trial he...testified to...a series of alleged acts of perversion.

But the testimony of Conley did not alone convict Frank. Nor did the circumstantial evidence. It was a combination of these with the outside influences. There was a strong religious prejudice against Frank. The atmosphere in the courtroom was obviously hostile.[186]

In the aftermath, Solicitor General Hugh M. Dorsey was elected governor of Georgia, Tom Watson was elected U.S. senator from Georgia, and the Ku Klux Klan was revived in Georgia.[187] Jim Conley was convicted of wife beating and arrested for public drunkenness and vagrancy. He was shot in the chest during a burglary attempt, and after his release from the hospital, he received a twenty-year sentence.[188] He had received a one-year sentence on a chain gang as an accessory after the fact to the murder of Mary Phagan.[189]

In 1982, when he was in his eighties, Alonzo Mann, who had been an office boy at the factory in 1913, came forward to unburden his conscience. He admitted what he had been too afraid to say at Frank's trial. On Saturday, April 26, shortly after 12:00, Mann walked into the factory and saw Jim Conley carrying a limp girl. Conley threatened to kill him if he told anyone. Mann went home and told his mother, who begged him not to get involved. The Board of Pardons and Paroles considered Mann's evidence in determining not to grant a posthumous pardon to Leo Frank, but decided that the evidence had little probative value, as Conley had admitted carrying Mary Phagan's body. The issue was whether he had done so as the murderer or as an accomplice.[190]

In 1986, in response to a request by the B'nai B'rith Anti-Defamation League through the attorneys Dale Schwartz and Charles Wittenstein, the Georgia Pardon and Parole Board granted a posthumous pardon to Leo Frank. In unanimously issuing the pardon, the members of the board said that too much time had gone by for them to state that he was innocent of the charges against him, but they were issuing the pardon because he did not receive a fair trial. The pardon was granted "in recognition of the state's failure to protect the person of Leo Frank" and to bring his killers to justice.[191] Thus ends the procedural sequence of a unique saga in the annals of American law, but the absence of conclusive proof of Leo Frank's guilt or innocence lingers as an intriguing conundrum for aficionados of legal and Jewish history.

Further Reading

Dinnerstein, Leonard. *The Leo Frank Case.* New York and London: Columbia U. Press, 1968; Atlanta: University of Georgia Press, 1987

Golden, Harry. *A Little Girl is Dead.* Cleveland: World, 1965; New York: Avon Books, 1965.

Lindeman, Albert S. *The Jew Accused: Three Anti-Semitic Affairs.* Cambridge: Cambridge University Press, 1991

Oney, Steve. *And the Dead Shall Rise: The Murder of Mary Phagan and the Lynching of Leo Frank.* New York: Pantheon/Random House, 2003

Notes

1. According to conservative estimates, approximately 4,752 people – 3,446 of them African-American – were lynched in the United States between 1882 (the first year reliable statistics were compiled) and 1968 (the year many scholars believe the classic form of lynching ended). Tim Walker, "It Happened Here," *Teaching Tolerance* (Southern Poverty Law Center), Fall 2003,

p. 52; Franklin E. Zimring, "Lynching," *World Book Encyclopedia* (1990), p. 539. Between 1884 and 1900, fifty-one women were lynched in the United States; 2,080 people were lynched in the South and 436 in the North. Of the lynchings that occurred prior to 1884, two-thirds of the victims were accused of petty offenses, such as shoplifting and public drunkenness. Of the lynchings that occurred between 1889 and 1930, four-fifths of the victims were African-American men; less than one-sixth were accused of rape (www.spartacus.schoolnet.co.uk.) The Tuskegee Institute found that in almost half of the cases of lynchings of African-American males, the victim was castrated prior to being killed. Harry Golden, *A Little Girl Is Dead* (New York: Avon Books, 1965), p. 122. Nineteen Italians were lynched in Louisiana in the 1890s because they appeared to have fraternized with African-Americans. Leonard Dinnerstein, *The Leo Frank Case* (New York: Columbia University Press, 1968), p. 65. At the time Leo Frank was arrested.,approximately three African-Americans per week were lynched in the South (PBS Online, http://afroamhistory.about.com).

2. Steve Oney, *And the Dead Shall Rise: The Murder of Mary Phagan and the Lynching of Leo Frank* (New York: Random House 2003), p. 16.

3. Albert S. Lindemann, *The Jew Accused: Three Anti-Semitic Affairs: Dreyfus, Beilis, Frank, 1894–1915* (Cambridge University Press, 1991), p. 240.

4. Harry Golden, *A Little Girl Is Dead* (New York: Avon Books, 1965), pp. 22–23.

5. Lindemann, quoting Steven Hertzberg, *Strangers Within the Gate City: The Jews of Atlanta, 1845–1915* (Philadelphia: Jewish Publication Society, 1978), p. 180.

6. Dinnerstein, p. 2.

7. Golden, pp. 59–60.

8. Ibid., p. 19.

9. Ibid., p. 65.

10. In the preceding years there were eighteen unsolved murders of black women in Atlanta and the Atlanta police were viewed with skepticism. Lindemann, p. 242; Oney, p. 100.

11. Governor Slaton's Commutation Order, quoted in Golden, p. 337.

12. Ibid., quoted in Golden, p. 335.

13. Oney, p. 318.

14. Lindemann, p. 243.

15. Pierre van Paassen, *To Number Our Days, An Autobiographical Memoir* (New York: Charles Scribner's Sons, 1964), pp. 237–238.

16. Golden, pp. 66–67.

17. Oney, pp. 389, 405.

18. Oney, p. 88; Golden, pp. 67–68.

19. Golden, pp. 60–61, 107.

20. Ibid., p. 145.

21. Ibid., p. 60.
22. Oney, p. 114.
23. Golden, p. 68.
24. Oney, p. 341.
25. Golden, p. 68.
26. Oney, pp. 482–483.
27. Golden, p. 5.
28. Oney, p. 494.
29. Golden, pp. 56, 63.
30. Ibid., pp. 81–84, 121.
31. Dinnerstein, pp. 6–7.
32. Ibid., p. 6.
33. Golden, pp. 64, 78.
34. Governor Slaton's Commutation Order, quoted in Golden, p. 333.
35. Oney, p. 498.
36. Dinnerstein, pp. 20–21, 29; Golden, pp. 87–88.
37. Oney, p. 134.
38. Ibid., p. 136.
39. Governor Slaton's Commutation Order, quoted in Golden, pp. 327–330.
40. Golden, pp. 90–91, 130.
41. Governor Slaton's Commutation Order, quoted in Golden, pp. 328–332, 337.
42. Oney, p. 139.
43. Governor Slaton's Commutation Order, quoted in Golden, p. 330.
44. Lindemann, p. 236.
45. Ibid., pp. 229-231, 233–234.
46. Golden, p. 53.
47. Harry Golden dedicated *A Little Girl Is Dead* to the city of Atlanta, "which suffered the most of all southern cities in the 1860s. In the 1950s Atlanta led the South in the resolution of the desegregation crisis, and in the 1960s it led the nation in the reapportionment process." In contrast, in 1905, out of a total population of 115,000, Atlanta police arrested 17,000 people, largely for drunkenness and disorderly conduct, and Atlanta arrested more children for disturbing the peace than any other city in the United States. Moreover, from 1889 through 1928 more people were lynched in Georgia than in any other state in the country, (Dinnerstein, pp. 8, 148). A foreign visitor to Atlanta recalled: "There is scarcely a trace left today of the unimaginable squalor of Atlanta's Negro quarters. Under... Roosevelt's New Deal all the shanty towns and slums were wiped out and replaced with modern dwellings. In 1922, though, the city's Negro sections were labyrinths of unpaved narrow streets, tumble-down shacks with corrugated iron roofs and a teeming population.... on Monday mornings... the number of arrests sometimes ran up to a hundred or more as a result of the raids carried out

by the police in the Negro section on Saturday nights. The prisoners were not even asked whether they pleaded guilty or not. But seldom were they represented by counsel, and even more rarely was anyone discharged as not guilty. It was the sheerest travesty of justice" (van Paassen, pp. 233–234, 237).

48. Lindemann, p. 232.
49. The South became industrialized later than the North. In order to revitalize the local economy, Southern leaders encouraged Northern industrialists to build factories in the South, where labor was relatively cheap. At the turn of the twentieth century Atlanta was one of the fastest-growing cities in the South. The chamber of commerce's slogan was "Watch Atlanta Grow," which replaced the previous year's slogan "Balance Agriculture with Industry." However, the shift to an industrial economy was occurring because the price of crops was falling, small farms were failing, and farmers and their families provided a source of cheap labor. Under the crop lien system, farmers mortgaged their future harvests to merchants who supplied seed, food, and clothes (Golden, pp. 22, 207). Marginal Southern farmers lost not only their family farms, but also their way of life, as women and even children had to leave their homes and work in factories in order to help support their impoverished families. It was commonly feared that bosses would take advantage of young girls in the factories where they had to work. Reformist efforts to abolish child labor, shorten the workday for women, and pay higher wages were unsuccessful. In the aftermath of the trial, Tom Watson wrote in the *Jeffersonian*, "The National Pencil Factory, owned by Frank's people, fought our Child Labor bill fiercely, and helped to kill it – and... it cost the Superintendent his life" (Oney, pp. 73, 599).

One of Frank's lawyers said of the National Pencil firm, "The factory is no better and no worse than any other factory of about that size in the city of Atlanta" (Oney, p. 317). Thus was his client damned with faint praise. In contrast, the prosecution was able to use the factory conditions against Frank, as when F.A. Hooper commented in his summation, "As a citizen of Atlanta, I am not proud of conditions that existed in that factory!... The factory was under the control of this man Frank" (Golden, pp. 177–178).

50. Dinnerstein, p. 202.
51. Lindemann, p. 239.
52. Ibid., p. 264.
53. Golden, p. 218.
54. Lindemann, pp. 247–248.
55. Golden, pp. 3, 314.
56. Ibid., pp. 106–107.
57. Dinnerstein, p. 18.
58. Golden, p. 56.
59. Ibid., pp. 218–219.

60. Lindemann, p. 264.
61. Governor Slaton's Commutation Order, quoted in Golden, p. 314.
62. Lindemann, p. 258.
63. Golden, p. 105.
64. Oney, p. 237.
65. Dinnerstein, pp. 189–190.
66. Golden, p. 114; Oney, p. 227.
67. Dinnerstein, p. 49.
68. Governor Slaton's Commutation Order, quoted in Golden, pp. 335–336.
69. Golden, p. 174.
70. Golden, p. 97; Oney, p. 166.
71. Oney pp. 167–170.
72. Ibid., p. 307.
73. Ibid., p. 82.
74. Ibid., pp. 372, 393–394, 407, 409.
75. Ibid., p. 416.
76. Ibid., pp. 422–423.
77. Golden, p. 97.
78. Lindemann, p. 246; Golden, pp. 108, 111; Oney, p. 47.
79. Golden, pp. 101–102; Oney p. 191.
80. Oney, p. 328.
81. Golden, p. 180.
82. Jim Conley had been fined several times for drunk and disorderly conduct. He had also been arrested for rock-throwing and attempted robbery and had served two sentences on a road gang. Three months prior to Mary Phagan's murder, Conley was jailed for shooting at a woman "I have been having intercourse with," grazing another woman in the process (Oney, pp. 119–120).
83. Oney, p. 408.
84. Ibid., p. 405.
85. *Frank v. State*, 80 S.E. 1016, 1031 (Georgia Supreme Court 1914).
86. Golden, pp. 125–127.
87. Ibid., pp. 128–129.
88. Lindemann, pp. 255, 269.
89. Governor Slaton's Commutation Order, quoted in Golden, p. 336.
90. Golden, pp. 170–171, quoting Frank's statement to the jury.
91. Governor Slaton's Commutation Order, quoted in Golden, p. 333.
92. Golden, pp. 127–128; *Frank v. State*, 80 S.E. 1016, 1034 (*dissent*).
93. Oney, p. 496.
94. Golden pp. 128, 236; Lindemann, p. 244.
95. Golden, p. 137.
96. Governor Slaton's Commutation Order, quoted in Golden, p. 338.
97. Golden, p. 153.

98. Oney, pp. 388–389.
99. Ibid., p. 414.
100. Golden, pp. 152–154, Oney, p. 286.
101. Lindemann, pp. 256–257; Oney, p. 318.
102. Dinnerstein, pp. 14, 18, 19.
103. *Frank v. State*, 80 s.e. at 1029; Golden, pp. 174–175.
104. Oney, p. 326.
105. Golden, pp. 184–185.
106. *Frank v. State*, 80 s.e. at 1031, 1032.
107. Ibid. at 1032.
108. Governor Slaton's Commutation Order, quoted in Golden, p. 332.
109. Oney, p. 339.
110. Golden, p. 182.
111. Oney, p. 340.
112. Golden, p. 196.
113. Ibid., p. 227.
114. Ibid., p. 237.
115. Lindemann, p. 259.
116. Golden, p. 216.
117. Lindemann, pp. 266–267.
118. Ibid., p. 267.
119. See Oney, p. 431.
120. Allen Lumpkin Henson, *Confessions of a Criminal Lawyer* (New York: Vantage Press 1959), pp. 61–66.
121. Oney, pp. 423–443.
122. Henson, p. 66.
123. *Frank v. State*, 80 s.e. 1016, 1034 (Georgia Supreme Court 1914).
124. Golden, p. 233.
125. Ibid., p. 147.
126. *Frank v. State*, 80 s.e. at 1033.
127. Golden, p. 147.
128. *Frank v. State*, 80 s.e. at 1020.
129. Ibid., p. 1026.
130. *Frank v. State*, 80 s.e. at 1027.
131. Ibid. 1016, 1041, Chief Justice William D. Fish and Justice Marcus Beck *dissenting*.
132. Ibid. 1016, 1035, Justices Fish and Beck *dissenting*.
133. Ibid. 1016, 1037, *dissent*.
134. Ibid. 1016, 1038 (*dissent*), quoting from *Cawthon v. State*, 110 Ga. 395, 46 s.e. 897.
135. *Frank v. State*, 80 s.e. 1016, 1040 (*dissent*).
136. Ibid. 1016, 1037 (*dissent*).
137. Ibid., quoting from *People v. Molineux*, 168 n.y. 264, 61 n.e. 286.

138. Ibid. 1016, 1040 (*dissent*).

139. Ibid. 1041.

140. Ibid. 1042, 1043.

141. Ibid. (*dissent*) at 1036.

142. Ibid.

143. Ibid. 1016, 1030.

144. Ibid. 1030.

145. Ibid. 1016, 1034.

146. Golden, p. 239, quoting Samuels, *Night Fell on Georgia*, p. 184.

147. Oney, pp. 376–377.

148. Golden, p. 242.

149. Oney, pp. 447–449, 460.

150. *Frank v. Mangum*, 237 U.S. 309, 59 L.Ed. 969 (1915).

151. Ibid. at 979, 980.

152. Ibid. at 980.

153. Ibid. at 332, 333, 336.

154. Ibid. at 338–340.

155. Ibid. at 344.

156. Ibid.

157. Ibid. at 345.

158. Ibid. 309, 346 (*dissent*).

159. Dinnerstein, pp. 151–156.

160. Golden, p. 246, referring to *Moore v. Dempsey*, 261 U.S. 86.

161. *Rideau v. Louisiana*, 373 U.S. 723, 726 (1963); see also *Shepard v. State of Florida*, 341 U.S. 50 (1951); *Sheppard v. Maxwell*, 384 U.S. 333 (1966).

162. Golden, p. 247.

163. Oney, p. 488.

164. Dinnerstein, pp. 123–124.

165. Henson, p. 68; Golden, p. 256.

166. Golden, p. 313, quoting from Governor John M. Slaton's Commutation Order.

167. Oney, p. 472.

168. Golden, p. 255.

169. Oney, p. 435.

170. Ibid., pp. 436, 439.

171. Dinnerstein, pp. 114–115.

172. Oney, p. 643.

173. Dinnerstein, pp. 169–170.

174. Oney, pp. 495, 497, 498; Governor Slaton's Commutation Order, quoted in Golden, p. 325; Golden, pp. 255, 257.

175. Oney, pp. 454–455.

176. Henson, p. 68.

177. Governor Slaton's Commutation Order, quoted in Golden, pp. 339–341.

178. Governor Slaton's Commutation Order, quoted in Golden, p. 346.
179. Dinnerstein, p. 129.
180. Ibid., p. 126.
181. Ibid., p. 132.
182. Lindemann, p. 270.
183. Golden, pp. 224–225.
184. Dinnerstein, p. 133.
185. Lindemann, pp. 271–272; Oney, p. 565.
186. Golden, Appendix c, pp. 343–346.
187. Dinnerstein, pp. 149, 150, 159, 160.
188. Oney, p. 612.
189. Ibid., p. 385.
190. Oney, pp. 644–645.
191. Ibid., pp. 648–649; *New York Times*, March 12, 1986, A16.

The Confirmation of
Louis D. Brandeis

PHILIP S. CARCHMAN*

The central event in the life and career of Louis Dembitz Brandeis occurred during the four months encompassing his nomination and confirmation to the United States Supreme Court. We examine the impact of anti-Semitism on the nomination and confirmation process of Brandeis as the first Jewish member of the Court.

Before dealing with the events of January 1916, it is important to have some overview of the ethnic climate of the United States at the beginning of the twentieth century. Before 1881, the Jewish population of the United States approximated 150,000 people, comprising the descendants of the original Jewish settlers during the colonial period and the early nineteenth century, whose numbers were significantly supplemented by the immigration of German middle-class Jews during the mid-nineteenth century. These immigrants were, for the most part, educated and, because of their small numbers, were generally accepted into the mainstream of American life. The year 1881 saw the beginning of a three-decade migration of over a million and a half East European Jews, of whom approximately 70 percent were from Russia and the territories it controlled. These immigrants were, by and large, less educated and more religious than the Jews already in the United

---

* The views expressed in this essay represent the views of the author only and not those of the New Jersey judiciary.

States; they were less familiar with the secular world and the ways of their new homeland. In 1917 Jews made up approximately 3.25 percent of the United States population. The primary population locations were the large urban centers, especially New York City. The Jews, joined by many other immigrants, including Italians and Slavs, were not unique per se, but formed a distinct group subject to the nativism, which served as the counterweight to their acceptance. With the vast number of immigrants came the inevitable threat to the established society, both economically and politically, and in the case of the Russian Jews, a feeling that they represented a radical force. In urban centers, the immigrant population was clearly an economic threat, while in the rural areas, the strangeness of the new immigrants created a social threat. Significantly for our later discussion, the well-established Yankees of New England felt the status quo threatened by these interlopers from foreign lands. In politics and in business, anti-Semitism took a subtle form. Direct anti-Semitism was less apparent than references to "greed," "materialism" and other similar expressions.

In addition, this period saw the rise of labor unions headed by Jews such as Samuel Gompers that reinforced the image of Jews as radicals. The rural area saw the rise of populism, which pitted the agrarian against the capitalist and further, provided a fertile ground for anti-Semitism. Jews presented an easy distant target for the ills of the population. In sum, there were three groups recognized as breeders of anti-Semitism in the early twentieth century: the patricians of New England, the farmers of the South and Midwest, and the economically threatened ethnic lower class.[1]

This period saw the creation of the American Jewish Committee, headed by German Jews like Louis Marshall, a prominent New York lawyer at Schiff, Salzberger, Strauss and Adler, who tried to deal with issues of anti-Semitism by establishing lines of communication between the Jewish community and governmental agencies. In addition, the Anti-Defamation League (then part of B'nai B'rith) was formed in 1913, in good measure as a result of an incident, which proved to be one of the most significant incidents evidencing anti-Semitism in this period. The incident would later be known as the American Dreyfus case. As fully discussed by Ms. Steinberg-Brent in the preceding essay, Leo Frank, the manager of a pencil factory in Georgia, was accused of murdering a fourteen-year-old girl by the name of Mary Phagen. Anti-Semitism was not dealt with in a subtle manner, but was openly discussed by Frank's attorney. Frank was convicted, but ultimately the governor of Georgia commuted his sentence. In response, Frank was taken from prison and lynched by a mob. The Southern reaction was not sympathy for Frank, but the heightening of strong anti-Semitic feelings throughout the agrarian South.

This was the sense of the country in the second decade of the twentieth century, and given the strong anti-Semitic feelings present throughout the country, the nomination of Louis Brandeis to the United States Supreme Court took on unique significance.

The Players

The drama that would result in the appointment of Louis D. Brandeis involved an interesting and diverse cast. Among the supporters were:

- Woodrow Wilson, twenty-eighth president of the United States, former governor of New Jersey, and former president of a "small obscure college" in central New Jersey (Princeton). Wilson was elected in 1912 by a plurality of 6 million out of 15 million votes, and not by a majority, in a three-way race with incumbent president William Howard Taft and former president Theodore Roosevelt, who had a combined vote of 7.5 million. Wilson was generally viewed as a progressive, and it was this view of him that attracted Louis D. Brandeis to Wilson's camp in 1912 when they met for the first time.
- Robert La Follette, Republican senator from Wisconsin and leader of the Progressive Party, whom Brandeis had supported prior to his support of Wilson. La Follette was to become a key vote in the Senate.

- Felix Frankfurter, professor at Harvard Law School and ultimately himself a justice of the Supreme Court. Frankfurter would later write numerous editorials supporting Brandeis.
- Norman Hapgood, editor of *Collier's Weekly*, a supporter of Brandeis, who would arrange a social meeting between Louis D. Brandeis and two senators, which ultimately ensured confirmation.
- Charles Elliot, president emeritus of Harvard and an important supporter of Brandeis.

The opposition was at least equally powerful. Among those opposed to Brandeis were:

- William Howard Taft, twenty-seventh president of the United States (1908–1912), a former judge of the Court of Appeals, and former president of the American Bar Association, who in 1916 had only one unattained aspiration left in his life – to be a justice of the United States Supreme Court.
- Henry Cabot Lodge, senior senator from Massachusetts, and the epitome of the "Yankee."
- The Boston 55, a group of fifty-five lawyers, businessmen, and educators who had one thing in common – they were all Yankees and opposed Brandeis.
- Lawrence Lowell, the current president of Harvard and the leading spokesman for the Boston 55.

The Court

In 1916, the United States Supreme Court, with the exception of two Catholics, was an all-WASP institution charged with the responsibility of interpreting the law as the highest tribunal in the United States. Its membership was interesting and consisted of Chief Justice Edward White of Louisiana, former United States senator and member of the Ku Klux Klan; Willis VanDevanter of Wyoming, a former railroad lawyer; Mahlon Pitney of New

Jersey, a conservative (there are Pitneys still practicing law in New Jersey); James McReynolds of Tennessee, Wilson's former attorney general, well-recognized as anti-Semitic. (When Benjamin Cardozo became the second Jew appointed to the Supreme Court, McReynolds reputedly never spoke a word to him during the years they served together); George McKenna of California, viewed as a swing vote; William Davis of Massachusetts, another swing vote; and Charles Evans Hughes, who would later run against Wilson as Republican presidential nominee in 1916. Not least, there was Oliver Wendell Holmes of Massachusetts, a conservative by nature but later identified with Brandeis on most significant issues coming before the court. There was one additional person who made this matter possible – an undistinguished Georgia jurist, Joseph Lamar, who died on January 2, 1916, and thereby created a vacancy on the Court.

On Friday, January 28, 1916, without consultation with any congressional or party leaders, President Wilson forwarded the following message to Capitol Hill: "To the Senate of the United States. I nominate Louis D. Brandeis of Massachusetts to be Associate Justice of the Supreme Court of the United States."

Brandeis was not unknown to Wilson, although their relationship had begun relatively recently. They first met in 1912 when Brandeis, impressed by Wilson's progressive views, worked in his campaign, and during the ensuing four years Brandeis became a key adviser to the president on critical issues. The drafting of the Federal Reserve Act, the Federal Communications Act establishing a Federal Communications Commission, and the Clayton Anti-Trust Act are attributable to Brandeis's counsel during Wilson's first term.

Who was the man Wilson chose to nominate as the first Jewish member of the United States Supreme Court? Brandeis was born in 1856 in Louisville, Kentucky. His parents, of course, were Jewish, but his only meaningful exposure to things religious was his uncle Lewis Dembitz, a Louisville lawyer, Jewish scholar, and early follower of Theodore Herzl. (It is generally accepted that Brandeis changed his middle name from David to Dembitz in honor of his relationship with his uncle, although Dembitz was also his mother's maiden name.) Brandeis was educated in Germany and Kentucky and graduated from Harvard Law School in 1877, achieving the highest grades ever recorded there. Dean Landis, in 1941, reported that Brandeis was the most brilliant student ever to have attended Harvard Law School. He practiced in Boston with a Harvard classmate, Samuel Warren, and his primary private practice representation was that of corporate and management interests. Within a decade of his entry into the private practice of law, Brandeis had achieved a degree of financial independence that allowed him to devote himself to social issues. He involved himself with the representation of unions and consumer issues, and in 1908 was retained in the case of *Muller v. Oregon*, where he defended an Oregon statute limiting the work hours of women in industry. The case was important for the principle of law espoused (*Muller* represented one of his most significant victories), but Brandeis's presence in the case created a new idiom for the lawyer's lexicon – the Brandeis Brief.

The Brandeis Brief

In upholding the validity of the statute, Brandeis relied less on the legal precedent – which was clearly against him, as courts had consistently set aside laws restricting work hours – than on descriptive and empirical information as to what actually occurred in the workplace. He incorporated life with the law and convinced the United States Supreme Court that the facts of life in the working place – that is, the danger to women's health, safety, and morals, and the social benefit that would derive from shorter work hours – transcended traditional legal arguments; the world had to recognize a modern, changing work environment, and the law would have to change with it. Of the 108 pages of Brandeis's brief, two pages were devoted to traditional legal arguments and the balance of over 100 pages was devoted to reports, statistical information, and other non-traditional matters. Justice Brewer, speaking for the majority, upheld the constitutionality of the statute and in the text of the opinion mentions Brandeis by name with reference to his brief. If he had done nothing else in his career, the Muller case and the concept of the Brandeis Brief would have established Brandeis as an important figure in national and legal circles. In 1910, Brandeis was called upon to assist in the settlement of the garment workers' strike in New York. The experience was unique because he was put in contact with large numbers of East European Jewish immigrants, both on the labor side and the management side. Here was a man who had never belonged to a synagogue or involved himself in any organized religion, but he later spoke of his involvement in the garment workers' strike as a critical period in his life. He said:

> throughout long years, which represent my own life, I have been to a great extent separated from Jews. I am very ignorant in things Jewish. But recent experiences, public and professional, have taught me this: I find Jews possessed of those very qualities which we of the twentieth century seek to develop in our struggle for justice and democracy: a deep moral feeling which makes them capable of noble acts: a deep sense of the brotherhood of man: and a high intelligence, the fruit of three thousand years of civilization.
>
> These experiences have made me feel that the Jewish people have something that should be saved for the world: that the Jewish people should be preserved, and that it is duty to pursue that method of saving which most promises success.[2]

In addition to this experience, a man befriended Brandeis by the name of Jacob De Haas, who had immigrated to Boston from London and had previously served as Herzl's secretary. De Haas was involved in Zionist affairs in the United States, and as a result of their friendship, De Haas urged Brandeis to become involved in Zionist affairs. Various commentators have indicated that it is the combination of this friendship with De Haas together with his experiences during the garment workers' strike that formed the commitment for Brandeis not simply to become involved, but to become enveloped by the Zionist movement.[3] It would be an understatement to say he became passionately involved; in 1912, he assumed the chairmanship of the Provisional Executive Committee of General Zionist Affairs. He traveled throughout the country, speaking and working on behalf of the movement. His involvement in Zionist affairs could be the topic of long hours of discussion, but of particular interest here is the fact that he was in an active leadership role. He would, at a later time, come in conflict with the leaders of the American Jewish Committee and still later with Chaim Weizmann. But he would also play an integral part in the promulgation of the Balfour Declaration of 1917.

While issues would be raised concerning Brandeis's involvement and commitment to Zionism, we can conclude simply that it was not a passing or obscure fancy, but a deep-seeded commitment to a cause that he felt was just. The late professor Alpheus Thomas Mason of Princeton reports, in his work on Brandeis, that during his lifetime Brandeis contributed in excess of $670,000 to Zionist causes.[4] In a speech in 1915 entitled "Zionism and Patriotism" that was to become a classic of its time, Brandeis said, "To be good Americans we must be better Jews, and to be better Jews we must become Zionists." This was clearly a man of deep-seated principle and commitment who faced, as a Supreme Court nominee, the most difficult time in his life.

The reaction to his nomination was mixed but definitive. The *New York Sun*'s headline said: "Wilson shocks Congress by naming Brandeis."[5] The United Press International's lead announcing the story said: "Wilson sent a bomb to the United States Senate... the bomb exploded."[6] The *Sun* reported:

> it is clearly apparent that if he were obliged to go before the senate purely on his merits he would be defeated. There is, however, danger that the racial issue will become involved in the struggle,

and in that event it would be difficult to predict how members of the senate would vote. Already there are evidences that this phase of the situation is influencing those who will be called upon to pass upon Mr. Brandeis' qualifications.[7]

Some democrats pointed out that as he is the first Jew to be nominated to the United States Supreme Court the circumstances would have a decided effect upon the attitude of the hundreds of thousands of Jewish voters in the United States toward President Wilson. This vote in New York is very large and without that state, President Wilson would fail of reelection.[8]

An editorial in the *Sun* was critical, and went on to say, "The stronghold of sane conservatism, the safeguard of our institutions, the ultimate interpreter of our fundamental law."[9] The Detroit Free Press, the Wall Street Journal, and the New York Times expressed strong opinions and opposition to the nomination. The Pulitzer-owned *New York World* and *Boston Globe* were more positive. On Friday, January 28, 1916, the press found William Howard Taft. His reaction, which was reported as one of disappointment, was "No comment."[10]

Ironically, this definitive statement was made after Taft was found in Trenton, New Jersey, addressing an audience at Rider College. Taft would later comment on the nomination at length.

The Senate

The nomination moved to the Senate, and it was up to the Senate to take action. In 1916, the Senate was controlled by the Democratic Party, but given this unique appointment, there was, among other things, the threat of the exercise of senatorial courtesy by Senators Lodge and Young of Massachusetts: the South was still reacting to the Leo Frank case in a way that was troublesome for Brandeis. The Frank case, rather than evoking sympathy, generated what can be categorized as the rise of redneck nativism. Some senators immediately indicated that they would vote for Brandeis. One

Southern senator – James Kimble Vardaman of Mississippi – was of particular interest. A well-known Senator who "played" on racial issues was ironically a critic of anti-Semitism and a strong supporter of the nomination.

It became clear early on that the strategy was to hold the party line, but no one failed to acknowledge that a fight was in store.

As its first order of business, the Senate established a Sub-committee of the Judiciary Committee to hold hearings on the nomination. Since the Democrats controlled the Senate, they in fact controlled the subcommittee, and its five members included three Democrats and two Republicans. The Democrats were the highly partisan Senator William Chilton of West Virginia; Senator Duncan Fletcher of Florida, who had absolutely no interest in the nomination or issues; and Senator Thomas Walsh of Montana, the youngest of three at age fifty-six. The two Republican members were Senator Clarence Clark of Wyoming, later replaced by John Weeks of California, and Senator Albert B. Cummins of Iowa, who had aspirations to be the Republican presidential candidate. Brandeis scholar Melvin I. Urofsky reports:

> The first few days of hearings were sheer chaos, with charges and rebuttals flying around the room. Clifford Thorne, Chairman of the Iowa Board of Railroad Commissions and reputed to be a reformer, led off the attack, charging Brandeis with being "guilty of infidelity, breach of faith, and unprofessional conduct in connection with one of the great cases of this generation.[11]

Thorne and the nominee had met before in a matter before the Interstate Commerce Commission in which Brandeis recommended higher shipping rates than Thorne proposed.

The hearings focused less on the positive aspects of the Brandeis nomination than on numerous witnesses presented to complain about Brandeis's conduct on a whole series of issues. The world learned more positive things about Brandeis from the negative presentations. It was obvious immediately that the string of witnesses called by the opposition was lawyers or litigants who at some time during their careers had confronted Brandeis and lost. In February, the opposition organized and hired Austin George Fox, a Wall Street lawyer, to represent the opposition view. The majority countered with the retention of George Anderson, an attorney practicing in Boston, to ensure what was categorized as a balanced presentation. The witnesses seemed to backfire. One witness, who was complaining about a conflict that turned out to be non-existent in a railroad case, testified that he had been advised that Brandeis would not represent him unless convinced of the justice of the position.

Another complaint, easily refuted, came from a lawyer who had opposed the nominee in an estate matter. The complainant was one of the Boston 55.

In the United Shoe Company case, Brandeis condemned the practices of a firm he had represented three years earlier. Critics found fault with his public criticism of a former client.

The hearings, which went on for weeks, resulted in a party line recommendation – three to two – supporting the nomination. Perhaps more germane to our inquiry was not what was going on inside the Senate, but outside.

Consider the distinguished Henry Cabot Lodge. Lodge's view of Brandeis can be found in many of his speeches and writings. As early at 1896 in a Senate speech, he said:

> more precious even than the forms of government are the mental and moral qualities that make what we call our race. While those stand unimpaired all is safe. When those decline all is imperiled. They are exposed to but a single danger, and that is by changing the quality of our race and citizenship through the wholesale infusion of races whose traditions and inheritances, whose thoughts and whose beliefs are wholly alien to ours and with whom we have never assimilated or even been associated in the past.

This attitude, which clearly did not change after the turn of the century and continued in 1916, might have resulted in Lodge's being outspoken in opposition to Brandeis's nomination. It did not, because Lodge had a very serious problem, a quirk of political fate that would muffle his public voice. In 1913, the states ratified the Seventeenth Amendment, requiring senators to be popularly elected rather than selected by the state legislature. Thus in November 1916, for the first time in his senatorial career, Lodge had to face the voters. This compelled Lodge to be cautious and strangely silent when dealing publicly with the nomination. Notwithstanding his lack of public statement, much is learned from Lodge's private writings. In correspondence with his close friend Arthur Hill, a Boston lawyer who was supportive of Brandeis, Lodge wrote:

> The principal reason that you give for supporting Brandeis seems to me to constitute the most serious objection to his nomination. For the first time in our history a man has been nominated to the Supreme Court with a view to attracting to the President a group of voters on racial grounds. Converting the United States into a government by foreign groups is to me the most fatal thing that can happen to our government....
>
> A man ought to be appointed without any reference to his race or religion, and solely on his fitness. If it were not that Brandeis is a Jew, and a German Jew, he would never have been appointed and he would not have a baker's dozen of votes in the Senate. This seems to me in the highest degree un-American and wrong.

Hill responded to Lodge as follows:

> I have never heard any reliable evidence of any conduct on his part which would make him unfit for a judicial position.
>
> His unpopularity at the bar, which undoubtedly exists, is the result, I think, of two things: first, that he has been always

an active radical, constantly attacking all sorts of established institutions, and thereby inevitably inciting considerable enmity; and second, a certain hard and unsympathetic quality which is largely racial.

He has no power of feeling or understanding the position of an opponent, and none of that spirit of playing the game with courtesy and good nature that is part of the standard of the Anglo-Saxon. He fights to win, and fights up to the limit of his rights with a stern and even cruel exultation in the defeat of his adversary. It is not for nothing that in the Old Testament there isn't a word from beginning to end of admiration for a gallant enemy.

Lodge was caught in a dilemma that would be resolved by working behind the scenes with Republican senators, the Bar Association, and the Boston elite. One of Lodge's most significant efforts in the nomination process was supporting a petition to the Congress signed by the Boston 55. A. Lawrence Lowell, president of Harvard, and Charles Frances Adams, a Boston lawyer, headed the campaign for the petition. Additional signatories included names like Putnam, Peabody, Thorndike, and Gardner, all stalwarts of Boston Brahmin society. The petition read:

We, the undersigned citizens of Massachusetts, are opposed to the appointment of Louis D. Brandeis to the vacancy in the Supreme Court of the United States. An appointment to this court should only be conferred upon a member of the legal profession whose general reputation is as good as his legal attainments are great.

We do not believe that Mr. Brandeis has the judicial temperament and capacity that should be required in a judge of the Supreme Court. His reputation as a lawyer is such that he has not the confidence of the people.

For these reasons we express the hope that the senate will not confirm his appointment.[12]

Needless to say, Lowell's intervention carried with it the imprimatur of the establishment. Melvin I. Urofsky states it directly:

> Proper Boston resented this outsider, this Jew, who adhered more closely to the old Massachusetts principles than they did, who was too successful (i.e., not "gentlemanly") in his profession, and who had defeated them time after time. J. Butler Studley, a lawyer in Brandeis' office, drew up a chart showing how all fifty-five were interconnected through private clubs, corporate directorships, Back Bay residences, and intermarriage.[13]

But there was a response from persons who did not have the same status as the Yankees. For example, Joseph Pelletier, a product of public schools and Catholic Boston College, pointed to the privileged patrician background of the Brahmin signers. He had the temerity to suggest that the opposition was founded on the nominee's religion.

There is little question as to the views or the perspectives of the Boston 55 or the motivating factors. But consider now the views of former President William Howard Taft.

William Howard Taft

One of the great controversies in the nomination process pertains to the role of William Howard Taft, and specifically, whether he was motivated by anti-Semitism or simply reacting to his disappointment at not being the nominee to the Supreme Court. Examine some of his statements and actions, starting with the premise, which is not disputed, that he desperately wanted the seat and there was an active campaign with Wilson on his behalf to have Taft appointed after the death of Lamar and prior to the nomination of Brandeis. Taft and Brandeis had met before. The Ballinger-Pinchot affair was one of the most significant aspects of Brandeis's career.

In 1909, a young civil servant, Louis P. Glavis, charged that his superior, Secretary of the Interior Ballinger, had let public land fall prey to private coal-mining interests, and he documented his accusation. The secretary went to President Taft, who, on the advice of Attorney General Wickersham, cleared him and fired Glavis. Glavis then published his charges in *Collier's Weekly*, edited by Norman Hapgood. A congressional committee was convened to consider the now public charges, and Brandeis was retained for Glavis and *Collier's*. He demonstrated, in protracted hearings, Taft's laxity and showed Secretary Ballinger to be a rogue. Ballinger soon resigned. The president's reputation had suffered a severe blow at the hands of Brandeis.

Taft's initial reaction to the nomination, after a "no comment,"[14] was, one of feeling "wounded." Taft would later suggest that Brandeis used Judaism and Zionism for political gain and questioned whether because of his conflicts with some Zionist leaders, Brandeis had the depth of Jewish support for the nomination. Some commentators dispute whether Taft was motivated simply by desire for the position or by a deep-seated anti-Jewish belief. Consider the circumstantial evidence:

Taft clearly aligned himself with Lodge and his efforts, including the protests of the Boston 55 – although ironically much of the correspondence between Lodge and Taft contained disclaimers of prejudice. They protested too much.

Taft and his former attorney general, Wickersham (the attorney general during the Ballinger episode), organized a letter opposing the nomination that was ultimately signed by Taft, Wickersham, Elihu Root, and five other former presidents of the American Bar Association. While the letter from these estimable gentlemen was of some concern, it was pointed out that nine former American Bar Association presidents refused to sign, thus spiking that gun.

Wickersham's motivation was without question. A review of his correspondence with Taft contains such phraseology as a reference to critics of Taft as "a bunch of Hebrew uplifters of the same stripe as Brandeis." Such messages were clear and unmistakable. Taft was probably not overtly anti-Semitic but represented a prevalent mind-set. Ironically, his later service with Brandeis on the Court would prove cordial.

To combat these efforts, Brandeis's allies Frankfurter and Roscoe Pound of Harvard Law School marshaled their resources and forwarded petitions of support from the law school faculty and student body.

Frankfurter gained notoriety not only as a ghostwriter of numerous pro-Brandeis editorials, but also as a careful composer orchestrating the support by Jews in favor of Brandeis. Frankfurter was keenly sensitive to the issues raised by Brandeis's religion and took care not to apply pressure or have it apply where he felt its value was outweighed by its potential for prejudice.

And to deal with the impact of Lawrence Lowell, Charles Elliot, president emeritus of Harvard University, communicated with Congress, effectively neutralizing Lowell's presence on the scene.

The subcommittee of the Senate Judiciary Committee hearing recommended the nomination three to two. The matter had to be voted on by the Judiciary Committee before the full Senate could consider it. Democrats controlled ten votes out sixteen. Of their ten votes, five Democrats refused to commit in favor of the nomination.

As the vote approached, politicians went into high gear. Wilson, who had remained relatively quiet, was informed that the nomination was in jeopardy. On May 5, Wilson wrote to Senator Charles A. Culberson of Texas, chairman of the committee, praising his nominee and noting that he had "tested" Brandeis, the president declared, "by seeking his advice upon some of the most difficult and perplexing public questions." In every instance Brandeis had provided "counsel singularly enlightening, singularly clear-sighted and judicial, above all, full of moral stimulation."[15] The man he had named to the nation's highest court was "a friend of all just men and a lover of the right." In tone and substance the president made it clear that he wanted the nomination approved.

Slowly, the Democrats on the subcommittee, such as Senators Smith and Reed, who met the nominee through an arranged meeting at the apartment of Hapgood, fell into line. While the last uncommitted vote, John Knight Shields of Tennessee, proved to be no problem by this time, the two penultimate votes proved more problematic. And again the fates intervened; creating unrelated circumstances that would ensure the success of the nomination.

The first event took place in England. Urofsky reports it this way:

> A British court-martial passed a sentence of death on Jeremiah Lynch, a naturalized American citizen and New York resident who had returned to his native land to participate in the Irish struggle for independence. Lynch's sentence was to be carried out at midnight, and Senator O'Gorman, the pride of New York's Irish community, suddenly forgot all his old grievances against Woodrow Wilson and sought his help in preventing Lynch's execution. The next day's papers told the story of how Wilson, at O'Gorman's request, had cabled the American Ambassador in London directing him to make every possible effort to save Lynch and as a result the death sentence was commuted to ten years in prison. O'Gorman, now a hero in New York, recognized his political debt to Wilson; one more vote for Brandeis' confirmation.[16]

And a few days later, in response to a plea by North Carolina Senator Lee Overman, a tired Wilson disembarked a train, celebrated the Mecklenburg Declaration of 1775 while extolling the virtues of the local senator, and ensured yet another vote for Brandeis.[17]

The vote was scheduled for May 24, and on that date the party line held and the Judiciary Committee voted generally along party lines in favor of the nomination.

During this process, Brandeis never appeared in the Senate or before any committee. He refused to talk to the press. True to his character, of course, he knew what was transpiring and successfully fixed strategy.

On June 1, 1916, shortly before 5:00 P.M., the Senate voted 47 to 27 in favor of the nomination of Louis D. Brandeis, the first Jewish member of the Supreme Court.

Only three Republicans, all Progressives, including La Follette, voted in favor of the nomination, and one Democrat voted against.

Brandeis's response to the Senate action was perhaps less conciliatory to those who opposed him and more a harbinger of things to come.

He said: "The struggle certainly was worthwhile. It has defined the issues. It has been a great education to a large number of people; perhaps even to judges. And I trust it may prove possible for me to render service of real value on the bench."[18]

Was anti-Semitism a factor in the confirmation process? Clearly this is an issue that will be debated on and on. While we cannot forget that the acceptable language of 1916 would not be tolerated in the twenty-first century, we must wonder whether the underlying views and beliefs or prejudices of the Hodges and Wickersham and perhaps even the Taft's would be different today. We can never know.

Brandeis, after his appointment, went on to fulfill the expectations of both his supporters and the opposition. He represented a bold departure from the courts of the past. In matters of social reform and free speech he spoke with the convictions of his past practice and beliefs. He would join with Holmes in dissenting on matters that in a more enlightened time might have become the law. To his detractors he was as evil as they had anticipated.

Of the rest of the cast of the drama there were some ironies: Wilson would be reelected in 1916, soundly defeating former justice Charles Evans Hughes. Much had been made of Wilson's political consideration in appointing Brandeis to ensure the Jewish vote and capture New York in the 1916 election, but in fact Hughes easily defeated Wilson in New York. Frankfurter, as we know, would be the third Jew appointed to the Supreme Court – appointed by Franklin D. Roosevelt to succeed Benjamin Cardozo, the second Jewish appointment. William Howard Taft would realize his life's ambition when he was ultimately appointed as a justice of the Supreme Court. It is reported that he and Brandeis established a friendship of respect and admiration.

Finally, Brandeis would surprise those critics who claimed that his commitment to Zionism was political opportunism. While Brandeis would resign his leadership role in what ultimately became the Zionist Organization of America after a dispute with Chaim Weizmann, his efforts were continually channeled to economic assistance to Palestine and a commitment to a homeland for the Jewish people. He was a remarkable man in a remarkable time.

Further Reading

Dawson, Nelson L., ed. *Brandeis and America*. Lexington: University Press of Kentucky, 1989.

Gerstle, Gary. *American Crucible*. Princeton, N.J.: Princeton University Press, 2001.

Goldman, Solomon. ed., *The Words of Justice Brandeis*, New York, Henry Schuman, 1953.

Gross, David C. *A Justice for All the People: Louis D. Brandeis*. New York: Lodestar Books, 1987.

Mason, Alpheus Thomas. *Brandeis, A Free Man's Life*, New York, Viking Press, 1956.

Paper, Lewis J. *Brandeis*, Englewood Cliffs, Prentice Hall, Inc., 1983.

Stern, Ellen Norman. *Embattled Justice: The Story of Louis Dembitz Brandeis*. Philadelphia: Jewish Publication Society, 1971.

Strum, Phillippa. *Louis D. Brandeis: Justice for the People*. Cambridge, Mass.: Harvard University Press, 1984.

Todd, Alden. *Justice on Trial: The Case of Louis D. Brandeis*. New York: McGraw-Hill, 1984.

Urofsky, Melvin I., Oliver Handlin, ed. *Louis D. Brandeis and the Progressive Tradition*. Boston: Little, Brown, 1981.

Notes

1. For an excellent analysis of this period, see Gary Gerstle, *American Crucible* (Princeton, N.J.: Princeton University Press, 2001).
2. Solomon Goldman, editor, *The Words of Justice Brandeis*, (New York, Henry Schuman, 1953) at 108.
3. *See, e.g.*, Lewis J. Paper, *Brandeis*, (Englewood Cliffs, Prentice Hall, Inc., 1983) at 202.
4. Alpheus Thomas Mason, *Brandeis, A Free Man's Life*, (New York, Viking Press, 1956).
5. A.L. Todd, *Justice on Trial*, 69, (New York, Mc-Graw Hill, 1964).
6. *Id., at 69.*
7. *Id.*, at 70.
8. *Id.*, at 71.
9. *Id.*, at 71.
10. *Id.*, at 75.
11. Melvin I. Urofsky, Oscar Handlin, Editor, *Louis D. Brandeis and the Progressive Tradition*, 110, (Boston, Little Brown and Company, 1981).
12. As reported in Mason, at 472–73.
13. Urofsky, at 113.
14. *See*, fn. 12, *supra*
15. Todd, at 213
16. Urofsky, at 117–18.
17. *Id.* at 118.
18. *Id.* at 118.

The American Republic vs. Julius and Ethel Rosenberg

BRUCE AFRAN

> I felt good that this was strictly a Jewish show.
> It was Jew against Jew. It wasn't the Christians hanging the Jews.
> – Vincent Lebonitte, Jury Foreman[1]

The words quoted above encapsulate the true spirit of the trial of Julius and Ethel Rosenberg, an American show trial intended to expose not the guilt or innocence of the defendants but the nefarious reach of the Soviet Union into the deepest secrets of the United States. It was a trial intended to buttress the commitment of the United States to the hunting of communists and the continued development of nuclear weaponry with little regard for due process or constitutional protection.

While their guilt is today assumed by many, little is said any longer about the trial itself, which rivals the case of Dreyfus in France or the Doctors' Trial in the Soviet Union for the undercurrent of anti-Semitism that tainted the constitutional process. Perhaps reflecting the great success of the diaspora in the United States, the anti-Jewish overtones of *United States v. Julius and Ethel Rosenberg* were fomented not by Jew-haters but by American Jews who occupied positions of power and influence in the secular republic and were the prime movers of the prosecution.

A "strictly Jewish show" it was, with a Jewish judge, Jewish prosecutors, Jewish defense lawyers, and Jewish defendants. One wonders at the confluence of Jewish actors who came together to bring forth this most emotive and searing of criminal cases. One looks back at the silence of American Jewry, imprisoned by fear during the many months of the Rosenberg epic, while the full brunt of the U.S. government was brought to bear upon a Jewish family tried in a courtroom cloaked with an atmosphere of Jewish and communist hatred, masked all the while in the neutral cloth of due process.

The frenzy that surrounded the trial of the Rosenbergs was animated by two men, Senator Joseph McCarthy and Roy Cohn, since charged (and convicted) by history with distortion and invention in the service of demagoguery. Cohn's role as a prosecutor of the Rosenbergs was far more significant than his later role as sidekick to Senator McCarthy. Junior to the lead prosecutor, Irving Saypol, Cohn was by far the more aggressive in courtroom argument and lent his deviant talents in full to the government's case.

Cohn's presence brought to the trial an overt connection with the anti-communist abuses of the 1950s, but contemporary discussion of the case centers on the Rosenbergs' guilt or innocence, not the fairness of the proceedings. History assumes that the McCarthyite investigations had little or no factual validity, but no such presumption has been extended to the popular view of the trial of Julius and Ethel Rosenberg despite the preeminent role played in the prosecution by Cohn, who, it is widely understood, invented evidence used in McCarthy's investigations.

Just why Cohn's presence on the prosecution team has not tainted the verdict against the Rosenbergs is a mystery that owes more to Jewish fears than to the quality of the evidence presented at trial. As shown by the tepid defense of Jonathan Pollard, an American sentenced to life imprisonment for spying for Israel three decades later, American Jews since the Rosenberg trial have been rendered immobile at the barest hint of dual loyalty, a concern that appears completely absent from gentile views of American Jewry but nevertheless pervades the psyche of the American Jewish community.

An episode reported by the civil rights lawyer Arthur Kinoy confirms that even Jewish appellate judges were afraid to intervene in the Rosenberg case. Kinoy, who filed an application for a stay of execution before the U.S. Court of Appeals for the Second Circuit, was rebuffed by Judge Jerome Frank, a Jew and a great liberal jurist. "If I were as young as you are," Frank told Kinoy, "I would be sitting where you are now and saying and arguing what you are arguing. You are right to do so. But when you are as old as I am, you will understand why I...why I cannot do what you ask. I cannot do it."

Kinoy understood that Frank would not jeopardize his position "as a liberal, as a progressive – even, I thought, as a progressive Jew," by intervening to stop the Rosenbergs' execution. The forces of anti-communist paranoia were strong, so strong that not even a life-tenured federal judge felt free to act. Judge Frank's words reflect the haunting melody of Jewish fear that fifty years after the Rosenbergs' electrocution paralyzes Jews into silence in the face of injustice.[2]

Midwives to Espionage

Julius and Ethel Rosenberg were arrested in July 1950. The government's case was built on the claim that Julius was the leader of a Russian spy ring centered in New York City, where Julius and Ethel lived with their two young sons. Their arrests followed several others, including Ethel's brother David Greenglass, a former army machinist who had worked at the nuclear research facility at Los Alamos, and Harry Gold, an American who served as a Soviet courier. It was Gold who led government investigators to David Greenglass, telling FBI agents that he had met Greenglass in New Mexico to accept a delivery of notes about scientists working on the atomic bomb project.

After his arrest and interrogation, Greenglass told the government that he had been recruited into spying for the Soviet Union by his brother-in-law, Julius Rosenberg. Greenglass identified his sister, Ethel Rosenberg, as a participant in the conspiracy, although he later recanted his accusations against Ethel, telling a *New York Times* reporter, Sam Roberts, that he had lied about Ethel's involvement to protect his wife, Ruth, from prosecution.[3]

Ruth and David Greenglass were the principal witnesses against Ethel and Julius Rosenberg. They were the only witnesses to directly link Julius and Ethel to the theft of information from Los Alamos. Ruth testified that in November 1944 Julius asked her to recruit her husband, David, to steal information from the Los Alamos labs in New Mexico. David was assigned to the machine shop at Los Alamos. Julius told Ruth that David was working on the atomic bomb, the most destructive weapon ever imagined, and that it was unfair for the United States not to share this technology with its wartime ally, the Soviet Union.[4] Ruth duly conveyed Julius's request to David, who said at trial that he agreed to give Julius a description of the bomb, along with drawings of the lens mold used to focus the explosive force inward toward the radioactive core. David's notes were never reproduced in court, but his reproduction of the drawings of the lens mold became court exhibits.

Ethel typed. That is to say, her role in this espionage ring was to type David's notes, but she was charged as a co-conspirator and sentenced to death along with Julius. Ruth, who said she had enlisted David to steal Los Alamos secrets for Julius, played a far more material role in the conspiracy than Ethel, but Ruth was never charged with any crime. Ruth, who recruited her husband to spy, went free. Ethel, the typist, was executed.

Within days of their arrests the "Atomic Spies" had become the most notorious criminals in American history. The Rosenberg epic was an American family drama, with husband and wife the twin demons of the Russian enemy informed on by their own brother and sister, David, a traitor to his uniform, and Julius, the evil extension of the Soviet arm. Julius's idiosyncratic moustache, owl-eyed spectacles, natty suits, and floral ties, along with Ethel's unrelenting look of poised stoicism, were images seared into the world's stock of notorious figures, the Goebbels and Himmler of their day.

That the defendants were Jews merely imbued the already sensational with an overlay of the exotic.

But it was drama infused with pathos. From the moment of their arrest, Julius and Ethel never again breathed free air and were cut off from their two small sons, whose parents had instantly and ineradicably become the most notorious human beings alive. Two boys, Michael and Robert, who had known only the middle-class life of New York City boredom, were thrust into a maelstrom of anti-communist, anti-Jewish ferment.[5] Julius and Ethel became, for most Americans, the incarnate image of world communism. Through them, the specter of the lurid, manipulative Jew, once buried in the world's subliminal conscience, rose again.

Julius Rosenberg is said to have gained the secret of the atom bomb from his brother-in-law, David Greenglass, a machinist in the army with a high school diploma. Greenglass, who rose no higher than corporal and had no scientific background, became the source of the greatest technological secret ever possessed by a nation-state, a secret so well kept that President Harry Truman, on taking office in 1945, was ignorant of its very existence. In a coincidence of astounding magnitude, David, the brother-in-law of a master Soviet spy, was assigned by random chance to the machine shop of the Los Alamos laboratories where the atom bomb was built. If the trial testimony is to be believed, the greatest military secret in human history was betrayed by an untrained corporal who, by the sheerest chance turn of events, happened to be the brother-in-law of a Soviet master spy.

Tens of thousands of men, perhaps hundreds of thousands, worked as machinists in the United States in 1944. How did David Greenglass, a known communist and brother-in-law to an alleged Soviet spy, happen to be assigned to Los Alamos, the most sensitive machine shop in the world? Just how did Julius learn that his brother-in-law was working on the atom bomb? David's work at Los Alamos was secret. No evidence has ever emerged that David told Julius or Ethel, or even his own wife, about the nature of his assignment to Los Alamos. So how did Julius know? Was he told by the Soviets that his brother-in-law was working on the atom bomb? But if the Soviets had such intimate knowledge of Los Alamos as to know that Julius Rosenberg's brother-in-law was assigned to the project, why did they need Julius (or David) to extract secret information?[6] The coincidence of Julius Rosenberg, an alleged Soviet spy, having a brother-in-law assigned by random chance to work on the atom bomb is simply too much. If these facts are true, then no spy in history had such stupendous luck as Julius Rosenberg.

We are forced by such questions to examine anew the case of the atomic spies.

A Judge as Prosecutor

America in the 1950s was a nation gorged on suspicion and choking on the bile of fanaticism. The trial of Julius and Ethel Rosenberg reflected the obsession with communism that was sweeping American life; the United States was a society in which whispered innuendo brought down careers, where neither celebrity nor anonymity protected the citizen from the ultimate charge of disloyalty.

The judicial system was not immune to this contagion and, too often, was the medium for its spread. If truth is the first casualty of war, then due process is the first casualty of national paranoia.

From its opening minutes, the trial of Julius and Ethel Rosenberg degenerated into an American analogue of the infamous Soviet show trials.

Judge Irving Kaufman, the youngest person ever appointed to the federal bench and one of only a few Jewish federal judges, was injected into a career-breaking crucible of intense public focus. A gifted lawyer, Kaufman had graduated from Fordham Law School at the age of twenty. Considered a prince of the law, Kaufman was widely thought destined for greatness on the Supreme Court, a prophecy almost certainly doomed by the execution of the Rosenbergs.[7] But in the spring of 1951, when *United States v. Julius and Ethel Rosenberg* came before him, Kaufman was at the apex of legal grandeur, with nothing but accolades seemingly ahead; even after fifty years, the arrogance of youthful power leaches through the trial transcript. Far from being immune to the political bias of the day, Kaufman was a part of the establishment that fed that bias and nourished its incubation. Kaufman's actions from the bench harnessed the emotive power of anti-communist hatred to constitutional process; in his lower Manhattan courtroom, paranoia became the blood brother of due process.

Bias raised its head early. In an American federal court, the trial judge questions prospective jurors to weed out those whose life experience or personal views make them unfit to be objective triers of fact. This is the *voir dire*.[8] A common tactic of trial lawyers is to put questions to jurors that seem intended to weed out prejudice but are really meant to insert bias in the juror's mind. The alert lawyer sees such tactics for what they are, and the court ordinarily excludes them.

But in the most sensitive criminal trial of the twentieth century, this process failed. Judge Irving Kaufman used jury selection, the *voir dire*, to instill prejudice into the court and to install an atmosphere of fear of communism, bias, and hatred in the minds of the jurors.

Kaufman recited to the jurors a list of the names of dozens of publications and organizations, nearly all of which contained the words "Soviet," "Russian," "Russia," "communist," "labor," or "socialist." He asked the juror if they read, worked, or did business with any of these publications or groups. While the list began harmlessly enough with five or six mainstream New York daily newspapers, Kaufman almost immediately began reading names such as *Counterattack, Red Channels, Daily Worker, Communist Political Affairs, New Masses, People's World,* and *Soviet Russia*

Today and continued through nearly 200 publications and groups with communist, socialist, labor, or Russian titles. For good measure, he threw in the Soviet embassy as a "suspect" group.[9] In the climate of the early 1950s, with its red-baiting and blacklisting of "communists" on the slightest pretext, it is inconceivable that any juror would not be intimidated by this litany of communist and socialist journals and organizations. In a case charging defendants with spying for a communist state, little could be more prejudicial than to confront jurors with a list of the most radical socialist publications and organizations in the nation and demand to know whether the juror was "affiliated" with these groups.

Kaufman then proceeded to a second list of organizations that he told the jury "are contained on a list published by the Attorney General pursuant to a presidential order."[10] Kaufman was referring, of course, to the famous list of "subversive" groups compiled by the attorney general and known at that time by every literate American to refer to communist "front" organizations. Kaufman agreed to delete the word "subversive" from the question, but rejected defense counsel demands that jurors be told the list had never been subject to hearings as to whether any of the groups were actually subversive or communist. The list reads like an official registry of disloyalty containing more than 100 groups, almost all with names including the words "Marxist," "Soviet," "Russian," "anti-fascist," "Negro," "Jewish," "Social," "Labor," "Workers," "Communist," "Youth," "Socialist," "Civil Rights," and the names of many East European nations and ethnic groups.

Few in the courtroom failed to get the message that this trial involved people and events disloyal to the United Sates and the American way of life. Not surprisingly, not a single prospective juror said he or she had any association with any of these groups or had read any of the journals on the first list.

Having infused a living sense of the "red menace" into the case, Kaufman proceeded upon a series of questions to jurors that rivaled anything in the congressional inquisitions of the 1940s and 1950s:[11]

Has any juror such prejudice or bias against the House Committee on Un-American Activities...that you would be unable to arrive at a just and honest verdict?

Have you or anyone you know ever testified before or given information to the House Committee on Un-American Activities?

Has anybody got prejudice or bias against the government's loyalty program?

Has any juror...ever attended an educational institution which was supported...by either the Russian Government, the Communist Party or any affiliated Communist Party association or Communist Front Organization?

Does any juror believe in or belong to any organization which is dedicated to or teaches or advocates the overthrow of the Government of the United States by force and violence?

Has any member of the jury at any time indicated support of the Communist Party or signed a Communist Party petition...?

Was any juror born in...Russia or any of the Russian satellite countries ...?

Has any juror...ever worked for the Russian Government... or any Russian relief agency?

Have you at any time been a member of, made contribution to or been associated in any way with any religious or business organizations or labor organizations or organizations of any character which were supported either directly or indirectly by the Communist party?

With these questions, the jury's attention was riveted on the titanic battle between American democracy and Russian communism. Kaufman might just as well have asked, "Are you now or have you ever been a member of the Communist Party?" the famous interrogatory shibboleth of the House and Senate Un-American Activities Committees. No reasonable juror in 1951 would have answered yes to any of these questions in a federal courtroom, and none did. As defense lawyer Edward Kuntz argued to no avail, it is difficult to see any legitimate purpose to this inquiry other than to instill a spirit of bias (and fear) in the jury. By the time Kaufman had finished reciting the lists of subversive and communist publications and groups, asking the jurors whether they had any connections with the Communist Party or Communist front organizations or whether they opposed the government's loyalty program, anti-communist fear and paranoia had become the dominant theme of the trial. The guilt or innocence of the Rosenbergs was secondary.

Irving Saypol's opening statement for the government hammered relentlessly at the theme of the defendants' loyalty to communism and Soviet Russia.[12] "Their loyalty was to the cause of world communism," Saypol told jurors. "The evidence will show that the loyalty and the allegiance of the Rosenbergs was not to our country, but that it was to Communism, Communism in this country and Communism throughout the world." Saypol liberally called the defendants "traitors," David Greenglass "a modern Benedict Arnold," the defendants' acts as "treasonable," and Julius Rosenberg as having "devoted himself to...betraying his own country." The defendants were moved by "a worship of the Soviet Union" and by "rank disloyalty to our country," Saypol told jurors, and had "joined...in a conspiracy to deliver to the Soviet Union the information and the weapons which the Soviet Union could use to destroy us." These accusations cemented in the jury's mind a presumption of guilt before the first witness had even taken the stand.

Saypol made a subtle, indelible call upon the vocabulary of anti-Semitism in his appeal to the jury. The stereotype of the international Jew, grasping and manipulative, appeared in the guise of Julius and Ethel Rosenberg, who, Saypol said, "*reached* into wartime projects and installations of the United States government," "*reached* in to obtain...from people in positions of trust secret information," engaged in a "*ceaseless* campaign to recruit promising members for their Soviet espionage ring," "*ever on the lookout"* for sympathetic souls to steal, possessed of "a *constant* concern for recruiting Americans," this last thrust as if Julius and Ethel were not themselves Americans. But the FBI "broke through the darkness of this insidious business," Saypol said, and brought "these culprits before the bar of justice" (emphasis added throughout).

No longer New Yorkers, no longer the parents of two young boys, no longer Americans, Julius and Ethel Rosenberg were less than human; they were, in Saypol's words, "insidious culprits," purveyors of "darkness," corruptors of youth, grasping as they "reached into" our nation's deep secrets, ceaselessly on the prowl to betray our nation.

Smoother than the Nazi propagandists with their primitive reliance on fevered adjectives, Saypol, a Jewish prosecutor from New York, married the images of anti-Semitism to the impersonal text of American criminal law. With this stratagem, calling upon the tired image of the overreaching, grasping Jew, Saypol injected into the mind of the jury that fear of conspiratorial world Jewry that lives, even today, in the not-so-hidden reservoirs of the Diaspora.[13]

Judge Kaufman refused to strike a single line of this attack.

Only after repeated demands by the defense lawyers did he instruct the jurors that the defendants were *not* on trial for being members of the Communist Party, an instruction that merely hardened the presumption of disloyalty and communist sympathy that already operated as the prosecution's principal storyline. Kaufman's supposedly "cautionary" instruction actually told jurors that the defendants *were* members of the Communist Party, a fact that was the jury's to decide and which was never plainly proven at trial.

Kaufman's bias was manifest in other ways as well. Out of the jury's hearing, the judge agreed that the government must show "a *causal* connection" between Communist Party membership and the alleged acts of espionage. Seconds later, Kaufman softened this ruling, telling jurors that the government had to prove "*some*" connection between communism and conspiracy to commit espionage. Nothing better illustrates Kaufman's subliminal bias than the alteration of "*causal* connection" to "*some* connection," a much lower standard of proof. In any event, the tepid instruction could do little to cleanse the courtroom of the anti-communist rhetoric put there by Kaufman's own jury examination. The government lost no time following the judge's lead.

With their first question to their first witness, Max Elitcher, Saypol and Cohn launched a direct attack on the Rosenbergs' communist beliefs, asking Elitcher whether the defendants were members of the Communist Party. Elitcher was a graduate of City College of New York, where he had known Julius Rosenberg and co-defendant Morton Sobell. Elitcher testified that he had been recruited to the Communist Party in the 1930s by Sobell and joined a communist cell. At this point, again in response to defense counsel objections, Kaufman told the jury that it should disregard the *fact* that defendants were communists: "I want you to understand right at the outset that the *fact* that they *were* members of the Communist Party does not establish the elements necessary to prove them guilty of the crime charged" (emphaisis added).

Twice, then, in the guise of cautioning the jury *against* prejudice, Kaufman told the jury the defendants *were* communists, a fact each denied. At a time when thousands of Americans – tradesmen, bus drivers, actors, school teachers, union members, lawyers, professors, and many others – had lost their jobs because of mere suspicion of communist sympathy, much less membership, these were astoundingly prejudicial statements by an American judge to a jury in an American courtroom.

John Derry, an intelligence officer, was called by the government to testify about the importance of the information that David Greenglass had leaked to his brother-in-law, Julius Rosenberg. Greenglass's transmission of Los Alamos secrets was at the core of the espionage charges against Julius and Ethel. Derry's testimony was essential to establishing whether the Rosenbergs had passed to Russia information damaging to the national defense of the United States. In front of the jury, before Derry had uttered a word, Kaufman declared that the information leaked by Greenglass had damaged the national security. "[I]t might be in the interest of the country that we do not hear certain portions of testimony," Kaufman told the jury before ordering the court cleared of all spectators but the press. Again in front of the jury, Kaufman ordered the court stenographer not to transcribe Derry's testimony.

Later, as Derry began to speak directly about the atom bomb, the operation of which was by then familiar to every high school physics student, Kaufman again warned the press: "May I at this point say to the members of the press that I do hope that they will exercise the same good judgment that they exercised in publishing the information as it came from the lips of Mr. Greenglass," sending the plain message to the jury that it was the *defendants* who had failed to use good judgment when they leaked the information to the Soviets.

Kaufman's intervention left the jury with the firm belief that the information allegedly stolen by Greenglass damaged the national defense, the very question the jury was there to decide.

In his summary of the evidence for the jury, Kaufman gave remarkable emphasis to the government's case and ignored most of the Rosenbergs' defense. For example, the government called a photographer, one Ben Schneider, who said that in June 1950, shortly before their arrest, Ethel and Julius had come to him to have passport photos taken, a claim the government made to show that the defendants intended flight. This testimony would tend to discredit Julius and Ethel – any plan to flee the country, including taking passport photos, would show consciousness of guilt. But Schneider admitted on cross-examination that the photos included *group* pictures of the Rosenbergs *with their children*, a fact brought out by the defendants to show that the photos were never intended for passports but were ordinary family pictures.[14] When he summarized this testimony for the jury, Kaufman left out any reference to Schneider's admission, leaving the jury with the impression that Schneider's claim that the Rosenbergs had come to get passport photos had not been disputed. Considering the inflammatory nature of the photographer's evidence, the lack of balance in Kaufman's summation is astounding.

This omission must be seen in light of Kaufman's instruction to the jury that Morton Sobell's flight to Mexico following the arrest of the physicist Klaus Fuchs, who had passed secrets from the Manhattan Project to the Soviets, could be considered as evidence of a preconceived plan by *all* the defendants (including the Rosenbergs) to flee the country. Kaufman did not tell the jury that Julius, Ethel, and David Greenglass had remained in the United States until they were arrested, making no effort to leave the country. The three did not even have passports, though they were supposed to be leading members of a Soviet espionage ring. If Kaufman believed Sobell's flight was important enough to stress to the jury, he should also have told the jury that the Rosenbergs' continued presence in the United States until their arrest, and their lack of passports, should be considered evidence of a lack of an intent to flee and a lack of consciousness of guilt. But he didn't.

Schneider's testimony itself is subject to extreme doubt.

Julius and Ethel's arrests made them the most notorious living Americans in July 1950, just two months after Schneider claimed they had come to his shop. Despite their fame, the photographer apparently did not recognize his recent clients from their front-page newspaper photographs, which no New Yorker at the time could have avoided seeing.[15]

Having made no connection in his mind between the Rosenbergs as public figures and his recent customers, Schneider never came forth and brought his information to the FBI or the United States attorney. So nervous was the government about his reliability as a witness that FBI agents twice brought him to the courtroom on the afternoon before he testified to identify Julius and Ethel; at the time Julius was in the witness box and Ethel sitting at counsel table, a fact never revealed until after the trial.[16]

When he testified, though, Schneider denied having seen the Rosenbergs at any time since the previous spring, even though, at the instigation of the FBI, he had seen them surreptitiously in court on the previous afternoon.[17]

Presented with this evidence after the trial, Kaufman remained unmoved, finding the deception an insufficient basis on which to vacate the judgment, even though Schneider's testimony was fulsomely used by Kaufman in his summation to the jury as evidence of the defendants' intent to flee, a critical argument in favor of conviction.

In an American criminal trial, a defendant is presumed innocent and the government must prove its case beyond a reasonable doubt. The first duty of an American judge is to protect that presumption of innocence, but in this case the trial judge told the jury that the defendants, simply because they were defendants, had a motive to lie. "The greater a person's interest in the case," Kaufman said, "the stronger is the temptation to falsify testimony, and the interest of the defendants who took the stand [i.e., the Rosenbergs] is of a character possessed by no other witness.... they have a vital interest in the outcome of the case.... you may find that a defendant is telling the truth despite his obvious interest in the outcome, but you may consider a defendant's temptation to falsify."[18]

Rather than protect the Rosenbergs' presumption of innocence, Kaufman told the jurors that the Rosenbergs could not be trusted to tell the truth because they were defendants and had a motive to lie. Kaufman's bias was so manifest that even while acknowledging the defendants "*may*" be telling the truth, he told jurors that this would be "*despite* their *obvious* interest in the outcome" of the case (emphasis added). In so many words, Kaufman told the jury that it could presume that Julius and Ethel were lying. Though David Greenglass and Harry Gold had already pled guilty to espionage and admitted they were hoping for leniency in exchange for their cooperation, Kaufman never warned the jury that Greenglass and Gold might have been tempted to falsify their testimony. Actually, Kaufman told that jury that even though Gold and Greenglass were "accused of being accomplices," this did not mean they "are not to be believed. If this were so, many cases in this court could not be proven."[19]

Strange justice was practiced here. As to the Rosenbergs, who were presumed to be innocent, Kaufman told the jury to assume they had a motive to lie, and as to Greenglass and Gold, who had already pled guilty, Kaufman said this was not a reason to disbelieve them. In Irving Kaufman's court, the presumption of innocence was turned on its head.

Julius and Ethel gained an important admission when David Greenglass said on cross-examination that he hoped by testifying to avoid prosecution for Ruth and prison for himself. David and Ruth Greenglass were the prime witnesses linking the Rosenbergs to the theft of atomic secrets, and their credibility was essential to the government's case. Ignoring David's powerful admission that he was hoping for leniency by testifying, Kaufman told the jury *only* of the Rosenbergs' belief that Greenglass was lying because Julius owed him money for his share of profits in the family's contracting business, a separate (and weaker) challenge to David's credibility. When the defense lawyers demanded that Kaufman tell the jury about Greenglass's admitted hope for leniency, a far more powerful argument than the limp claim that he had lied because of a financial dispute with Julius, the judge refused, saying he had already added the phrase "and other reasons," which somehow covered David's admission that he was looking for leniency by testifying.[20]

The claim that David accused Julius of espionage because Julius owed him money was surely a weak argument; few people would condemn their sister and her husband to death simply because of a family debt. Kaufman chose to emphasize this weakest link of the Rosenberg's attack on the Greenglasses' credibility while refusing to remind the jury of David's truly potent admission that he was testifying to save Ruth, the mother of young children, from prosecution and himself from imprisonment. When considered alongside Kaufman's earlier instruction to the jury that

Julius and Ethel had a reason to lie because they wanted to avoid conviction, Kaufman's refusal to fairly describe the Rosenbergs' challenge to the Greenglasses' credibility is a shocking lapse.

Over and over Kaufman omitted crucial parts of the Rosenbergs' defense. On no occasion did the judge elaborate on the defendants' contentions. He never gave emphasis to them and ignored most of their most compelling evidence, while indulging the government's case at length. Kaufman's summation of the government's case consumed 248 lines in the trial transcript, compared to the 77 lines he devoted to the defendants' claims.[21] So unbalanced was Kaufman that he simply cut off his discussion of the defense evidence with the curt declaration to the jury: "You have heard their summation and therefore I will not discuss their contentions further."[22] The jury had also heard the government's summation, but that didn't stop Kaufman from emphasizing the government's case.

Twice Kaufman stressed how broad the government's case was, that it went beyond the theft of atomic secrets. "Bear in mind – please listen to this, ladies and gentlemen – that the Government contends that the conspiracy was one to obtain not only atomic bomb information but other secret and classified information."[23] Having stressed this point once – "*bear in mind – please listen to this*" – Kaufman a second time told the jurors, "Again I want to emphasize that the conspiracy in this case is a conspiracy to obtain secret information pertaining to the national defense.... It is not a conspiracy to obtain information *only* about the atom bomb"[24] (emphasis added). Why stress this point at all, and why repeat it? The government's case as to the theft of atomic secrets was weak, depending upon the testimony of two admitted spies, David and Ruth Greenglass. Perhaps Kaufman understood the weakness of the government's principal claim and for this reason emphasized that the government had other, broader claims of injury to national security beyond the theft of atomic secrets that did not depend on the Greenglasses' testimony.

Finally, and ingloriously, Kaufman, reaching the apex of

prejudice, made the truly titanic declaration to the jury that the Rosenbergs were "proven traitors."

Irving Saypol had luridly and lavishly laid on the claim that Julius and Ethel had committed treason. In the popular mind, the Rosenbergs were indeed executed for treason, but they were never charged with treason – and for good reason: treason is defined in the U.S. Constitution as giving "aid and comfort" to the enemy, and in 1944 and 1945, when the atomic thefts supposedly took place, the Soviet Union was an ally of the United States. Treason was legally impossible. In spite of Saypol's repeated denunciations to the jury, the Rosenbergs could not be traitors, since the information they stole was given to an ally, not an enemy.

Lacking treason for a charge, the trial judge defined the crime of espionage in terms that virtually invited the jury to convict:

> Espionage, reduced to essentials, means spying on the United States to aid a foreign power. Because of the development of highly destructive weapons and their highly guarded possession by nations existing in a state of tension with one another, the enforcement of the espionage laws takes on a new significance. Our national well-being requires that we guard against spying on the secrets of our defense, whether such spying is carried on through agents of foreign powers or through our own nationals who prefer to help a foreign power. [25]

Perhaps realizing he had gone too far, Kaufman warned the jury that the mere use of the word "espionage" does not justify "convicting innocent persons," but then he added the truly amazing comment, "however, irrational sympathies must not shield proven traitors."[26]

Proven traitors! These are the words of a federal judge to a jury about to deliberate on the defendants' guilt or innocence. If Kaufman's comments could be interchanged with the closing argument of prosecutor Irving Saypol, few would notice anything amiss. The Rosenbergs were not charged with treason, not yet found guilty, but trial judge tells the jury that their "sympathies must not shield *proven traitors*." Who were those "proven traitors"? Why would a federal judge use such language if not to impress a jury with the need to convict? For good measure, Kaufman made it plain that any juror harboring such sympathy would not only be wrong, but "irrational."

The trial of Julius and Ethel Rosenberg was America's showplace judicial effort against communism. Judge Kaufman's every action was observed by millions in America, in Europe, in the Soviet bloc. So poisoned was the political and judicial climate that Kaufman retained only the form of due process; he abandoned the substance, replacing the presumption of innocence with a presumption of traitorous guilt. A play straight from the Soviet judicial playbook, Kaufman's condemnation of the defendants as "proven traitors" not only invited but instructed the jury to convict. And convict they did.

Whether Julius and Ethel Rosenberg were guilty or innocent, their judge, their Constitution, their judiciary, turned against them.

Never in American jurisprudence had so great a calling failed so grandly.

The Myth of Julius and David

Twentieth-century legend treats Julius Rosenberg as the Soviet Union's "Master Spy." Rosenberg's supposed insight and perspicacity featured heavily in the government's case against Julius and Ethel. The United States went to great lengths to show Julius to be a deviant genius in the service of Russia.

In truth, a guilty Julius Rosenberg was but a small-time operative with the great good fortune to have a brother-in-law assigned to the most sensitive military laboratory in the world, a piece of luck that is both inexplicable and astonishing.[27] Much of what is attributed to Julius has the air of prophecy about it, such as Ruth Greenglass's testimony that on May 24, 1950, Julius told her that Harry Gold had been arrested and David Greenglass would be next. "The next arrest will probably take place between June 12th and June 16th," Ruth quoted Julius as saying.[28] David *was* arrested on June 15, 1950, in the same four-day period that Ruth said Julius had identified. Saypol and Cohn used such testimony to create the image of Julius Rosenberg as the mastermind of a Soviet spy ring – Julius was either prophetic or had access to the deepest secrets of the United States government.

A question never raised at the trial was just how Julius could have known such information at all, let alone three weeks before the actual arrest? Even the KGB could not have known the nearly exact date on which the FBI was to arrest a suspect. The timing of David Greenglass's arrest ultimately depended on when Harry Gold would identify David as a collaborator, something that could not be predicted at all, let alone with mathematical precision three weeks in advance, as Ruth claims Julius did. No one, including Julius, could have had such insight, and it is a fair conclusion that Ruth's testimony was contrived after the fact to fit the date of David's arrest, bolstering the impression that Julius was the mastermind of a Soviet spy ring with access to secret information.

Ruth raises a second time the specter of Rosenberg as a man with strange access to a nation's deepest secrets. Ruth testified that in November 1944 Julius came to her and said that "he knew David was working on the atomic bomb.... he said that his friends had told him that David was working on the atomic bomb, and he went on to tell me that the atomic bomb was the most destructive weapon used so far, that it had dangerous radiation effects."[29] But much rings false about this testimony. Who were Julius's friends, and how could they have learned that Julius's brother-in-law was working at Los Alamos? Just as Ruth makes the unlikely claim that Julius prophesied the precise date of David's arrest, here she claims that Julius's unnamed "friends" somehow managed to make the connection between David Greenglass and Julius Rosenberg.

Ruth quotes Julius as speaking about the bomb in the past tense: "the atomic bomb *was* the most destructive weapon *used* so far" (emphasis added). But the bomb was not even tested until

July 16, 1945, the Trinity test, eight months *after* the conversation took place. Since the atom bomb had never previously been used and its existence was unknown to the public, Julius would not likely have spoken of the weapon in the past tense. The term "atomic bomb" did not even come into the language until *after* the Hiroshima attack in August 1945. John Lansdale, the security chief at Los Alamos, testified that the words "atomic" and "bomb" were never used at Los Alamos, not in conversation, not in correspondence, not even to or by the president, and the same held for related terms such as "nuclear fission."[30] Like Shakespeare's clocks in *Julius Caesar*, Ruth used terms and references that were anachronistic. They could not have been in use in November 1944 when the conversation with Julius supposedly took place. Here again her testimony seems to have been created after the fact, unconsciously using post-Hiroshima terminology about the atomic bomb that was not in use in November 1944, when, so she said, Julius came to her with the story of David's secret work.

Strange, unlikely occurrences characterize the saga of the Rosenbergs and the Greenglasses.

We have seen the inexplicable coincidence of a Russian "master spy" learning that his brother-in-law has been assigned, completely at random, to the machine shop at Los Alamos making models of the atom bomb. We have seen Greenglass's claim that, while working in the most secret facility in the world, he managed to acquire, as an untrained machinist with no scientific knowledge, the detailed plans for the operation of the atom bomb. Only a high school graduate, he claims to have understood and transmitted to Julius Rosenberg the principles of the lens mold, an innovation designed to focus the force of a conventional explosive inward upon a nuclear core, setting in motion an immensely powerful nuclear chain reaction.

Everything we know about Los Alamos tells us that this was impossible.

Lansdale, the security chief, testified that Los Alamos was rigidly compartmentalized. Workers knew no more than necessary for their task, and even highly placed scientists knew nothing of the true nature of the project. "Only the people in the upper levels of the project were actually told what they were working on," Lansdale told the court. "Compartmention" meant that each aspect of the project was segregated from all others, with workers in "one compartment not knowing what the other one was doing."[31]

Greenglass worked in a machine shop at Los Alamos making models of what later turned out to be the lens mold for the atom bomb. Under Lansdale's security rules, Greenglass would not have known the purpose of his work; as a non-scientist he would never have been told the nature of the project. Nor would this information have passed from scientists to lower-ranking workers. Nobel Prize winner Richard Feynman, assigned to Los Alamos as a young physicist, recalled in his memoirs that senior scientists spoke only with each other about their work and not to the non-scientific staff.[32] As Feynman recalls, even the scientists at the Oak Ridge labs, where the uranium was separated, did not know "exactly how it worked or anything. The people underneath didn't know at *all* what they were doing," Feynman wrote, "and the army wanted to keep it that way, There was no information going back and forth."[33]

Logically, Greenglass should have known next to nothing about the work he was doing at Los Alamos. If, as Feynman believed, even the scientists separating the uranium knew nothing about the operation of the bomb, it strains credulity to think that Greenglass, an untrained machinist, would have possessed such information. Lansdale's "compartmentation" meant that Greenglass certainly could not have filled a dozen pages of detailed notes on the operation of the atom bomb, as he claimed he gave to Julius.[34]

Greenglass said that he knew nothing about the nature of his work at Los Alamos or the atom bomb before November 1944, when Ruth told him about her conversation with Julius. In his testimony he confirmed Lansdale's "compartmentation," the security system that should have blocked him from acquiring any substantive secret information:[35]

Q.   Were you told anything about the nature of those duties [at Los Alamos] and the nature of the work at Manhattan Project?

A.   I was.

Q.   What were you told?

A.   I was told that it was a secret project.

Q.   Were you told at that time what was going on at that project, what was being constructed?

A.   No.

Q.   You were told nothing about that, is that correct?

A.   Nothing at all.... I was told just as much as was necessary to do my job.

Q.   And nothing more?

A.   Nothing more.

These were the Lansdale security rules in operation. But despite the rigid compartmentalization, David claimed he was later able to learn not only the function of the lens mold, but the nature of the atomic weapon, its operation, and the code names of leading scientists in the project, enough to fill a dozen pages of typed notes. All of this should have been unavailable to him under the Los Alamos security rules. What happened at Los Alamos that David suddenly gained access to secret information that had been unavailable to him before November 1944? Why did the security apparatus suddenly cease to work?

Strangely enough, such questions were never asked or raised at the trial. Both the lawyers and Judge Kaufman assumed that the information Greenglass said he had given to Julius had damaged the security of the United States. No one seemed perturbed that the strict rationing of scientific information at Los Alamos should have made it impossible for Greenglass to acquire such information. Equally surprising, Judge Kaufman called no independent scientific witness to evaluate whether the information Greenglass claimed he had given to Julius was real or whether it could have damaged national security.

The espionage careers of Julius Rosenberg and David Greenglass were strange wonders to behold.

Macbeth and the Atom Bomb

To a trial lawyer, nothing rings more of fabrication than witnesses whose testimony of events years earlier match with perfection and without deviation. The Rosenbergs were tried in April 1951, at least six years after the crucial events in 1944 and 1945. All of the major witnesses were testifying to events that were at least six years old. Despite the passage of time, on at least four crucial points the testimonies of Ruth and David Greenglass are so consistent and match so closely that, when read in transcript, they seem to have been scripted for the trial.

David Greenglass testified that Julius was to send a courier to meet him at the Greenglasses' New Mexico apartment to retrieve intelligence. David asked how he would know the courier, and from this question was born the most enduring symbol of the trial: a cut Jello box whose matching halves were to be used to identify Julius's messenger. In the tradition of an espionage thriller, this was to be their "signal." David claimed that when he asked Julius how he would be able to identify the courier, Julius, Ruth, and Ethel all went into the kitchen of the Greenglasses' apartment, leaving David alone in the living room. David testified that they returned bearing the cut Jello box.[36]

> Well, Rosenberg and my wife and Ethel went into the kitchen and I was in the living room; and then a little while later, after they had been there about five minutes or so, they came out and my wife had in her hand a Jello box side....
>
> And it had been cut, and Julius had the other part to it, and when he came in with it, I said, "Oh, that is very clever," because I noticed how it fit, and he said, "The simplest things

are the cleverist."

Ruth's testimony about this incident matches David's nearly word for word.

> Well, the three of us walked into the living room [from the kitchen] and I showed David the half of the Jello box and I told him that Julius had given this to me to identify me to the other party who was going to come to get the information....

David said it was very clever; and Julius said "The simplest things are always clever."[37]

One wonders at this consistency six years after the alleged event. The sequence of answers is nearly identical; Ruth and David preserved in their memories not only David's statement that the Jello box design "was very clever" but Julius's response that "the simplest things are always clever." Such consistency between witnesses under stress recalling long-ago events is rare if not astounding. But what could be excused as a one-off event cannot be ignored where there are multiple occurrences of identical testimony as to key elements of the government's evidence.

When testifying about Harry Gold's visit to the Greenglasses' apartment in New Mexico, David and Ruth both spoke about Gold's producing the Jello box section to identify himself as Julius's courier.

When asked by the prosecutor "Where did you last see this other side [of the Jello box] on that night?" David testified, "In Julius' hand."[38]

When Ruth was asked the same question, she replied, "In Julius Rosenberg's hand."[39]

It is the striking specificity of these answers six years after the fact that is suspect. A far more natural answer to the question "Where did you last see the Jello box?" would have been, "In Julius' apartment." While a good prosecutor might lead the witnesses to the ultimate conclusion that they had last seen the Jello box "in

Julius' hand," such an answer would not normally be reached at the outset and certainly not by *two* witnesses in a row. Scripting is the only possible conclusion.

Testifying as to Harry Gold's appearance at their doorstep in New Mexico, David and Ruth (and Harry) again testify in identical detail. David's testimony:

> There was a knock on the door and I opened it. We had just completed eating breakfast, and there was a man standing in the hallway who asked if I were Mr. Greenglass, and I said yes. He stepped through the door and he said, "Julius sent me," and I said "oh," and walked to my wife's purse, took out the wallet and took out the matched part of the Jello box.[40]

Ruth's testimony matches David's verbatim:

> We had just finished breakfast and someone knocked at the door. My husband opened it and he said he bore greetings from Julius. He came into the apartment and ... he produced half the Jello box side. Then my husband went to my wallet and got the other half and they matched them and they fit.[41]

Harry Gold's testimony matches perfectly:

> I knocked on a door. It was opened by a young man about 23 with dark hair. He was smiling. I said, "Mr. Greenglass?" He answered in the affirmative. I said, "I came from Julius." I showed him the piece of cardboard that had been given me by Yakovlev in Volks' Café. He asked me to enter. I did. Greenglass went to a woman's handbag and brought out from it a piece of cardboard. We matched the two of them.[42]

Harry Gold does include David's age and hair color, but otherwise his answer follows the same facts and in the same order as Ruth and David's. And the additional facts, "a young man about 23 with dark hair," seem stilted, too formal for mere recollection, as if included purposefully to give credibility to Gold's answer.

Thus, six years after the fact, three witnesses testified in the precisely same manner as to the crucial facts about the meeting at the Greenglasses' apartment, each including the banal act of David's walking to Ruth's handbag and removing the Jello box piece. Why should three people each remember the act of walking to a handbag six years later? The testimony of each witness ends with the same statement that the Jello box pieces were matched and that they fit, an uncanny sequence. Witnesses do not behave like this; they deviate on material points and in the sequence of their answers. Even David and Ruth's joint recollection at the beginning of their answer that they had just finished breakfast (when Gold knocked at the door) is too much after six years had passed. David's strained phrase, "we had just *completed* eating breakfast" seems artificial, pre-planned (emphasis added). The coincidence of detail and sequence of answers is too great to overlook. David, Ruth, and Harry Gold's testimony bespeaks scripting, not recollection.

A final episode underscores the appearance of contrived testimony by the Greenglasses. In September 1945, David returned home on furlough from his Los Alamos assignment. Ruth had stayed in New York: this was their first time together in many months. Meeting with Ruth at Julius and Ethel's apartment, David said he produced a handwritten summary describing the operation of the atomic bomb. David and Ruth each testified as to Julius's reaction to the summary. David's testimony:

> Well, he [Julius] stepped into another room and he read it and he came out and he said "This is very good. We ought to have this typed up immediately." And my wife said, "We will probably have to correct the grammar involved," because I was more interested in writing down the technical phrases of it than I was in correcting the grammar.[43]

Ruth's testimony is again indistinguishable from David's.

David gave Julius the written information. Julius said he was very pleased to get it and he went into another room to read it over, and after he wrote it he said this had to be gotten out immediately and he wanted Ethel to type it right away....

Ethel was typing the notes and David was helping her when she couldn't make out his handwriting and explained the technical terms and spelled them out for her, and Julius and I helped her with the phraseology when it got a little too lengthy, wordy.[44]

David and Ruth again recalled events in nearly identical sequence: Julius stepped into another room to read the notes, he was very pleased, Julius said it had to be sent out "immediately," he wanted Ethel to type it, and David was more concerned with the "technical" phrases, a term used by *both* David and Ruth. Ruth and David recall levels of detail *in identical sequence* far beyond what would be reasonable for people under immense stress after a span of more than six years.

These episodes reveal what may well have been a common plan of designed or scripted testimony used by the government in Julius and Ethel's trial. The testimony of each witness matches the others word for word, sequence for sequence. In the real world of a criminal trial, such identicalness has only one explanation: testimony has been scripted or designed by the prosecution.

Death of a Typist

Julius and Ethel Rosenberg are the only Americans executed for espionage in the past hundred years.

"They die tonight," screamed headlines, and all America seemed poised to count down their burning deaths on Sing Sing's electric chair. The electrocution of Julius and Ethel, a husband and wife, mother and father, is the reason their case won't die. Even those who accept their guilt question the fairness of their punishment. That two young boys had to say farewell to their parents in the death house impels us to question its very humanity. That a single person, Judge Irving Kaufman, held this power of life and death causes us to question its justice.

Ethel Rosenberg's part in the conspiracy, according to the trial testimony, was the least of any of the major figures. At worst, she typed David Greenglass's notes, an act that by no stretch of reasoning deserved the death penalty, especially when viewed in light of the far more damaging acts of Julius, David, and Ruth. Julius, if the trial testimony is believed, transmitted to the Soviets the notes and drawings originally stolen by David. Ruth Greenglass, by her own admission, recruited David as a Soviet agent. These acts far eclipse Ethel's prosaic act of typing, which David Greenglass later said never happened and for which he admitted he perjured himself to save Ruth from prosecution.[45]

David Greenglass's admitted perjury inevitably alters the context of the trial. The government's case depended almost entirely upon Ruth and David's testimony. No other witnesses could have linked Julius and Ethel to the theft of atomic or military secrets from Los Alamos, and if their credibility had ever been in doubt, the prosecution would almost certainly have dissolved. David's testimony about Ethel was bound up with the charges against Julius. To put it simply, if David lied about Ethel, there is reason to doubt his claims against Julius and greater reason for the jury to accept Julius and Ethel's version of events. But David's admission that he lied about Ethel's involvement in the conspiracy came decades after the executions, too late to help Julius and Ethel.

David's notes were at the core of the espionage for which Julius and Ethel Rosenberg were found guilty and executed. Inexplicably, his testimony and notes were never evaluated by any independent scientist at trial; neither the government nor the defense called any scientific witnesses who were not employed by the federal government. Robert Oppenheimer and other physicists were on the government's witness list, but never testified. Oppenheimer and others later argued that Greenglass could not have had the expertise to provide worthwhile data to the Soviets.[46]

The value of much espionage is overblown. With his sparse

scientific background, can it be assumed that Greenglass's notes were sufficiently compromising or scientifically important to justify a death sentence? His drawing of the lens mold, a childish scribble laughable by any technical standard, would not have done much to enlighten Soviet physicists already familiar with the principles of implosion,[47] and who apparently already knew more about the goings on at Los Alamos than President Truman, who had come to office completely ignorant of the Manhattan Project's very existence.

In modern courts, sentence cannot be imposed unless the substance of the act is known. Judge Kaufman, having no independent scientists to advise him of the value of Greenglass's stolen data, nevertheless accepted that an undisclosed, unverified "summary" of the operation of the atom bomb by a high school–educated machinist compromised a nation's secrets to the point where the parents of two young children had to be executed. Can we accept such reasoning, and should we? Kaufman accepted uncritically the testimony of government agents that Greenglass's information was of value to the Soviet Union and damaged America's national defense without having heard testimony from a single independent scientist or any member of the Los Alamos scientific staff. Judge Kaufman, in essence, pulled the switch without ever having seen the facts.

In 1946, Congress passed the Atomic Energy Act, which required that in any case involving the theft of atomic secrets, only a jury could recommend a sentence of death. Although the 1946 law had been in force for five years before the Rosenbergs' trial, Kaufman (and the lawyers for the defense and the prosecution) assumed it would be the trial judge who would decide the sentence. Only after the conviction and death sentence had been upheld on appeal did Julius and Ethel's lawyers argue that the 1946 law required that any death sentence be imposed by the jury. Kaufman, however, refused to vacate the sentence, reasoning that the law covered only offenses committed *after* 1946 and that the theft of nuclear secrets by Greenglass took place in 1944, two years earlier.

Here Kaufman was unquestionably on thin ice. In his original sentencing judgment, Kaufman declared that he was sentencing Julius and Ethel to death based on acts of conspiracy that had continued into 1948 and 1950, long after the 1946 law went into force. Julius and Ethel deserved death, Kaufman reasoned, because these continuing acts occurred after the Soviet Union had ceased to be an ally and had become hostile to the United States. With this reasoning, Kaufman created a closed circle of contradiction: he refused to permit a jury to decide upon the death sentence on the ground that the theft of atomic secrets took place *before* the 1946 law requiring jury sentencing went into effect, but sentenced the Rosenbergs to death for secondary acts of conspiracy occurring *after* 1946. If Kaufman believed that the post-1946 acts of conspiracy were so substantial as to necessitate a death sentence, he should have permitted the jury to decide the question under the 1946 law.

Supreme Court Justice William O. Douglas was impressed by the force of this argument and actually ordered a stay of execution on June 17, 1953, just days before the Rosenbergs' death date. Justice Douglas was concerned that the 1946 law might prohibit Kaufman from imposing a death sentence and that the Rosenbergs had been denied their right to trial by jury.

Ordinarily, Douglas's stay would have continued in force until the case came up on the Supreme Court's docket, but the furor surrounding the Rosenbergs was so intense that the full Supreme Court was called into special session two days later, on June 19, 1953, in a blistering Washington summer. This unprecedented act meant the recall of Justice Hugo Black from the hospital, where he was preparing for elective surgery, to consider Douglas's stay. After a two-day delay, the stay was reversed. Never before had American justice been so rushed.[48]

Every defendant in an American courtroom is entitled to

"plead the Fifth," to invoke the Fifth Amendment right against self-incrimination. Under the Constitution, no person can be required to give evidence that will injure his or her own interests in a criminal case. Fifth Amendment freedoms are a bedrock of our constitutional liberties, but the trouble with constitutional liberties is that they often go unrecognized until a defendant has been unjustly convicted and executed.

At trial, Ethel testified that she had never spoken with David or Ruth Greenglass about David's work at Los Alamos. This was a key question for the jury, since the answer could establish whether Ethel intended to solicit military secrets. Ethel's denial would go far in supporting Julius and Ethel's case, because no other evidence linked her directly to the theft of national secrets.

Months earlier, when she appeared before the grand jury that was considering indicting Julius and David, Ethel had refused to answer these same questions, invoking her Fifth Amendment right against self-incrimination. Saypol pounded relentlessly on this point, demanding in front of the jury to know why Ethel had earlier told the grand jury that the answers would incriminate her but now said at trial that she had never had the conversations with Ruth and David. Saypol reeled off dozens of questions that Ethel had refused to answer at the grand jury but which she later answered in a non-incriminatory way at trial. Each time, he recited her statement to the grand jury that she was refusing to answer on the grounds that the answer would tend to incriminate her. Saypol's point was obvious: if Ethel had not spoken to Ruth and David about David's work at Los Alamos, as she said at trial, there would have been no reason for her to refuse to answer the same questions when she was at the grand jury. Like the blunt trial lawyer he was, Saypol was suggesting that Ethel's original refusal to answer the questions at the grand jury meant that she did have the incriminating conversations with Ruth and David and was now lying at trial when she denied having such conversations.[49]

Like thousands of defendants before her, Ethel was only following her lawyer's advice when she refused to testify at the grand jury, a routine instruction by a cautious criminal attorney. Even witnesses who are completely innocent are often advised by their lawyers to refuse to speak to a grand jury for fear of unfounded perjury charges being filed later on. Political defendants in the 1950s, such as Alger Hiss and William Remington, were convicted of perjury for their denials of communist associations before the grand jury, even though their actions had been perfectly legal and protected by the Constitution. Ethel's lawyer had good reason to tell her to remain silent at the grand jury even if she was innocent of any illegal acts. But by disclosing her previous use of her Fifth Amendment right against self-incrimination, a perfectly proper exercise of her constitutional rights, Saypol made it appear that Ethel was now lying to the trial jury when she said that she had had no discussions with Ruth and David about David's work. By demanding repeatedly to know why Ethel felt she could now answer questions that she could not answer when she was before the grand jury, Saypol put her in a difficult tautological bind that would confuse even the most seasoned trial lawyer: a high school–educated housewife was simply in no position to deal with this onslaught.

In 1951 such tactics were legal. Federal prosecutors were permitted to bring out a defendant's *previous* use of the Fifth Amendment if the defendant later testified at trial. Sadly for the Rosenbergs, the Supreme Court did not declare such practices unconstitutional until 1957, four years *after* Ethel and Julius were executed.[50] The highly damaging confrontation between Ethel and Saypol, which would have been illegal four years later, was one of the most dramatic moments of the trial and was probably the single greatest factor in undermining Julius and Ethel's credibility before the jury.

In many other ways, Kaufman stacked the deck against the Rosenbergs and their co-defendant Morton Sobell, even to the point of effectively wiping out the "reasonable doubt" test that protects all criminal defendants.

After discussing at length the government's claims, Kaufman

told the jury: "Now, on the other hand, the defendants' version of this case is as different as night is from day. The two versions are not reconcilable. You must determine which one you believe."[51]

In other words, the jury had to believe *either* the Greenglasses or the Rosenbergs, *but not both*. Kaufman's instruction wiped away six hundred years of the reasonable doubt test on which all of our criminal law rests. In British and American courts, a jury is never required to believe only one side but may well find both sides to be credible – and if so is required, for that very reason, to acquit the defendants. That is the very meaning of reasonable doubt! Kaufman, by telling the jury it *must* believe one side or the other, effectively did away with the reasonable doubt test, virtually mandating conviction. The jury may well have believed *both* the Rosenbergs and the Greenglasses and have been unable to decide between them; in that case, reasonable doubt would have required the jury to find the defendants "not guilty."

Judge Kaufman's instruction forced the jury to choose only one version of the testimony, even if they found both sides credible. In light of Kaufman's unbalanced summation, which overtly favored the government's case and omitted major parts of the defense claims, and his declaration that the Rosenbergs were "proven traitors," this final instruction dictated the jury's verdict and sealed the Rosenbergs' and Sobell's fate.

Justice failed in Judge Irving Kaufman's court. In its place, fear triumphed, the Constitution was abandoned, and presumption of guilt was raised as the standard for judgment in political cases.

Where Do Morals Lie?

Julius and Ethel Rosenberg were the victims of the failure of due process, of intolerance and legal paranoia. Time passed them by: charged with spying for a wartime ally, they were tried amidst the cold war anti-communist hysteria that ultimately came to dominate American life and thought. [52] As Judge Kaufman meaningfully remarked to the jury, "Unhappily the status of a foreign power may change."[53] The theft of secret information to aid an ally in the war years came to be seen, in a later and different political climate, as treason, a theme that overwhelmed the trial of the Rosenbergs. Many communist sympathizers changed their views of the Soviet Union after its takeover of Eastern Europe following the defeat of Germany, but the Rosenbergs were judged for their earlier wartime sympathies at a later time when the Soviet Union was perceived as an enemy, no longer an ally.

As epitomized by Irving Saypol's repeated accusations of treason, the trial of the Rosenbergs was conducted in the setting of the cold war, when any communist sympathizer was presumed to be a traitor, not during the wartime alliance when the atomic secrets were stolen, a time when the Russians were allies and brothers-in-arms. The disconnect between the wartime acts of conspiracy and the later cold war mentality is best illustrated by Judge Kaufman's declaration to Julius and Ethel at their sentencing: "I believe your conduct in putting into the hands of the Russians the A-bomb years before our best scientists predicted Russia would perfect the bomb has already caused, in my opinion, the communist aggression in Korea, with the resultant casualties exceeding 50,000, and who knows but that millions more of innocent people may pay the price of your treason."[54] In other words, Kaufman attributed to the Rosenbergs' wartime theft of atomic secrets the later growth of the cold war, the onset of the Korean War, and the potential casualties of future nuclear confrontations between the United States and communist Russia. He seemed blind to the anomaly of equating the wartime theft of atomic secrets on behalf of an ally to the later growth of international tension and enmity between that former ally and the United States.

The connection Kaufman drew between the theft of atomic secrets and the Korean War is not only tenuous but contrary to the true state of mid-twentieth-century geopolitics. Kaufman's suggestion that the Soviets were emboldened to fight in Korea because of their possession of nuclear weapons made possible by the Rosenbergs' theft ignored completely the Soviet Union's aggression in post-war Eastern Europe in the years before it possessed an atom bomb. Kaufman's comments demonstrate the linkage with the cold war mentality that came to be the determinative way of viewing the Rosenbergs.

Looking back from a place beyond the cold war and encroaching communism, beyond the emotional hysteria of the era, beyond the irrational fear of Russian infiltration in all areas of American life that animated the conviction and death of the Rosenbergs, can we today judge them in a more sympathetic light than their crime and their times would suggest?

Many have decried the atom bomb as a crime against humanity and depict the scientists who built the bomb as morally stricken men, riven by internal conflict over the power they helped to unleash. Julius and Ethel Rosenberg may well have been guilty of espionage, but by leveling the American nuclear monopoly, they may have prevented further and greater human catastrophe. Can we assume that the United States, in that tense, angry world of the 1950s, would not have again used the atomic weapon, this time against the communist bloc, if it still possessed a nuclear monopoly?

The moral weight of a crime often bears little resemblance to the law that is broken. Certainly, espionage and the theft of secrets must be punished by governments, but by their particular crime the Rosenbergs and the Greenglasses may have stopped the bomb. If guilty legally, are they guilty morally?

Perhaps the moral balance has not yet been calibrated. What is terribly clear in the case of the American Republic v. Julius and Ethel Rosenberg is that the foreman of the jury, quoted in the epigraph to this essay, was right. As much a failure of due process, as much a matter of legal paranoia, it was a repellent case of Jew against Jew.

Further Reading

Meeropol, Robert and Michael Meeropol. *We Are Your Sons*, Boston: Houghton Mifflin, 1975.

Nizer, Louis. *The Implosion Conspiracy.* New York: Doubleday, 1973.

Radosh, Ronald and Joyce Milton. *The Rosenberg File: A Search for the Truth.* New York: Holt, Rinhart & Winston, 1983

Roberts, Sam, *The Untold Stroy of Atomic Spy David Greenglass and How He Sent his Sister, Ethel Rosenberg, to the Electric Chair.* New York: Random House, 2001.

Schneir, Walter and Miriam Schneir. *Invitation to an Inquest.* Garden City, N.Y., Doubleday, 1965.

Sharp, Malcom. *Was Justice Done? The Rosenberg-Sobell Case.* New York: Monthly Review Press, 1956.

Notes

1. Quoted in Ronald Radosh and Joyce Milton, *The Rosenberg File: A Search for the Truth* (New York: Holt, Rinehart & Winston, 1983), p. 288.
2. Arthur Kinoy, *Rights on Trial* (Cambridge, Mass.: Harvard University Press, 1983), pp. 123–124.
3. Sam Roberts, *The Untold Story of Atomic Spy David Greenglass and How He Sent His Sister, Ethel Rosenberg, to the Electric Chair* (New York: Random House 2001), pp. 482–484.
4. *United States v. Rosenberg,* Trial Transcript, pp. 679–682.
5. Soon after their parents' execution, Michael and Robert were adopted by the Meeropol family. The two boys, now Michael and Robert Meeropol, lived anonymously until the 1973 publication of Louis Nizer's *The Implosion Conspiracy,* which drew heavily on Julius and Ethel's letters to their sons. The Meeropols revealed their identities after *The Implosion Conspiracy* was published to counter what they believed were false suggestions in the book about their parents.
6. The NSA's Venona intercepts, the transcripts of KGB communications from the 1940s that purport to identify Julius as a KGB agent, give no indication of the source that made the connection between Julius Rosenberg and David Greenglass.
7. Justice Felix Frankfurter reportedly refused to retire from the Supreme Court because of the prospect of Kaufman getting his seat: "I despise a judge who feels God told him to impose a death sentence. I am mean enough to try to stay here long enough so that K [Kaufman] will be too old to succeed me" (Roberts, p. 489).
8. *Voir dire* literally means "speaking truth" and refers to the duty of prospective jurors to answer truthfully the questions of the court or the parties. *Ballantine's Law Dictionary,* 3rd ed. (1969), p. 1349.

9. Trial Transcript, pp. 64–66. References to the pages of the trial transcript correspond to the printed transcript filed with the Rosenbergs' and Morton Sobell's petition to the United States Supreme Court for review of their case. On October 13, 1952, the Supreme Court denied their petition for certiorari, meaning that it refused even to hear their case, bringing to an end the Rosenbergs' and Sobell's right of appeal on the merits. See Radosh and Milton, p. 330.

10. Trial Transcript, pp. 69–71.

11. Ibid., pp. 74–77.

12. Saypol's opening statement to the jury can be found on pp. 177–184 of the Trial Transcript.

13. Saypol and Cohn, both Jews, were plainly not beyond using anti-Semitism as a trial tactic. Indeed, they were harshly criticized by the U.S. Court of Appeals for the Second Circuit, which covers Manhattan, for their vicious cross-examination of a Jewish witness, Bernard Redmont, who testified in the trial of William Remington, a Commerce Department official accused of perjury for denying his membership in the Communist Party. Saypol repeatedly attacked Redmont on the stand for having changed his last name to hide his Jewish roots. As the Court of Appeals noted, such an attack "could only serve to arouse possible racial prejudice on the part of the jury." See discussion in May, *UnAmerican Activities* (New York: Oxford University Press, 1994), p. 272.

14. Schneider said that while separate photographs of Julius and Ethel had been taken, he took no individual pictures of the children, a fact that the defense brought out to demonstrate that these were not passport photos. Trial Transcript, pp. 1424–1440.

15. Trial Transcript, pp. 1431–1432

16. Radosh and Milton, pp. 264–265.

17. Trial Transcript, p. 1429; Roberts, p. 366.

18. Ibid., p. 1565.

19. Ibid., pp. 1565, 1568.

20. Ibid., p. 1561.

21. Ibid., pp. 1542–1567.

22. Ibid., p. 1562.

23. Ibid., p. 1557.

24. Ibid., p. 1560.

25. Ibid., p. 1550

26. Ibid.

27. Sam Roberts reports that Greenglass was ordered transferred to Los Alamos the day before his battalion was to be shipped overseas, a truly remarkable occurrence for an army private whose brother was alleged to be a master Soviet spy. See Roberts, p. 6.

28. Trial Transcript, p. 709.

29. Ibid., p. 679.
30. Ibid., pp. 889–890.
31. Ibid., pp. 888–889.
32. Richard Feynman, *"Surely You're Joking, Mr. Feynman"* (New York: Bantam Books, 1986), p. 103 [emphasis in original].
33. Ibid.
34. Greenglass admitted on cross-examination that while attending Brooklyn Polytechnic Institute for six months he had failed *all* eight courses that he took. Trial Transcript, pp. 610–611.
35. Ibid., pp. 398–400.
36. Ibid.
37. Ibid., p. 690.
38. Ibid., p. 448.
39. Ibid., p. 700.
40. Ibid., p. 457.
41. Ibid., pp. 699–700.
42. Ibid., p. 825.
43. Ibid.
44. Ibid., p. 704.
45. Roberts, loc. cit.
46. Ibid., pp. 432–434.
47. Radosh and Milton, pp. 438–439.
48. See discussion in Radosh, pp. 402–411.
49. Trial Transcript, pp. 1372–1402
50. *Grunewald v. U.S.*, 353 U.S. 391 (1957).
51. Trial Transcript, p. 1560.
52. In conversation with the author, New Jersey constitutional lawyer Falk Engel has described this as a shift in the "geo-political landscape."
53. Trial Transcript, p. 1553.
54. Quoted in Stanley Yalkowsky, *The Murder of the Rosenbergs* (New York, 1990), p. 428.

The Punishment of
Jonathan Jay Pollard

JOYCE USISKIN

On September 2, 2003, the United States District Court in Washington, D.C., heard oral arguments on motions brought by lawyers for Jonathan Jay Pollard seeking to reopen the penalty phase of Pollard's trial for espionage. The question before the court was not whether Pollard was entitled to release, but whether he was entitled to reconsideration of the life sentence imposed. A year later, the motion remains undecided. The lengthy period of judicial deliberation attests to the troubling controversy surrounding the Pollard case and the procedural and political web in which Pollard is entangled. Public opinion is easily torn by indecision.

Mention of the name of Jonathan Jay Pollard is met with reactions ranging from rabid passion for his release or against his release, stoic silence, ambivalence, or unfamiliarity with the details of the case. Unlike the other subjects in this series, the Jonathan Pollard story is still unfinished. He is alive and has been incarcerated for more than eighteen years, and the issue of a possible release is still pending. He remains a controversial subject and represents a politically sensitive issue. In the case of Jonathan Jay Pollard, the issue is the sentence, not the conviction.

First, let us consider the bare-bone facts as to what he did, together with the legal steps and missteps that constitute such a big part of the procedural history. Next, we will review the history of his attempts to get a presidential pardon. Third, we will take a hard look at the response of Jewish leaders, Jewish organizations, and the State of Israel, the beneficiary of Pollard's misdeeds.

Finally, we would be remiss to ignore what was happening on the world stage at the time of Pollard's arrest, and we must attempt to fathom why the United States government has been so impassioned in its prosecution – or some would say, persecution – of Pollard.

In 1979, Pollard began his employment with the U.S. Navy as a civilian naval intelligence analyst, GS-12, earning approximately $40,000 per year.[1] He held top secret clearances, but these did not entitle him access to codes or cryptological information. Initially, he received favorable reviews for his work performance and, in 1984, was assigned to the Anti-Terrorist Alert Center as a watch officer and then as a research analyst. His assigned specialty was the Caribbean, but members of the intelligence community were given access to classified documents outside their specialty so as to keep abreast of developments in other parts of the world.

Pollard gravitated toward Middle Eastern operations on his own and became aware that the normal flow of intelligence information to Israel had been cut off after Israel bombed Iraq's nuclear reactor in 1981, an event opposed by the United States, which then had a pro-Iraq policy. In the wake of the Iranian hostage crisis and the Iran–Iraq war, the United States was furious with Iran. Although the Reagan administration maintained a neutral posture on the conflict between Iraq and Iran, which lasted from 1980 to 1988, the war unleashed considerable bureaucratic infighting. One faction, of which Oliver North was a part, was arming Iran, leading to the clandestine exchange of arms for hostages and diverting the profits to the Nicaraguan contras. Another faction, led by Defense Secretary Casper Weinberger, supported Iraq and supplied it with the weapons systems that later became the subject of the 2003 invasion of Iraq. George Herbert Walker Bush straddled both sides and claimed, during his 1988 presidential campaign, that he had not been in the loop.[2] Israel favored Iran over Iraq – a position diametrically opposed to the Weinberger position and the overt U.S. policy. Israel maintained that Iraq's Saddam Hussein, not the Ayatollah Khomeini, posed the greater threat to the security of the Gulf region. To this end, it sold American weapons to Iran and bought oil from Iran.

After 1981, Israel was cut off from the flow of intelligence information, and Pollard, unilaterally, determined to redress this omission. When he questioned his superiors about the reasons why Israel was being denied information on the Soviet's chemical buildup, he claims that they told him, "Jews are paranoid about gas."

On his own, he set out to correct the deficiency by supplying Israel with classified documents, satellite photos, and intelligence on Arab weapon systems, Soviet deliveries to Arab states, and other message traffic concerning Arab leaders, their political intentions, and the like.[3] He had only top secret clearance, not higher, and hence only had access to documents and photos classified as top secret. The trial court later found that Pollard was motivated to aid Israel by ideological rather than mercenary reasons. For approximately eighteen months, from June 1984 to November 1985, Pollard removed U.S. intelligence information, had it copied, and delivered it to agents of the Israeli government. Initially he was not paid, but during the last year he met regularly with his Israeli handlers to receive instructions and between $1,500 and $2,500 per month for his efforts.

The classified information about Iraq's chemical warfare production capabilities transmitted to Israel by Pollard included satellite photos and maps showing the location of production factories and storage facilities. Some of these factories and facilities were constructed by Bechtel, Inc., Casper Weinberger's former company.

In November 1985, agents of the FBI and the Naval Investigative Service interviewed Pollard in furtherance of an investigation into his unauthorized removals. He was given permission to call home and telephone his wife, Anne Henderson Pollard, using the prearranged code word, "cactus" which alerted her to remove all of the copied documents from their apartment and to contact the Israeli handlers. This was the extent of Mrs. Pollard's involvement.

The interviewing continued for two days, during which Pollard stalled and kept secret his involvement with two Israeli handlers, allowing time for one of them to leave the country. On November 21, 1985, the Pollards sought asylum at the Israeli embassy. They were turned away. Pollard was arrested and charged with violation of two U.S. statutes, one for espionage and the second for conspiracy to commit espionage. Mrs. Pollard was arrested a day later, charged as an accessory. Although Pollard admitted that he had lied in earlier interviews and had been delivering classified documents to a foreign country, he refused to identify the government or the names of their agents. His other Israeli handler left the United States during this time.

The Pollards were jailed immediately upon their arrest and denied bail. Mrs. Pollard suffered from a gastrointestinal disorder that had been misdiagnosed and she was very ill during her stay in the D.C. jail. In February 1986, she was released on bail.

Meanwhile, Pollard's family had hired an attorney, Richard Hibey, a former U.S. attorney. Plea discussions with the government began. Both the prosecution and the defense saw the advantage of a plea agreement. The government wanted to avoid a trial that would reveal its covert operation to arm Iraq. Pollard hoped to avoid a life sentence and reduce his custodial period to the four to seven years generally given for espionage activities on behalf of a friendly nation. No agent before Pollard had ever served more than fourteen years for spying on behalf of a friendly nation.

That fourteen-year sentence had been meted out to a U.S. State Department employee named Stephen Lalas who had spied for Greece. The court, in his case, noted that his sole motivation was greed and that he had turned over about 700 highly classified documents, including papers describing U.S. activities in Bosnia. Moreover, he had exposed the identities of U.S. agents operating in the Balkans. He, too, entered into a plea agreement with the government, which the government honored, but he didn't. He did not cooperate, failed to reveal which documents had been turned over, and failed two polygraphs. The government eventually learned of the document transfer from the Greek government. Unlike Pollard, who passed polygraph tests, did not identify U.S. agents, and cooperated with the government, Lalas was dealing with a government that honored its plea bargain. In another case, an Egyptian-American rocket scientist named Kader Helmy, who illegally shipped ballistic missile technology to Egypt, got less than four years. Egypt later gave Iraq that information, which increased the range of Iraq's Scud-B missiles.

Israel refused to acknowledge Pollard as an agent but secretly paid his attorney. It was not until 1995 that Israel granted Pollard Israeli citizenship. Not until 1998 did it publicly acknowledge that he had acted as an agent for Israel.

The plea agreement, in essence, provided for the following: Pollard would plead guilty to the lesser of the two charges – conspiracy to commit espionage. He would cooperate in the government investigation and refrain from speaking to the press without authorization from the director of naval intelligence. In exchange, the government agreed not to seek a life sentence, to limit its argument before the court to the facts and circumstances of the offenses committed, to bring to the court's attention the nature, extent, and value of Pollard's cooperation with the government, and further, not to recommend a particular sentence but to ask the court to impose a substantial period of incarceration and a monetary fine. The government further promised lenient treatment for Pollard's wife if she would plead guilty as well. She did.

In May 1986 Pollard signed the plea agreement, and on June 4, 1986, he entered his guilty plea to one count of conspiracy to commit espionage. Sentencing was delayed until March 1987, nine months later.

Two things happened after the plea agreement was struck and before sentencing. First, in November 1986, Pollard allowed himself to be interviewed by Wolf Blitzer, then a reporter for the *Jerusalem Post*. He did not obtain clearance from the director of naval intelligence. Nor did he inform his attorney prior to the interview. The government later claimed that he had breached the plea agreement. In a later declaration before the court, Pollard claimed that since Blitzer have been given access to the prison, he had assumed that Blitzer must have obtained authorization from someone in the government.

The Blitzer interview did not help Pollard. The story was titled "Pollard: Not a Bumbler, But Israel's Master Spy." The article went on to describe what types of documents he had given to Israel and why he had felt compelled to help Israel in this way. But the label "Master Spy" conveyed the notion that here was an experienced operative who knew his way around. No remorse was expressed in the article, a fact noted by the government and brought to the court's attention. Actually, Pollard was so naive that he never asked to proofread and approve the copy prior to its publication. The article appeared in the *Washington Post* on February 15, 1987, about two weeks before sentencing.

The second occurrence was the intervention of Casper Weinberger, secretary of defense under Reagan. Weinberger submitted two declarations. The first was a 46-page document of classified information allegedly cataloguing the damage Pollard had done and labeling it substantial and irrevocable. Approximately 30 pages of this document have been sealed from public view under a protective order entered by the trial judge, Judge Aubrey Robinson Jr. Even Pollard's subsequent lawyers have not had access to this document. Pollard and his first attorney did have access to it, and Hibey claims that he did read it and did show it to his client. This first declaration was submitted along with the government's principal pre-sentencing memoranda, which downplayed Pollard's cooperation. Despite its agreement to confine its arguments to the facts and circumstances of the offenses, the government told the district judge that Pollard's expressions of remorse were belated and hollow, grounded in the fact that he had been caught; he was a recidivist who was contemptuous of the court's authority, unworthy of trust.

The day before sentencing, Weinberger filed a second declaration. This was four pages and was made public. In it, Weinberger stated that "the punishment imposed should reflect the perfidy of his actions, the magnitude of the treason committed and the needs of national security." Even the Court of Appeals, which denied Pollard's later petition, admitted in its majority opinion that Weinberger's repeated use of superlatives and his reference to treason constituted a plea for the maximum sentence that could be imposed under the statute, life imprisonment.

An act of treason requires the aiding and abetting of an enemy of the United States – acts for which the death penalty can be imposed. Weinberger's barrage equated Pollard's acts to treason and implied that the heaviest possible sentence was the only just one. Further, Weinberger made reference to 1986 as the "year of the spy," by implicating associating Pollard with Walker, Whitmore, and Pelton, all of whom had been convicted of espionage for the Soviet Union, an enemy state. All had received life sentences seven months prior to Pollard's sentencing date. Weinberger was suggesting that Pollard deserved no less a sentence. Weinberger, of course, was later indicted for perjury. The first indictment was quashed by the appellate court on technical grounds. After the procedural matters were cured, a second grand jury indicted him, and this time he escaped trial after a pardon by the first President Bush.

The reaction of Pollard's counsel to Weinberger's intervention was inexplicable. Even a law clerk should have known enough to not only object to these unsupported declarations, but to demand an evidentiary hearing as to their veracity. Hibey did nothing. He did not even request an adjournment of the sentencing for the purpose of studying these papers further and analyzing their implications for the fate of his client.

Nor did Hibey express outrage after hearing the government's statements in support of sentencing, knowing full well that the terms of the plea agreement were violated when DiGenova and Lipper, the prosecutors, went beyond the facts and circumstances of Pollard's confession, failed to credit Pollard for cooperating in the investigation, and failed to confine the case to the actual transmittals made by Pollard. The transcript is replete with inflammatory comments by the prosecution implying that Pollard had played a more significant and sinister role than he actually did. Hibey did not object to these comments. On his own part, he acknowledged that Pollard had deviated from the agreement by allowing himself to be interviewed by Blitzer without checking with his attorney. Consequently, the portrait painted by the prosecution of an arrogant, contemptuous defendant who could not be controlled by his attorney was actually reinforced by his own attorney.

Pollard received the maximum sentence of life imprisonment on March 4, 1987.[4] No monetary fine was levied because Judge Aubrey E. Robinson, Jr. did not find his actions mercenary, and in any event, it was inconceivable that any fine could be collected. Anne Henderson Pollard received concurrent sentences of five years. Mrs. Pollard was released on parole after serving three years in prison. In August 1990 she moved to Israel and divorced Pollard.

But the wrath of the government was not assuaged by the severe sentence. After sentencing, when the press asked the prosecutor, Joseph DiGenova, how long he thought Pollard would actually serve, he replied that Pollard would never see the light of day. And indeed, for his first seven years of confinement, he was held three stories below ground in a basement cell, separated from the rest of the prison population. Neither Walker nor his cohorts nor Aldrich Ames, who was arrested in 1988, received such treatment. Ames had admitted giving the Soviets the names of virtually every Western agent, and at least twelve double agents had been executed by Russia as a result. Pollard's transmittals have never been shown to have endangered any U.S. operatives.

Following Pollard's sentencing, Hibey filed the usual motion to reduce the sentence. Predictably this was denied. A judge who has just imposed a sentence is quite unlikely to reverse himself without any new information. The entire purpose of such a motion is normally to preserve the issue for appeal. But again, Hibey acted inexplicably. He neither filed a direct appeal from the sentence, nor did he file an appeal from the denial of his motion to reduce the sentence. He appears to have dropped the case like a hot potato, and it is hard to believe that a seasoned lawyer like Hibey could have been so incompetent without receiving instructions to do so. It has been suggested that Israel, the fee payer, may have asked him to abandon Pollard. It is known that on March 10, 1987, six days after sentencing, Morris Abram, then chairman of the Conference of Major American Jewish Organizations sent a letter to Secretary of State George Schultz indicating that the Pollard affair would awaken no protest from the leaders of the American Jewish community. After complimenting Schultz on his stewardship of the Mideast situation, he wrote, "In my judgment, and I believe in yours as well, it would be contrary to the interest of the United States were the Pollard affair allowed to unravel, in any respect, what you have so painstakingly developed."

Then Abram went on to write, "I am off to Israel Saturday, where I shall convey the feelings I have expressed in the enclosed statement to the Prime Minister and others in the Israeli government." In this statement he tells the leaders of Israel that the American Jewish community on which they rely wants Israel to abandon Pollard. Was it Israel who gave instructions to Hibey? All we know is that for three years nothing happened. No appeal, no motion – nothing!

Three years later Israel, again secretly, hired a new attorney for Pollard. He was Hamilton Fox III, another former U.S. attorney and, like Hibey, a member of the District of Columbia bar specializing in the defense of white-collar criminals. By this time, Pollard had no timely recourse to the courts. Fox filed a habeas corpus motion. *Habeas corpus* in Latin literally means "produce the body." When applied to a sentencing issue, it means "Justify my sentence. If you can't, then vacate it or correct it." Fox raised all the right issues but one. He asked the trial judge to recuse himself, he sought access to the classified documents filed by Weinberger, he argued that the government had breached the plea agreement, and he argued that the guilty plea should be withdrawn because the government had obtained the agreement improperly by linking or wiring Pollard's wife's plea to Pollards's. But Fox failed to raise the issue of ineffective assistance of counsel by Hibey.

Fox presents the court with a curious affidavit from Alan Dershowitz, a Harvard law professor frequently involved in liberal causes. Though not representing Pollard, Dershowitz said that he had asked retired Supreme Court Justice Arthur Goldberg to inquire as to the reasons for Pollard's stiff sentence. According to Dershowitz, Goldberg discussed the matter with Judge Robinson. He reported back that the judge had told him that the Weinberger documents disclosed that Pollard had provided Israel with information about American knowledge of the details of the Israel–South African defense cooperation, and that this disclosure had weighed heavily in the sentence. Arthur Goldberg died on January 18, 1990 and therefore no affidavit of his could corroborate Dershowitz's statements.

In district court, Judge Robinson rejected all of Pollard's claims without a hearing. Then Fox referred the matter to Theodore Olsen to take the appeal from this rejection. Ted Olsen, an experienced appellate lawyer, subsequently became solicitor general of the United States.[5]

Even in his brief, which is well reasoned, Olsen makes derogatory comments about his client that do not aid his case but belittle his client in the eyes of the judiciary. He wrote: "There is no doubt that the government decided that Mr. Pollard was an offensive and thoroughly unpleasant individual who deserved the nastiest punishment." He went on to say, "But they [the government] bargained away their right to have it imposed."

Why did Olsen make this statement? Was it necessary to

discredit his client in order to argue that a deal is a deal and the government did not live up to the bargain it made?

Olsen argued the case for Pollard before the District of Columbia Court of Appeals. Sitting on the bench were Ruth Bader Ginsburg, now a Supreme Court justice, Laurence H. Silberman, who wrote the majority opinion on behalf of himself and Ginsburg, and Stephen Williams, the lone dissenter. The majority affirmed Judge Robinson for mainly procedural reasons. They did state that they might not have disposed of the matter without a hearing had a *timely* appeal been filed. But on a habeas corpus motion three years later, a higher standard was necessary to disturb a sentence. Judge Williams, the only non-Jew on the panel, wrote a rather impassioned dissent, describing the breach of the plea agreement and finding the vituperative arguments of the government so fundamentally flawed that it required vacating of the sentence and a remand for resentencing. Judge Williams went so far as to quote from Shakespeare's *Macbeth*, saying that the case reminded him of Macbeth's curse against the witches whose promises led them to doom:

> And be these juggling fiends no more believed
> That palter with us in a double sense,
> That keep the word of promise to our ear,
> And break it to our hope.[6]

That was how he viewed the government's promises in their plea agreement.

But the dissent did not free Pollard. The case was appealed to the U.S. Supreme Court, which declined to hear it. That was in October of 1992.

It was not until eight years afterward, on September 20, 2000, that Pollard's third set of lawyers, Eliot Lauer and Jacques Semmelman, filed a renewed motion for resentencing, again under §2255, the old habeas corpus petition. Here they raised for the first time the issue of ineffective assistance of counsel by both previous counsels. Pollard submitted a declaration in support of the motion, stating that he had not known that he had a right to appeal the sentence directly and only learned it belatedly from a fellow inmate. As for the second counsel, Hamilton Fox, the new motion addressed the perceived collegiality between the few members of the District of Columbia white-collar criminal defense bar that would inhibit any of them from soiling the reputation of another. Therefore Fox would have been loathe to criticize Hibey.

Before these arguments were heard, Pollard's lawyers filed a second motion in December 2000 to unseal the classified documents that were used to sentence Pollard and allow access to his present counsel, both of whom had top security clearance. The ACLU asked leave to file an amicus (friend of the court) brief in support of Pollard's motion to unseal the record. It took only one month for the district court, now Judge Norma Hathaway Johnson presiding, to deny these applications on January 12, 2001. She noted that the motion to unseal the records had been made by Fox and had been denied by Judge Robinson. There was no new evidence.

A review of the transcript of the hearing before Judge Johnson discloses that Pollard's present counsel waived any right to the classified materials for the pending motion for resentencing or for any future motion under §2255, the habeas corpus motion. Why? Now they have filed yet another motion for habeas corpus, and they are seeking access to these documents for that. The government, in response, can note that they once said they did not need it.

The purpose of the motion in January 2001 was to have access to these documents solely for the clemency petition then before President Bill Clinton in his final days in office. If that was the sole purpose of the motion, then the government's rejoinder is clear. Why would you need access to show Clinton? He was the president of the United States. He had top clearance. He and his staff could get anything they needed, and indeed, he could show the document to you if he chose. There is no judicial oversight of an application for executive clemency. One has nothing to do with the other. Judge Johnson evidently agreed.

The other motion, the one for resentencing, was heard and denied by Judge Johnson on August 7, 2001. The reason for this denial was that the statute of limitations had run.

Since that time, Pollard's lawyers have filed a flurry of motions, including motions for reconsideration of the denial of access to the classified materials, a motion for modification of the order of denial, a motion for a status conference and, on May 9, 2002, a motion to enlarge the scope of the pending motions based on newly discovered evidence. The new evidence was the disclosure in a letter from a U.S. assistant attorney general to a congressman that between November 19, 1993 and January 12, 2001 the government had authorized access to these sealed documents twenty-five times, meaning that the government had determined that *someone* had a need to know the contents. In addition, Pollard filed an appeal from the district court denial of his motion for access to the sealed documents. That appeal, though still pending, is unlikely to be heard before the motion for reconsideration is dealt with by the trial court.

What delayed the hearing on these motions? First, a new judge had been assigned. Judge Norma Hathaway Johnson fell ill, and the new chief judge, Thomas Hogan, reassigned the case to himself. But the second reason for the delay is the lack of response of the government. The government, in response to these motions, simply sat on their hands. Normally, a response is mandated because without one the court can treat the motion as unopposed and grant it. But in a case of this magnitude, no court is going to free Pollard without considering the opposition papers. So on January 21, 2003 Judge Hogan had to resort to ordering the government to respond. The motion was finally heard on September 2, 2003.

The parole situation is equally dim. In 1995 an attorney by the name of Benson Weintraub, apparently hired by the family to advise as to parole possibilities, wrote a memo strongly urging Pollard not to apply for a parole hearing at that time. The parole file contains so many letters from top-level government personnel urging the parole commission to deny any relief that Weintraub wrote the family, "The consensus of informed opinion among the post conviction attorneys with whom I have reviewed this scenario is that it would be ill advised to proceed." Instead Weintraub encouraged Pollard to pursue political solutions.

During the next eight years, Pollard married a Canadian woman, Elaine Zeitz of Toronto, who now is Esther Pollard.[7] She was working in Israel for the Ministry of Justice during the summer of 1990 and saw an advertisement in an Israeli paper urging people to write to Pollard and offer him compassion. She was not familiar with the case because the Canadian coverage was sparse. She wrote to Pollard; he wrote back, and after a lengthy correspondence, she visited him at the federal prison in Butner, North Carolina, where had had been transferred in 1993, and she married him there. Her field is special education and she gives lectures on stress management.

During the eight years of legal inactivity, there was political activity. Up to now, the information presented in this essay has been gleaned from the original court affidavits, pleadings, decisions, and so forth, all of which are fairly reliable in their recitation of the facts. Entering the political arena, we are faced with many sources of information, some of it conflicting and much of it hearsay. A digest of the political maneuvering from various sources may be useful.

As we know, the president of the United States has, under the Constitution, the absolute right to grant a pardon with or without a cogent reason. When Reagan and the first Bush were in office, such a possibility was remote. But during Clinton's presidency, Israel acknowledged its responsibility for Pollard. They granted him citizenship in 1995, although not publicly admitting that he was an Israeli agent until May 1998.

Clinton saw himself as the architect of a peace in the Middle

East, and to that end Yitzhak Rabin, began to negotiate for Pollard's release as early as 1995. According to some sources, Rabin exacted a personal promise from Clinton that he would free Pollard as part of a Middle East settlement, a quid pro quo. Then Rabin was assassinated and Clinton did not feel compelled to honor this personal commitment. Shimon Peres, Rabin's successor, made an ineffective attempt to link Pollard's release with the peace process.

Clinton later came to the realization that linking Pollard's release with his own goals for the Middle East might be workable. In September 1998, just before the mid-term congressional elections, Clinton was facing impeachment hearings and needed a public relations foreign policy victory. He asked Prime Minister Benjamin Netanyahu to attend a three-way summit with the Palestinians at Wye River, Maryland. The success of this meeting would help congressional Democrats in the election and would help Clinton personally. Apparently Netanyahu had some reservations about attending such a conference at that time. Republicans in Congress, understanding Clinton's motives, tried to discourage Netanyahu from agreeing to the conference before the election.

As an inducement to Netanyahu, Clinton offered to release Pollard within the context of the summit. Netanyahu had his own re-election bid coming up and needed a sweetener like the release of Pollard to sell any kind of peace deal to his electorate. He attended the Wye summit.

The talks at Wye broke down over the release of Palestinians in Israeli prisons and over Israel's request for the extradition of Ghazi Jabali, the chief of police in Gaza. To break the stalemate, so it has been reported, the Palestinians suggested that Pollard be released in return for the release of the jailed Palestinians and immunity for Jabali. A deal was reached along these lines.

According to accounts, the details of the agreement were worked out by President Clinton personally and Israeli and Palestinian representatives in a late-night session. A signing ceremony was scheduled for the next morning in Washington on October 23, 1998. The release of Pollard was not to be made public, however, until after the congressional elections. Therefore, the guarantee by Clinton to release Pollard was to be sent to Netanyahu in a side letter, not as part of the written agreement, and would provide for Pollard's release on November 11, 1998, one week after the congressional elections. This side letter was one of about thirty side letters the United States promised Israel in return for its support of this peace proposal.

All of the side letters arrived on the morning of the signing except the one promising the release of Pollard. Netanyahu threatened not to attend the signing ceremony. Conflicting reports have surfaced as to what happened next. Some news media reported that the CIA chief George Tenet threatened to resign if Pollard was released. Other reports indicated a rush of hostile messages to the White House from government enforcement agencies, notably the FBI and the CIA, when the terms of the side agreements were leaked. The agencies took the position that no release of a defendant in jail for espionage should occur without their consent or at least their investigation.

Further reports indicate that George Tenet, the CIA chief, in an effort to torpedo the deal leaked the news of Pollard's imminent release to the media, which published it. Further, he is said to have enlisted the support of key congressional members in denouncing the release.

Meanwhile, at the Wye plantation, Clinton negotiated a fall-back position to keep Netanyahu at the signing ceremony. Clinton would publicly promise a speedy review of the Pollard case. Some reports claim that Clinton promised to free Pollard at the same time 750 Palestinians were freed. Yitzhak Mordecai, then the Israeli minister of defense (later tried in Israel for sexual assault) and Netanyahu accepted Clinton's private side deal and attended the signing ceremony. When Netanyahu got back to Israel, he freed 200 Palestinian common criminals, not the political prisoners the Palestinians had bargained for. The Americans joined in the protest, and Netanyahu reminded them that the agreement did not specify which prisoners were to be released.

Some have concluded that Netanyahu was sending a message to Clinton not to double-cross him on the side promise to release Pollard. The Netanyahu government fell in the next Israeli elections, and Ehud Barak took office. The side agreements, if they existed, were history.

When Clinton left the presidency in 2001, Pollard was not included among the 140 for whom clemency was granted. Clinton had no incentive, monetary or political, to grant a pardon at that time. Politically, there was no outpouring of concern from credible Jewish leaders or the liberal press. The *New York Times* published an editorial urging Clinton not to release Pollard. Certainly there have been defenders of Pollard in the rabbinic community, advocates in Israel, including five prime ministers and two presidents of Israel, and, of course, many defenders in the Jewish press.

But the most influential organizations promoting Jewish issues (like the American Jewish Committee and B'nai B'rith) have either declined to comment on the Pollard affair or have opposed his release. The *New York Times* editorials counseled against his release. As late as April 25, 2001, B'nai B'rith International sent a letter to President George W. Bush, signed by two of its presidents, Richard Heideman and Seymour Reich. If the letter was intended to help Pollard, its contents showed the Bush administration the basic lack of concern by Jewish community leaders. The letter said that Bush's eight years in office were drawing to a close and noted that he had granted amnesty to Puerto Rican terrorists. Obviously, this was a recycled letter, initially sent to Clinton, and was of such little moment to the authors that they neglected to read it, edit it, or approve it before it was sent by some underling.

Why have Jewish leaders been so reluctant to speak out about Pollard? Even those who support his release have not joined in any crusade to free him. There is clearly a response by the Jewish community – to be silent and to do nothing. There are at least three reasons for this inaction.

First is the old-fashioned Jewish response to upsetting developments. Don't appeal for his release. Let the issue remain quiet.

Second, there is a fear that a Jewish communal appeal would be misconstrued as condoning Pollard's crime. Third, and allied to the second, is the further fear that the protestors' loyalty would be questioned. American Jews have been burdened by being classified, not by place of origin, but by religious beliefs. Much work by Jewish organizations has been motivated by a need to counter that classification and to win acceptance for American Jews as American nationals with a Jewish religious heritage. Consequently, the responsible, credible, and politically potent Jewish community seems to have made a conscious decision to leave Pollard to his fate.

Further Reading

Abram, Morris B. Letter to Secretary of State George P. Shultz. FOIA DOC: Conference of Presidents of Major American Jewish Organizations Letter, March 10, 1987.

Black, Edwin. "Casper's Ghost." *New York Jewish Week*, June 14, 2002.

Blitzer, Wolf. "Pollard: Not a Bumbler, But Israel's Master Spy." *Washington Post*, February 15, 1987.

Goldenberg, Elliot. *The Hunting Horse: The Truth Behind the Jonathan Pollard Spy Case.* New York: Prometheus Books, 2000

"How the U.S. Armed Iraq." *New Yorker Magazine*, November 14, 2002.

Koppel, Ted. "How U.S. Arms and Technology Were Transferred to Iraq." ABC News, *Nightline*, Show 2690, September 13, 1991.

Loftus, John. "The Truth About Jonathan Pollard." *Moment Magazine*, June 2003.

Miller, Bill. "A 14 Year Sentence for Selling Secrets (The Steven Lalas Case)." *Washington Post*, September 16, 1993.

"Pardoning Pollard: The *Times* Points The Way." *Jewish Press* (New York), editorial, December 29, 2000.

Patterson, James. "Weinberger Memo Was Hatchet Work." *Indianapolis Star*, December 15, 2001.

Phelan, Wesley. "The True Motives Behind the Sentencing of Jonathan Pollard; An Interview with Angelo Codevilla." *Washington Weekly*, January 11, 1999.

Rosenblum, Jonathan. "New Hope for Jonathan Pollard." *Jerusalem Post*, November 3, 2000.

"U.S. Had Key Role in Iraq Buildup." *Washington Post*, December 30, 2002.

Waas, Murray, and Craig Unger. "In the Loop: Bush's Secret Mission." *New Yorker*, November 2, 1992.

Weintraub, Benson B. "Report on Parole." Letter to Nancy Luque, Esq. June 20, 1995.

Internet reference: www.jonathanpollard.org.

Legal Texts

1. *United States of America v. Jonathan Pollard* Crim. No. 86-0207. 747 F. Supp 797 (D.D.C. Sept. 11, 1990) 959 F.2d 1011, 295 U.S. App. D.C. 7 (D.C. Cir. 1992) Argued Sept. 10, 1991, Decided March 20, 1992, Order Amending Opinion May 28, 1992. Cf. *Pollard v. United States of America* 506 U.S. 915, 121 L.Ed. 2d 242, 113 S. Ct. 322 (1992) Denial of Petition for Certiorari on October 13, 1992.161 F. Supp. 2d 1 (D.D.C. August 7, 2001).

2. Richard Hibey Esq., *Jonathan J. Pollard 2ⁿᵈ Memorandum In Aid of Sentencing* Submitted February 27, 1987.

3. Richard Hibey Esq. *Rule 35 Motion for Reduction of Sentence* Filed July 1, 1987.

4. Theodore Olsen, Esq. *Reply Brief for Appellant Jonathan J. Pollard* (D.C. Cir. 1991).

5. *Motion to Unseal the Pollard Record*, December 6, 2000.

6. *Unopposed Motion of the American Civil Liberties Union of The National Capital Area for Leave to File a Brief as Amicus Curiae in Support of Defendant's Emergency Motion to Add to List of Defense Counsel Authorized to Access Sealed Docket Materials Pursuant to Protective Order* December 6, 2000.

7. *ACLU Amicus Brief* – December 6, 2000.

8.   *Transcript of Court Hearing on Motion to Unseal the Record* Before Hon. Norma Holloway Johnson, Washington, D.C., January 11, 2001.

9.   *Declaration of Jonathan Jay Pollard in Support of Motion for Resentencing,* September 20, 2000.

10. *Motion for Modification of the January 12, 2001 Memorandum Order* filed August 16, 2001.

11. *Motion for Reconsideration of the August 7, 2001 Memorandum Opinion and Judgment, or in the Alternative, for Issuance of a Certificate of Appealabililty Pursuant to 28 U.S.C. 2253(c)* Filed October 5, 2001.

12. *Declaration of George N. Leighton in Support of Defendant's Motion for Reconsideration of the Court's August 7, 2001 Memorandum Opinion and Judgment* Filed October 5, 2001.

13. *Memorandum of Law in Support of Jonathan Jay Pollard's Section 2255 Motion for Resentencing* Filed September 20, 2000.

14. *Government Response to Pollard's 2255 Motion,* November 28, 2000.

15. *Defendant's Supplemental Reply Memorandum,* Filed December 6, 2002.

16. *Court Orders Government to Respond to Pollard Motions –* Order of February 8, 2002.

Notes

1.   Information about Pollard's employment is restricted to court documents filed by his attorneys, *United States v. Pollard* Crim. No. 86-0207 Second Memorandum in Aid of Sentencing, submitted February 27, 1987, as excerpted January 18, 1999, on the official website established by Jonathan and Esther Pollard (www.jonathan pollard.org/2000/011800.htm), pp. 1–4

2.   It is clear that Pollard unwittingly fell into a firestorm of political intrigue arising from the administration's overt neutrality during the Iran–Iraq war and its covert operations arming both sides. See Murray Waas and Craig Unger, "How the U.S. Armed Iraq" and "In the Loop: Bush's Secret Mission," *New Yorker,* November 2, 1992 (www.Jonathanpollard.org/2002/111402.htm), p. 1.

3.   Without a trial, there is no definitive evidence as to precisely what docu-

ments were transferred by Pollard. Nor was Pollard convicted of theft. Rather the plea provided for conviction of conspiracy only. The Weinberger memos implicating Pollard in more egregious acts, including naming U.S. operatives, have been discredited by the later arrest of Aldrich Ames, the later statements of government prosecutors, and even the words of Weinberger himself, who, when asked why he omitted mention of Pollard from his memoirs, replied that "the Pollard matter was comparatively minor. It was made far bigger than its actual importance."

4. Pollard's parents did not attend the court hearing but waited in his attorney's office. Since then Pollard's mother has died, but his father and sister still attend meetings in support of his release.

5. In November 2000 Olsen argued the case of *Bush v. Gore* before the U.S. Supreme Court, representing Bush. Olsen's wife died in the September 11, 2001, Pennsylvania crash of the plane headed for the Pentagon.

6. *United States v. Pollard,* 959 F, 2d 1011, 1039 (D.C. Cir. 1992).

7. The marriage has created a rift in the family. Pollard's father and sister have been cut off from the legal aspects, which are now supervised by Esther and Jonathan alone. A public relations videotape, *The Case of Jonathan Pollard,* was produced by Eram Preas and Amirann Amitai with the cooperation of Pollard's father and sister but without the approval of Esther Pollard.

The Holocaust on Trial:
David Irving vs. Penguin Books Ltd. and Deborah Lipstadt

MICHAEL J. BAZYLER

I.

To normal-thinking people, it undeniable that approximately six million Jews[1] were murdered at the hands of the Nazis and their sympathizers through a systematic policy of extermination during World War II.[2] We not only have as proof the testimony of the survivors and the confessions of the perpetrators but also mounds of records created by the fastidious Germans to meticulously document their work. It is, therefore, surprising that there are both individuals and groups that make it their life's work to deny the reality of the Holocaust.

In 1994, Penguin Books published in England the paperback version of an academic treatise describing this movement. The book, *Denying the Holocaust: The Growing Assault on Truth and Memory*, was written by an American professor, Deborah Lipstadt, who holds the Dorot Chair in Modern Jewish and Holocaust Studies at Emory University in Atlanta. In the book, Lipstadt named an Englishman, David Irving, as one of those who fit the label of "Holocaust denier."[3]

Irving did not take kindly to the characterization. He sued for defamation, claiming that his professional reputation had been damaged by the book. While ostensibly a case for libel (the written form of defamation, as opposed to slander, the oral form), the case became both a history lesson and a forum in which the reality of the Holocaust could be proven using legal rules of evidence. As characterized by one writer, the lawsuit of *David Irving v. Penguin Books Ltd. and Deborah Lipstadt* became a forum for putting the Holocaust on trial.[4]

II.

David Irving is the author of nearly thirty books on Hitler and related subjects. His book-writing career began in 1963 with *The Destruction of Dresden,* focusing on the British air force fire-bombing of the German city in February 1945. At this stage, Irving did not yet question the Holocaust. What he did was to wildly exaggerate the death toll at Dresden, using the figure of 250,000 rather than the more accepted number of around 35,000.[5] He also began to question the number of Jews killed during the war. As he later stated, "The Holocaust at Dresden really happened. That of the Jews in the gas chambers of Auschwitz is an invention. I am ashamed to be an Englishman."[6]

Irving's great success came in 1977, when he published *Hitler's War.* The book was hailed as a innovative look at World War II, focusing on the war from the view of the perpetrators. In the first edition of the book, Irving did not dispute the Holocaust as a historical fact. In fact, he describes Auschwitz as a "monstrous killing machine." However, one of Irving's major aims in *Hitler's War* was to show that the Holocaust occurred without Hitler's knowledge. As Irving likes to point out, no specific order has ever been found signed by Hitler directing the implementation of the Final Solution.[7] In 1983, Irving emboldened his view of Hitler's clean hands in the Final Solution by offering $1,000 to anyone who could prove that Hitler knew about the Holocaust.

By the time the second edition of *Hitler's War* came out in 1991, all references to the Holocaust had been excised. And Auschwitz was now referred to merely as "a slave labor camp."

Irving proudly hailed the change. "You won't find the Holocaust mentioned in one line, not even a footnote, why should [you]? If something didn't happen, then you don't even dignify it with a footnote."[8]

In 1988, Irving became the star witness in the criminal trial in Canada of Holocaust denier Ernst Zündel. Irving's role in the trial was to confirm the accuracy of the report of Fred Leuchter, a quirky American engineer who had visited Auschwitz and, after testing the chemical residue on the inner walls of Crematorium II, issued a report that no traces of Zyklon-B, the cyanide poison gas used by the Nazis to exterminate the Jews at Auschwitz and other death camps, could be found there. Leuchter concluded from this finding that the use of this poison gas at Auschwitz was a myth. The Leuchter lie, as will be discussed below, became an important element in the defamation trial against Lipstadt.

Inviting further controversy, Irving began also to speak before neo-Nazi and right-wing groups worldwide. Seemingly pandering to these groups, his statements became increasingly incendiary. Before a group of extremists in 1991 at a rally in Calgary, Canada, he announced:

> I don't see any reasons to be tasteful about Auschwitz. It's baloney. It's a legend....I say quite tastelessly, in fact, that more women died in the back seat of Edward Kennedy's car...than ever died in a gas chamber at Auschwitz. Oh, you think that's tasteless, how about this?...I'm going to form an association of Auschwitz Survivors, Survivors of the Holocaust and Other Liars, or the A.S.S.H.O.L.S.[9]

His outrageous statements, both at these appearances and in his writings, led the German, Austrian, Canadian, and Australian governments to ban him from entering their countries.

By the time Liptstadt wrote her book, Irving was already a notorious figure on the Holocaust denial scene. What made him different from others calling the Holocaust a lie was that he was an author whose works were published by prominent publishing houses. Despite his bizarre pronouncements, he was still viewed by some as a respected military historian. This, according to Lipstadt, made Irving "one of the most dangerous spokespersons for Holocaust denial."[10] He was "familiar with historical evidence," she wrote, and "bends it until it conforms with his ideological leanings and political agenda."[11] Lipstadt goes on to describe Irving as a "Hitler partisan wearing blinkers" and an "ardent admirer of Hitler."[12]

III.

Irving first complained about Lipstadt's book in November 1995, when he wrote to Penguin Books asking that the statements about him be retracted. Penguin stood by the account. In September 1996, he filed suit against Lipstadt, Penguin, and four Waterstone's bookstores in London that carried the book.[13] (Irving later dropped the action against the bookstores).

By that time, Irving's career had already been going downhill. Earlier that year, St. Martin's Press had retracted its offer to publish Irving's next book, a biography of Nazi Propaganda Minister Joseph Goebbels.

Irving's suit triggered an intensive three-year period of pretrial discovery. During this stage, Irving was forced to turn over voluminous materials, including all his speeches, other writings, and even his private diaries. The latter proved critical at trial, showing Irving's racist and anti-Semitic mindset.

The final and most critical act of the saga began on January 11, 2000, with the start of the actual trial. On a gray English morning, in the Royal Courts of Justice in the Strand neighborhood of London, Courtroom 37 was packed. English newspapers had been reporting over the years about the suit, and elderly Holocaust survivors and Irving's extremist supporters mixed with reporters in the audience.

At the plaintiff's counsel table, Irving sat alone. Ignoring the old adage that only a fool would hire himself as a lawyer, he chose to represent himself.[14]

Lipstadt's lawyer was Anthony Julius of the firm of solicitors Mischcon De Reya, whose earlier claim to fame was representing Princess Diana in her divorce action against Prince Charles. Julius was also a scholar of sorts in his own right, having written a book on T.S. Eliot and anti-Semitism.

While Julius, representing Lipstadt, and Penguin's own set of solicitors had done the pre-trial discovery and all the background preparation for the case, the barrister arguing the case for both defendants, and the one who would actually face off with Irving at trial, was Richard Rampton, QC.[15]

The judge randomly chosen to hear the case was Mr. Justice Gray, who, as Charles Gray, QC, years earlier had won a £1.5 million libel judgment, at that time the largest defamation award in English history.[16] The losing barrister on the other side was Richard Rampton.

While the ancient trappings of English law were symbolized by the wigs worn by both the judge and Rampton, and the stilted "My Lord" and other English-language anachronisms of a bygone era, the small courtroom was surprisingly modern. Laptop computers were placed at the counsel table and before the judge.

Reveling in the limelight, Irving often appeared to be addressing the media as much as the judge. At one point, Judge Gray had to remind him that "this exercise is not entirely for the press."[17]

In contrast to the United States, trials by jury for civil suits have for the most part been abolished in England. One exception is suits for libel and slander. The rationale for allowing juries in such cases is that the value of a person's reputation – what is at stake in a defamation case – should be judged by a community of the person's peers as represented by a jury.

Plaintiffs prefer jury trials, because they hope that the jurors' reactions to defamatory statements and the injuries caused by them will lead the jury to issue damage verdicts much larger than would be issued by a more dispassionate judge. One might think, therefore, that Irving would have chosen to have his case heard by a jury of his peers, English men and women like himself, and especially when the litigant he was confronting was an American professor. Surprisingly, Irving did not take that route, agreeing with the defense lawyers to have the cases heard by a judge.

While Judge Gray often repeated that the trial was not meant to prove or disprove the existence of the Holocaust, and both Irving and Rampton seemed to agree with this view,[18] the existence or non-existence of historical facts about the Holocaust became the chief subject of the court proceedings. As aptly put by the foremost account of the trial, "Despite every determined attempt to usher it politely out the door of the courtroom, there will not be a single day in this trial when history is absent from the proceedings."[19] Another observer pointed out the strange significance of the fact that "the Holocaust was to be scrutinized in perhaps the most inappropriate place of all – a British court."[20]

Since Irving was the complaining party, he went first. Much of his long opening statement was taken up not with how his reputation had been damaged by Lipstadt, but with how he had been unfairly maligned by Jews, what he labeled an "international conspiracy" aimed to "destroy my legitimacy as an historian." In Irving's mind, the actual defendant in the case was worldwide Jewry. As he explained, "The Jewish community, their fame and fortunes, play a central role in these proceedings."[21] To Irving, the purported victims of the Holocaust were in fact the real victimizers.

> Anti-Semitism is both the most odious and overworked of
> epithets. Almost invariably it is wielded by members or repre-
> sentatives of that community to denigrate those outside their
> community in whom they find disfavor.... It does not seem to
> matter that the same community who thus labels him or her
> has conducted an international campaign of the most question-

able character in an attempt to destroy his legitimacy....If he
defends himself against these attacks, he is sooner or later to
be described as anti-Semitic.[22]

Rampton, in his opening statement, set the tone of the defendants'
case. As was to become clear during the course of the proceedings,
for the defendants the real party on trial here was going to be
David Irving, or more specifically, Irving in his purported role as
historian. This was emphasized early on when Rampton made it
known that Lipstadt would not even be testifying. As she later explained, as a woman never shy for words, keeping silent turned out
for her to be one of the most difficult parts of the case, since she
had to keep mum while her professional fate was being decided
around her. Also, no Holocaust survivor was called as a witness.
As Lipstadt later explained, "[This] would have exposed people
who have suffered mightily to denigration [by Irving]...which
none of us wanted when it was not necessary."[23]

Rampton's single-minded focus on Irving was also compelled
by the peculiarities of English libel law. In the United States, libel
law had undergone a revolution since 1964, when the United
States Supreme Court announced in a series of cases that it is the
plaintiff – here Irving – who bears the burden of proving both
that he has been defamed and that the statements made about
him are false. And the libel plaintiff's burden is even higher
than in an ordinary civil case, more closely akin to the burden
placed upon the prosecution to show guilt in a criminal trial. The
First Amendment protection freedom of speech, the Supreme
Court found in the renowned 1964 decision of New York Times
v. Sullivan, mandates this procedure.

English law, however, has no First Amendment. English libel
law is still mired in ancient judge-made rules going back to the
Middle Ages. All an English libel plaintiff has to show is that the
complained-of statements tend to expose him to "ridicule, hatred, or contempt." Once shown, the burden now shifts upon the
defendant to prove that the statements are either not defamatory

or true. Thus, Lipstadt and Penguin, to successfully rebut Irving, would have to show that he was in fact a "Holocaust denier."

Rampton went straight to that point.

> My Lord, Mr. Irving calls himself a historian. The truth is, however, that he is not a historian at all but a falsifier of history. To put it bluntly, he is a liar.... Lies may take various forms, and may as often consist of suppression or omission as of direct falsehood or invention, but in the end all forms of lying converge into a single definition: willful, deliberate misstatements of the facts. Mr. Irving has used many different means to falsify history: invention, misquotation, suppression, distortion, manipulation and not least mistranslation. But all of these techniques have the same ultimate effect: falsification of the truth.[24]

Using these methods, argued Rampton, Irving had consciously whitewashed both Hitler's knowledge of, and role in, the Final Solution and the scope of the murder of Jews during the war. This became the defense strategy during the trial. Devised by Julius, the defense would hire prominent Holocaust historians to investigate Irving's historical methods and to use his own words – in speeches, interviews, and diary entries – to show that he was a Holocaust denier.

Put under such close scrutiny, Irving was forced during the trial to concede a number of significant historical points that he had previously denied.

Before the trial, Irving had argued that there was no Nazi policy to exterminate the Jews through mass shootings after the German attack on the Soviet Union. At trial, he was forced to concede that he had been wrong: the mass shootings by the *Einsatzgruppen,* the German military's special-action killing squads, were part of a systematic extermination policy, and between 500,000 and 1.5 million men, women, and children were so murdered. Irving also was forced to concede that Hitler must have known of this mass-shootings policy after the German historian Peter Lonegrich entered into evidence a Nazi document ordering that "the Fuhrer should be presented with continuous reports on the work of the *Einsatzgruppen*."[25]

Irving also conceded that the next stage of the Holocaust – the use of carbon monoxide to gas Jews in trucks – was not "experimental" or "occasional," but systematic. This concession came when Rampton showed that in one instance, 97,000 Jews had been gassed over a period of three weeks in three such trucks.

As to Auschwitz, the most potent symbol of the Final Solution, Rampton demonstrated that the Leuchter report, which Irving so eagerly latched on as proof that there were no gas chambers in Auschwitz, was "bunk."[26] Irving had been so excited about Leuchter's "findings" that he had them published in England by his own publishing company and even penned a flattering introduction to the report.

To rebut the report, the defense presented the testimony of Robert Jan Van Pelt, a professor at the University of Waterloo, Canada, and the co-author of the definitive study of Auschwitz. The Dutch-born Van Pelt was commissioned by the defense to present a special study to counteract Irving's misstatements about the death camp. In both his study and trial testimony, Van Pelt indisputably showed that a million Jews were murdered at Auschwitz and that the gas chambers were the main instruments for the murders.[27]

The leading expert for the defense was Richard J. Evans, a distinguished professor of modern history at Cambridge University and a fellow of the British Academy and of the Royal Historical Society.[28] Evans was given the task of demonstrating that Irving was, as Lipstadt asserted, a falsifier of history. When first approached by Anthony Julius, Evans did not know Irving and had no prior opinion of his work. He also had never met Lipstadt.

Evans, with the assistance of two Ph.D. students, spent eighteen months researching Irving's books, other publications, and public speeches and, in a detective-like manner, checking his statements against his sources. His conclusion was unambiguous: Irving was, in fact, a Holocaust denier, and he was ready to so testify.

Evans found Irving's historiography – the methodology used by Irving to present a history of World War II based on a critical examination, evaluation, and selection of material from primary and secondary sources – to be seriously flawed.

His 740-page report showed that Irving's body of work had been built on "a tissue of lies...a shameless manipulation of text."[29] One example highlighted by the defense was a document reporting a telephone call by SS chief Heinrich Himmler to his deputy and right-hand man Reinhard Heydrich, dated November 30, 1941, which states, "Judentransport aus Berlin. Keine Liquidierung [Jew transport from Berlin. No liquidation]." Even though the document referred only to one transport of Jews from Berlin, and made no reference to Hitler, Irving, in his writings, seized upon this document as "incontrovertible evidence" from Himmler's private files that Hitler had issued an order protecting the Jews.

Evans testified that in undertaking a rigorous examination of Irving's writings, he had not been prepared for the "sheer duplicity which I encountered in Irving's treatment of the historical sources, nor for the way in which this dishonesty permeated [Irving's] entire written and spoken output. It is as all-pervasive in his early work as it is in his later publications."[30]

As Evans explained,

> It is clear...that Irving's claim to have a very good and thorough knowledge of the evidence on the basis of which the history of Nazi Germany has to be written is completely justified. His numerous mistakes and egregious errors are not, therefore, due to mere ignorance or sloppiness; on the contrary, it is obvious that they are calculated and deliberate. That is precisely why they are so shocking.[31]

Evans found that Irving's conclusion that "no decision was

ever taken, or that the Nazis did not undertake the systematic extermination of the Jews at all, or that very few Jews were in fact killed, lies wholly outside the limits of what is reasonable for a professional historian to argue in the light of the available evidence."[32]

According to Evans, Irving should not be considered a legitimate member of the historical profession.

Besides being a Holocaust denier, the defense also aimed to show that Irving was a racist and an anti-Semite. One of the most memorable portions of the trial came when Rampton recited before Judge Gray a "nursery rhyme" discovered in Irving's diary, which Irving taught his baby daughter.

> I am a Baby Aryan
> Not Jewish or Sectarian
> I have no plans to marry an
> Ape or Rastafarian.

Asked Rampton, "Racist, Mr. Irving? Anti-Semitic, Mr. Irving?" "I do not think so," replied Irving. Countered Rampton: "Teaching your little child this kind of poison?" All that Irving could muster was, "Do you think that a nine month old can understand words spoken in English or any other language?"[33]

In a video shown at trial, Irving is seen making a speech to a group of Neo-Nazis in Florida. In a reporter-like style, he poses to himself the following question, purportedly asked by a Jewish heckler in England at a speech a few days earlier, "Are you saying that we are responsible for Auschwitz ourselves?" Gleefully, he answers, "Well, the short answer is yes!"[34]

IV.

During the course of the two-month trial, Judge Gray heard from nine witnesses and sat through more than a million pages of testimony. He also had to wade through stacks of documentation and various expert historical reports. To help him make sense of all these, the defense provided the judge with a ninety-page document, setting out in detail each of the separate allegations of distortion in Irving's works presented during the trial.

On March 13, 2000, Irving and Rampton concluded their closing arguments. On April 11, 2000, following almost a month of deliberating, Judge Gray announced his verdict. Irving decisively lost every point of his case. Irving, Judge Gray found, was both a Holocaust denier and a racist.

Because this was a non-jury trial, Judge Gray, in his role as fact finder hearing all the evidence, issued a detailed opinion setting out his reasons for finding against Irving.

Judge Gray's 333-page opinion, in commenting on and evaluating the parties' respective arguments, added a critical document to the postwar evaluation of the Holocaust.

He wrote:

> It is my conclusion that the Defendants are justified in their assertion that Irving has seriously misrepresented Hitler's views on the Jewish question. He has done so in some instances by misinterpreting and mistranslating documents and in other instances by omitting documents or parts of them. In the result the picture which he provides to readers of Hitler and his attitude towards the Jews is at odds with the evidence.[35]

He further explained:

> In my opinion there is force in the opinion by Evans that all of Irving's historiographical "errors" converge, in the sense that they all tend to exonerate Hitler and to reflect Irving's partisanship for the Nazi leader. If indeed they were genuine errors or mistakes, one would not expect to find this consistency. I accept the Defendants' contention that this convergence is a cogent reason for supposing that the evidence has been deliberately slanted by Irving.[36]

Judge Gray found Irving's contention that "after 1933 Hitler lost interest in anti-Semitism or that he ceased to be anti-Semitic when he came to power" to be without support.

> Despite his increasing preoccupation with other matters, Hitler reverted time and again to the topic of the Jews and what was to be done with them. He continued to speak of them in terms which were both vitriolic and menacing.... It cannot in my view sensibly be argued that uprooting Jewish men, women and children from their homes and dumping them in often appalling conditions many miles away to the East was other than anti-Semitic. I therefore reject as being contrary to the evidence Irving's claim that Hitler ceased to be anti-Semitic from 1933 onwards.[37]

As to Auschwitz, Judge Gray rejected Irving's perverse conclusion, as Judge Gray characterized it, that the "killing by gas [there] was on a modest scale." Entirely accepting the historical record, Judge Gray held:

> It appears to me that the cumulative effect of the documentary evidence for the genocidal operation of gas chambers at Auschwitz is considerable.... What is to me striking about that category of evidence is the similarity of the accounts and the extent to which they are consistent with the documentary evidence.... My conclusion is that the various categories of evidence do "converge." ... My overall assessment of the totality of the evidence that Jews were killed in large numbers in the gas chambers at Auschwitz is that it would require exceedingly powerful reasons to reject it.[38]

The judge also found that the Leuchter report, upon which Irving had seized to deny the existence of gas chambers, was faulty and false. As Judge Gray explained,

In regard to the chemical analysis, Irving was unable to con-
trovert the evidence...that, because the cyanide would have
penetrated the brickwork and plaster to a depth of no more than
one tenth of the breadth of a human hair, any cyanide present
in the relatively large samples taken by Leuchter (which had to
be pulverised before analysis) would have been so diluted that
the results on which Leuchter relied had effectively no validity.
What is more significant is that Leuchter assumed, wrongly as
Irving agreed, that a greater concentration of cyanide would
have been required to kill humans than was required to fumi-
gate clothing. In fact the concentration required to kill humans
is 22 times less than is required for fumigation purposes....As
Irving was constrained to accept, Leuchter's false assumption
vitiated his conclusion....In the light of the evidence of van Pelt
and Irving's answers in cross-examination, I do not consider
that an objective historian would have regarded the Leuchter
report as a sufficient reason for dismissing, or even doubting,
the convergence of evidence on which the Defendants rely for
the presence of homicidal gas chambers at Auschwitz.

The most devastating part of the decision came at the end.

My conclusion [is] that Irving displays all the characteristics
of a Holocaust denier. He repeatedly makes assertions about
the Holocaust which are offensive to Jews in their terms and
unsupported by or contrary to the historical record.[39]

Echoing Lipstadt's original statements in her book, the judge
found

that Irving has for his own ideological reasons persistently
and deliberately misrepresented and manipulated historical
evidence; that for the same reasons he has portrayed Hitler in
an unwarrantedly favourable light, principally in relation to his
attitude towards and responsibility for the treatment of the Jews;

that he is an active Holocaust denier; that he is anti-Semitic and racist and that he associates with right wing extremists who promote neo-Nazism.[40]

In summary, the judge held,

> Irving is an antisemite and a racist... [who] associates regularly with extremist and neo-Nazi organisations and individuals. The conclusion which I draw from the evidence is that Irving is sympathetic towards and on occasion promotes the views held by those individuals and organizations.[41]

V.

A Canadian Holocaust historian, Gord McFee, cogently explains why Irving lost his suit and his right to be called a legitimate historian.

> The historian must above all present the truth. What Irving was found to have done violates that most fundamental principle.... The importance of this lay in the fact that the average reader... does not possess the time or the means to get to the bottom of these things and must therefore rely on the integrity of the historian. In Mr. Irving's case, as it turned out, readers have been seriously misled.

> David Irving lost his libel suit against Deborah Liptstadt for a variety of legal and historical reasons. But the seeds for that loss were sown long before, when he decided to manipulate history to make it conform with the facts as he wanted them to have been. Rather than reinterpret the past, Mr. Irving attempted to reinvent it.[42]

Having lost his case, Irving might have wished that he now was in an American rather than an English court. In England, unlike in the United States, the losing party does not have an automatic right to an appeal. Rather, an appeal is allowed only if it has merit. In Irving's case, the appellate court found no reason to review the case. In so doing, Lord Justice Stephen Sedley confirmed Judge Gray's findings, noting that "what might, in another historian have been casual misreadings of evidence, emerge in the applicant's case as sedulous misinterpretation all going in the direction of his racial and ideological leanings. Hence the verdict for the defendants."[43]

Even more critical, the losing party in England has to pay the attorney's fees of the prevailing party. Penguin spent £2 million in defending the case, and sought reimbursement from Irving. In May 2000 Irving was ordered to pay an interim amount of £150,000, which he failed to do. As a result, in March 2002, he was forced into involuntary bankruptcy, and two months later lost his flat in the posh Mayfair neighborhood of London, where he had lived for thirty years. His personal possessions, including furniture, computer disks, and research papers, were also seized.

Stripped of any remaining legitimacy he might have had before the trial, Irving was now left to cavort with his right-wing extremist friends. In December 2003, he was the featured speaker at the Institute of Historical Review, a Southern California–based pseudo-academic group dedicated to promoting Holocaust denial.

Lipstadt no longer had to keep silent. At a press conference after the trial, she explained, "David Irving has done a lot of evil things. The way he has denigrated survivors was truly horrible. The racism that he propagated in court was truly horrible and evil. I see this not only as a personal victory, but a victory for all those who speak out against hate and prejudice."[44] On the heels of her newfound notoriety, she went on a worldwide lecture circuit.

Penguin Books, for its part, never recouped the £2 million it spent on defense lawyers and experts. It did republish *Denying the Holocaust* soon after in paperback, with sales jumping significantly upwards from the 2,000 or so copies sold of the book before trial in England. Penguin also took the step of publishing the entire judgment in book form.[45]

The Irving judgment did not stop Holocaust deniers from spewing their poison. Nevertheless, it added an important tool to counteract their lies. An English judge, using evidentiary rules applied in a court of law, found the Holocaust to be a historical fact. Looking at the significance of the trial, The *Daily Telegraph* concluded that the "Irving case has done for the new century what the Nuremberg tribunals or the Eichmann trial did for earlier generations."[46]

Further Reading

Evans, Richard J. *Lying About Hitler: History, Holocaust and the David Irving Trial.* New York: Basic Books, 2001. Published in England as *Telling Lies About Hitler* (London: Verso, 2002).

Guttenplan, D.D. *The Holocaust on Trial.* New York: Norton, 2001. Published in England by Granta Books, 2001.

The Irving Judgment: Mr. David Irving v. Penguin Books and Professor Deborah Lipstadt. Toronto: Penguin Books Canada, 2000.

Lipstadt, Deborah. *Denying the Holocaust: The Growing Assault on Truth and Memory.* New York: Free Press 1993. Published in England by Penguin Books, 1994.

Schermer, Michael and Alex Grobman. *Denying History: Who Says the Holocaust Never Happened and Why Do They Say It?* Berkeley: University of California Press, 2002.

Taylor, Kate, ed. *Holocaust Denial: The David Irving Trial and International Revisionism.* London: Searchlight Educational Trust, 2000.

Van Pelt, Robert Jan. *The Case for Auschwitz: Evidence from the Irving Trial.* Bloomington: Indiana University Press, 2002.

For a website containing the *David Irving v. Penguin Books and Deborah Lipstadt* trial material see www.holocaustdenial ontrial.com.

Notes

1. The six million figure was first used at the Nuremberg trials in 1945, and has been corroborated by further research since the war. It is, however, an approximation. Raul Hilberg, the dean of Holocaust historians, puts the wfigure of European Jews murdered during World War II at 5.1 million.

2. As put by Deborah Liptstadt to an Australian television audience, "denying the Holocaust is equivalent to saying that 'the Earth is flat' or 'Elvis Presley is alive and well' or 'there was no slavery.'" Quoted in D.D. Guttenplan, *The Holocaust on Trial: History, Justice and the David Irving Libel Case* (New York: Norton, 2001), p. 58. The tape of the Australian TV program was played at trial.

3. The book was first published in 1993, in the United States. Penguin brought out the British edition a year later.

4. Guttenplan's *Holocaust on Trial* is the leading study of the *Irving v. Lipstadt* trial. The author is an American-born journalist based in London.

5. At trial it was shown that Irving based his figure of 250,000 on a typed copy of an alleged German document that later turned out to be a forgery, and of whose dubious origins Irving had been aware.

6. Quoted in Kate Taylor, "Irving in Denial: The Trial," in *Holocaust Denial: The David Irving Trial and International Revisionism*, ed. Kate Taylor (London: Searchlight Educational Trust, 2000), p. 11.

7. As Holocaust historians rightly point out, the absence of a "Hitler order" does not prove Hitler's lack of knowledge or direction. As early as 1925 in *Mein Kampf*, Hitler made known his hatred of the Jews. Historians have found various German documents connecting Hitler to the Final Solution. To cite just two: In a telling speech in January 1939 to the Nazi Party faithful, Hitler warned European Jews of their imminent destruction. And in a December 12, 1941, speech to the Nazi leadership, recounted in Goebbels's diary, Hitler states: "The world war is here, the annihilation of Jewry must be the necessary consequence."

8. Quoted in Taylor, p. 15.

9. Quoted in Taylor, p. 19.

10. Deborah Lipstadt, *Denying the Holocaust: The Growing Assault on Truth and Memory* (New York: Free Press, 1993), p. 181 (published in England by Penguin Books, 1994).

11. Ibid.

12. Ibid.

13. The formal method in England by which the suit was filed was the issuance by Irving of a writ against the defendants, accusing them of libel and demanding damages.

14. Putting up a spirited prosecution, Irving nevertheless committed some major whoppers. At one stage, in one of the most bizarre moments of the trial, Irving inadvertently addressed the trial judge as "Mein Führer."

15. QC designates "Queen's Counsel," the senior and most experienced level of barristers in England.

16. One chronicler of the trial describes Justice Gray as follows: "A patrician in fact as well as appearance (he was educated at Winchester and Trinity College, Oxford), Gray's handsome face, hound-dog eyes, and sash of office make him look like a leaner, more lugubrious version of Nigel Hawthorne, the actor who played the mad King George III." Guttenplan, p. 17.

17. Quoted in Taylor, p. 17.

18. "Judges," Judge Gray solemnly announced at the outset of the trial, "aren't historians." Rampton agreed: "This trial isn't about the Holocaust." Quoted in Guttenplan, p. 21.

19. Ibid.

20. Taylor, p.10.

21. Quoted in Taylor, p. 17.

22. Ibid, p. 18.

23. Richard J. Evans, *Lying About Hitler: History, Holocaust and the David Irving Trial* (New York: Basic Books, 2001), p. 282 (quoting Jan Colley, Cathy Gordon, and John Aston, "'Evil Racist' Irving Faces Libel Ruin," *Birmingham Post*, April 12, 2000, p. 7).

24. Quoted in Guttenplan, pp. 31–32.

25. Report of Peter Lonegrich, sec. 15.6.

26. Quoted in Taylor, p. 23.

27. Accordingly to Van Pelt, "It will be clear that by early 1947 there was a massive amount of evidence of the use of the camp as a site for mass extermination. This evidence had become available during the war as the result of reports by escaped inmates, had become more substantiated through eyewitness accounts by former Auschwitz inmates immediately after their liberation, and was confirmed in the Polish forensic investigations undertaken in 1945 and 1946....Finally, this evidence was corroborated by confessions of leading German personnel at Auschwitz during its years of operation... It is highly implausible that knowledge about Auschwitz was a wartime fabrication by British propagandists. In short, it has become possible to assert as moral certainty the statement that Auschwitz was an extermination camp where the Germans killed around one million people with the help of gas chambers." Van Pelt Report, Preface, available at http://www.holcaustdenialontrial.com.

    Van Pelt subsequently published his findings in a book. See Robert Jan Van Pelt, *The Case for Auschwitz: Evidence from the Irving Trial* (Bloomington: Indiana University Press, 2002).

28. Another prominent expert testifying at trial was the American Holocaust historian Christopher Browning, professor at the University of North Carolina and author of numerous works on the extermination policies of the Nazis. None of the experts testifying at trial were Jewish.

29. Evans Report, sec. 4.3(c)(ii)(D)1, (quoted in Taylor, p. 22) and available at
http://www.holcaustdenialontrial.com. Evans later published his report in
a book. See Richard J. Evans, *Lying About Hitler: History, Holocaust and
the David Irving Trial* (New York: Basic Books, 2001). The subsequent
publication history of Evans's book in England produced its own saga. It
also provides a good illustration of how anachronistic English libel laws
can dissuade publishers, even after the Irving judgment, from issuing
respected books for fear of being sued.

The original publisher, William Heinemann, Ltd., an imprint of Random House UK, the largest publishing house in England and part of the
German publishing media giant Bertelsmann, decided to pulp the book
after fearing another libel action from Irving. It earlier had advertised the
book in glowing terms. No other large publisher in England stepped up
to take over the publication. Even Basic Books, its American publisher,
declined to issue the book in England. Ironically, the publisher willing to
take the risk was Verso, a small publishing house known for its left-wing
works, including books critical of Israel. It published the book in 2002
under the title *Telling Lies About Hitler*. Irving, though threatening another
libel action, never sued Verso.

Irving, nevertheless, continued to make trouble for Evans. (On his
website, Irving refers to Evans as "the skunk," adding a skunk graphic
whenever he is mentioned.) As reported by the *London Guardian* newspaper, in early 2003, the online bookseller Amazon pulled Evan's book off its
UK website after Irving threatened to sue. According to Amazon, "We will
not list *Telling Lies About Hitler* or any other book over the objections that
the book contains defamatory content, at least not without a commitment
by the publisher to defend us in any legal action brought against us under
UK law." *Guardian*, March 8, 2003. Verso declined to indemnify Amazon.
Eventually, Amazon relented and returned the book to its website. Amazon
continues also to sell Irving's books. It drew the line, at least for a while, at
Hitler's *Mein Kampf*. It now offers a 2003 reprint of Hitler's book for sale,
however.

According to Amazon, "[English libel] law as it stands has 'a chilling
effect on free speech." Ibid. Evans, from his bitter experiences with *Telling
Lies About Hitler*, agrees. "There is a climate of fear in British publishing,
spread by this country's iniquitous libel laws....We badly need a reform
of the law that will put some burden of proof on claimants, and we need
legislation that will enshrine free speech as a basic human right. Otherwise
those who are unscrupulous enough to use the threat of invoking the law
to prevent criticism of their views and their actions will continue to be
able to intimidate publishers into silence, to the detriment of all." Richard
J. Evans, "The Real Cost of Free Speech," *Times* (London) *Higher Education*

Supplement, June 21, 2002 (relating Evans's circuitous journey to have the book published).

30. Evans Report, sec. 1.6.2.
31. Evans Report, sec. 1.6.2 (quoted in Guttenplan, p. 218).
32. Evans Report, sec. 1.6.6 (quoted in Taylor, p. 22).
33. Quoted in Guttenplan, p. 51.
34. Ibid, p. 205.
35. Judgment, sec. 13.31. The entire judgment is available at www.holocaustdenial ontrial.com and also at www.nizkor.org/hweb/people/i/irvinGodavid/judgment-00-00.html. Irving has also made it available on his publishing house's website, www.focal.org/judg.html. For legal scholars and others with access to Westlaw (www.westlaw.com), the judgment is reproduced at *2000 wl 362478*.
36. Judgment, sec. 13.142. Guttenplan, in his study of the trial, puts this finding by Judge Gray in plain terms that Irving himself raised during his questioning of Professor Christopher Browning. "Like the dishonest waiter in [Irving's own] example, Irving had been repeatedly caught giving incorrect change – always in his own favor." Guttenplan, p. 263.
37. Judgment, sec. 13.54–13.55.
38. Ibid., sec. 13.75.
39. Ibid., sec. 13.161.
40. Ibid., sec. 13.161.
41. Ibid., sec. 13.161.
42. Gort McFee, "Where Did David Irving Go Wrong?" (www.holocaust-history.org/irving-wrong).
43. Denial of Permission to Appeal, *Irving v. Penguin Books Ltd.* (Dec. 18, 2000), available at www.fpp.co.uk/Legal/Penguin/Appeal/refusal.html (website of Irving's publishing house).
44. Quoted in Taylor, p. 41.
45. *The Irving Judgment: Mr. David Irving v. Penguin Books and Professor Deborah Lipstadt* (Toronto: Penguin Books Canada, 2000).
46. "The Bad History Man," *Daily Telegraph* (London), April 12, 2000, p. 29 (editorial).

About the Authors

BRUCE AFRAN graduated from the State University of New York with a degree in history in 1982 and from Brooklyn Law School in 1985. He has practiced commercial and constitutional law, figuring prominently in New Jersey cases concerning voting rights, immigrant rights, and domestic relations. He has consulted on matters involving international human rights law, pensions, and securities law, and has argued cases in many states. As a civil rights lawyer in New Jersey, he has argued cases that established or led to major changes in state law and business practices.

He is also active as a consultant, notably regarding international human rights and represented the chief rabbi of Poland in a case against the former communist regime for violation of rights protected by international treaties and the United Nations Charter.

Bruce Afran lives in Princeton with his wife, a professor of family medicine and their two children.

MICHAEL J. BAZYLER is a professor of law at the Whittier Law School, Costa Mesa, California. The son of Holocaust survivors, born in the Soviet Union and raised in postwar Poland, he is an international law litigator and currently a visiting fellow at the Center for Advanced Holocaust Studies at the U.S. Holocaust Memorial Museum, Washington, D.C. He is also a research fellow of the Holocaust Education Trust in London, England.

Prof. Bazyler's book, *Holocaust Justice: The Battle for Restitution in America's Courts* (2003) was cited by the U.S. Supreme Court in both majority and dissenting opinions in an important insurance recovery case.

PHILIP S. CARCHMAN is a judge of the Superior Court of New Jersey, Appellate Division, and presently serves as acting administrative director of the courts. He previously served as Mercer County prosecutor and before that practiced law in Princeton with the firm of Carchman, Annich, Sochor and Shuster.

Judge Carchman is a graduate of the Wharton School of Business at the University of Pennsylvania and the University of Pennsylvania Law School. He resides in Princeton with his wife, JoAnn, and is the father of two daughters: Rebecca, a physician in Chapel Hill, North Carolina, and Jennifer, a television documentary film producer residing in Brooklyn. Judge Carchman has one granddaughter, Mia.

REBEKAH MARKS COSTIN is a graduate of the University of Rochester, where she majored in history, with a focus on American history. She has a law degree from Cardozo School of Law and a Master of Law, with a specialty in environmental law. As a practicing attorney, she represented the New Jersey Department of Environmental Protection. Her primary responsibility was to license "garbage guys" – haulers of solid waste.

Costin has taught American Jewish history at the Jewish Center of Princeton and received the Center's Fabian Award for Excellence in Teaching. She was also a curatorial assistant and researcher for the Princeton Historical Society's exhibit on Jews in Princeton.

MICHAEL CURTIS, a London-born scholar of modern politics, made the United States his home fifty years ago. Dr. Curtis has taught at Cornell, Yale, Oberlin, the Hebrew University, Tel Aviv

University, and the University of Bologna. He is distinguished professor emeritus of political science at Rutgers University, where he taught for thirty-eight years. Dr. Curtis is the author of several books, including *Religion and Politics in the Middle East, Three Against the Third Republic* (a discussion of French anti-Semitism after Dreyfus), and the recently published *Verdict on Vichy: Power and Prejudice in the Vichy France Regime*. He lives in Princeton, New Jersey, with his wife, the artist Judith Brodsky.

ROBERT A. GARBER, a tax lawyer who practiced in New York, received his B.A. in 1953 from Vanderbilt University, his LL.B. in 1955 from Vanderbilt Law School, and his LL.M. in 1960 from New York University. He is the author of *The Only Tax Book You'll Ever Need* and other titles relating to taxation and estate planning. Now retired, he lives with his wife, Eileen, in Princeton and reviews books regularly.

C.M. SILVER is a published author and translator of fiction. A son of a theatrical family, Silver fell under the spell of Shakespeare at an early age. He graduated from Oberlin College, and has an M.B.A. degree in finance from Columbia University Business School, as well as a Master of Fine Arts in Creative Writing from the New School, in New York. He has taught creative writing in private groups, and in the New York City prison system. He is also a teacher of Torah and rabbinic subjects, including stints teaching at the National Havurah Institute, where he presented a seminar on images of Jews in Elizabethan England. Silver is the managing director of an investment banking firm in New York. He resides in Princeton, New Jersey, where he teaches a weekly class at the Princeton Jewish Center.

SALLY STEINBERG-BRENT is a graduate of New York University. She received her law degree from Loyola University and was admitted to the New Jersey bar in 1978. She is a divorce mediator and labor arbitrator and also practices family and immigration law in Princeton, New Jersey, where she lives with her husband (with whom she practices law) and their three children.

JOYCE USISKIN was graduated from Barnard College with an A.B., received her M.A. in English literature from Boston University, and her J.D. from Rutgers University Law School.

In the public sector, she has served as a deputy attorney general of New Jersey, representing the Department of Human Resources and the Department of Education. She was a member of the research team for the Appellate Division of the New Jersey Superior Court, served as a legal adviser to the director of the Administrative Office of the Courts and was appointed by the late Chief Justice Wilentz to her present post, special master for mass tort litigation in New Jersey. She has handled fire retardant roof cases, diet drug cases, latex glove cases, tobacco cases, and blood serum cases among others.

Index